India in English Fiction, 1800-1970

An Annotated Bibliography

by

BRIJEN K. GUPTA

The Scarecrow Press, Inc.
Metuchen, N. J.   1973

Library of Congress Cataloging in Publication Data

Gupta, Brijen Kishore, 1929–
   India in English fiction, 1800–1970.

   Bibliography: p.
   1. English fiction—Bibliography. 2. India in
literature—Bibliography. 3. Indic literature—
Translations into English—Bibliography. 4. English
literature—Translations from Indic—Bibliography.
5. English literature—Indic authors—Bibliography.
I. Title.
Z2014.F5G86   823'.009'32   73–4194
ISBN 0–8108–0612–6

To my parents

ACKNOWLEDGMENTS

I owe my interest in fiction to my granduncle, the late Professor Bhupal Singh. A Survey of Anglo-Indian Fiction (London, 1934), which he wrote, was the single most important source in the preparation of this bibliography.

Financial support to prepare this work was provided by the Penrose Fund of the American Philosophical Society; intellectual encouragement came from my friend Ward Morehouse.

A large number of my students were involved in this project. Two who did the most work were Barbara Goldberg and Elaine Germano.

Successive drafts of the manuscript were typed by Linda Hodges, Karen DeVisser, Margaret Mesiti and Diana Wedel.

George Grella's preface is much better than my own effort.

To all of them, my sincerest thanks.

B. K. G.

CONTENTS

PREFACE

Passage O soul to India!
Eclaircise the myths Asiatic, the primitive fables.

Walt Whitman's great poem, "Passage to India," cele-
brates, among other things, Western man's continuing fas-
cination with and hopes for that various and magical subcontinent. As our present age daily demonstrates, that fas-
cination and those hopes have not diminished. It is appropri-
ate that at a time when Indian fashions in music, clothing,
religion, art, and (for want of a better word) sexology intrigue the popular imagination, we are now presented with a
comprehensive bibliography of English fiction about India.
To assess completely the impact of India on the Western
imagination or the meaning of India to Indians themselves is,
no doubt, an impossible task. A vast and populous land,
complicated by every apparent human difference--racial,
ethnic, religious, regional, political, linguistic--and haunted
by the ubiquitous spectres of pestilence, famine, and war,
India remains, in E. M. Forster's characteristically under-
stated words, "a mystery and a muddle." Although a pleth-
ora of studies in every possible discipline exists to instruct
us about the nation, the imaginative literature dealing with
India can perhaps tell us more than any textbook·or scholarly monograph. India in literature is a topic as large, as
varied, as potent as the nation itself; Mr. Gupta's bibliography provides a thoroughly detailed map of the enormous
territory he takes as his subject.

The sheer amount of fiction recorded in this volume
attests to the manifold reflections of India captured by
English, Anglo-Indian, and Indian writers. Initially, this
bibliography suggests the lasting results of colonialism on
any country. Conquest and colonization have marked many
nations, the conqueror as well as the conquered; none, perhaps, has been so deeply affected by the colonial experience
as the British Empire and its many territories, especially,
of course, India. The experience with India, that long
series of actions wise and foolish, gallant and craven,

benevolent and cruel, glorious and ignominious, may never cease influencing English culture, from the highest levels of government down to the retired colonel who dines on curry and thinks of himself as a pukka sahib. Whatever the appalling defects of Imperialism--and they could not possibly be recounted here--an important literature resulted from Britain's policy of international expansionism. Drawn from their little island to strange climes and peoples, English writers discovered new subjects far from home and were forced into artistry by what they found. Writers like Kipling, Conrad, Forster, Orwell, and Burgess depend in part on the history of England's encounter with exotic lands. The colonial novel, in all its avatars, stands as a permanent testimony to the sensitive Englishman's discovery of new areas of enchantment, mystery, and adventure, of new shapes for human relationships, and most of all, of himself as a stranger in a strange land; none of this could be revealed to him in his own country. Colonialism led numbers of extraordinary men to suffer and describe what today we call "cultural shock."

Whatever else it did, for good or for ill, England gave at least one bit of recompense for all it took from its conquered lands: the English language and its incomparably rich literary heritage. The English bequeathed to India, for example, the novel itself, not originally a native form. This bibliography, then, enumerates not only English novels about India, but Indian fiction in English; the two bodies of work, side by side, present perhaps as full a picture of the nation as one could hope to find. Juxtaposed with the viewpoint of the colonist is that of the colonized: together, both sides of that particular aspect of Indian life can be fully told. At least one great international adventure, ·the encounter between the powerful little island and the slumbering subcontinent, may be more completely represented in these pages than in any other place.

Because the history of England's encounter with India is, above all, a human story, it may be best told in the form of imaginative literature. Despite the mountains of data about India, facts cannot instruct us in the mysteries of the human spirit; we need truth as well as facts, and literature's great contribution is its presentation of the truth of the human heart, a very different thing from a compilation of data. Because it arises from and speaks to emotions, because it deals with the spirit of man, because it delights as well as instructs, fiction can help us know India in deeper and broader ways than the reports of scholars and scientists. Dozens of books about early twentieth-century Indian conditions of class, race, climate, and history cannot replace the world of Mosque, Cave, and Temple created in a novel like E. M. Forster's Passage to India. As that book beautifully demonstrates, art creates its own kinds of perceptions and can capture a range and significance of life that no discursive essay in any discipline could possibly match. If experiential knowledge shares a place with conceptual knowledge, then books like A Passage to India can be at least as valuable to the student of India as even the most comprehensive scholarly study. This bibliography will lead the student to discover what literature can contribute to his understanding of the subject; he will find himself entertained as well as enlightened. According to Aristotle, philosophy teaches by precept and history by example; literature, he suggests, teaches by combining precept and example, a dictum that this bibliography bears out.

Of course, not every novel about India approaches the excellence of Forster's masterpiece, but a great many writers have portrayed the life of India with sensitivity and power. The great name that everyone associates with India is Kipling, who is not usually a favorite of sophisticated literary scholars. Whatever the judgment on Kipling, there is no doubt that his novels and tales of India are the work of a master storyteller inspired by the immense vitality of his subject. Many readers have been introduced at an early age to India by novels like Kim; there are worse teachers than Kipling's exciting and perceptive exploration of the relationship between a half-caste boy and a learned priest, dramatized against the panorama of Indian life. Similarly, competent writers like Louis Bromfield, Rumer Godden, and John Masters have written intelligently and entertainingly about India. But one of the great discoveries for any student using this work is the sense of exploring the unknown: most of the writers listed here are familiar only to the most diligent readers of specialized literature or are programmatically neglected by serious scholars and critics. If India has engendered a significant and useful literature, it has also engendered a stirring and copious subliterature.

The obvious appeal of India to the popular imagination should not be discounted or ignored. Secondary literature can sometimes instruct us in matters that masterpieces omit, providing us with information about the unusual, the curious, the special aspects of life that great art sometimes neglects. One of the strong points of this bibliography is Mr. Gupta's steadfast refusal to discriminate between great and not-so-great literature; by mingling both the profound and the popular, he gives us a full sense of the varieties of Indian experience. The majority of novels about India seem to belong to the category of popular fiction. Like the great master, Kipling, many writers in this volume are chiefly known as authors of adventure yarns and other kinds of popular entertainment: mystery fiction, detective stories, juvenile fiction, spy novels, historical novels, "inside" peeks at particularly unusual Indian customs--concubinage, thuggee, the more mystical kinds of religions. One is tempted to ask why there should be anything wrong with this kind of literature about India. The popular imagination, rather an elusive concept to define, has always been attracted by the various genres of subliterature and by exotic places; if the two are combined as in the innumerable Indian adventure, mystery, historical, and juvenile novels, a literature with considerable selling power results. If many writers about India are undeniably popular, so much the better. Generations of readers have learned of India from Henty, Kipling, A. E. W. Mason, Talbot Mundy, and others. The enduring impressions of their works have formed certain images of India and have shaped the conventions of colonial literature in general. Anyone who delights in With Clive in India or King--of the Khyber Rifles can learn something of what India meant to the colonial imagination and can absorb a little of the romance that inspired Britain's long love affair with the largest and most exciting territory in her great empire. Though the thrilling popular stories of India may provide an antiquated and prejudiced view of the nation and its history, they also re-create some of the magic, glamor, and romance of a turbulent, tragic, engrossing period in the history of both countries.

Somewhere in between the masterpiece and the work of entertainment lies another area of fiction about India, perhaps the most interesting of all, the ordinary, everyday, more or less domestic novel. This is the novel that deals with some particular events in a particular place and time, some normal characters and some normal relationships, which are, after all, the materials of the novel as we know it. These works are probably the most neglected and the most rewarding of all. They cannot be ignored any more than the popular entertainment or the masterpiece. These commonplace, unsensational works of fiction may be instructive initially by providing a comparison with both the great and the sensational novels of India: comparative analysis of patterns, conventions, and techniques can suggest ways in which the Indian novel evolves. It can show the

degree of influence of English fiction on the Indian novel in
English. Comparison of subject and theme can reveal the
important similarities and differences between the two bodies
of fiction, and perhaps indicate the degree of authenticity
and verisimilitude of each. If we wish to know the history
of British attitudes toward India, a great many familiar
works are available; if we wish to know Indian attitudes
toward India and Britain, however, this bibliography tells us
where to look. These ordinary works of fiction also help in
understanding Indian life in ways that no other literature can.
If we want to know something of the experience of growing
up in Bombay or Calcutta, of what it is like to be a Sikh or
a Hindu or a Parsee or a Moslem, of what some of the
daily activities of certain segments of Indian life are like,
or how it is to live in a specific region or point of time in
India, these novels can re-create something of those experiences for us. They may not be great literature, but they
provide us with the incessantly fascinating details of human
life in a place many miles from our homes and light years
distant from our own heritage. Whatever English literature
has given us, it is incapable of presenting comprehensibly
the Indian mind, which seems always to have baffled Englishmen; these novels may assist in understanding and repre-
senting whatever is meant by that concept, may give us
some picture of the humanity of India.

The possibilities for study that this bibliography
generates are manifold and fascinating. One obvious task
would be the categorization of various subgenres of the
Indian novel. Another, already mentioned, is the analysis
of works on the basis of shared techniques and patterns. A
third is the study of reciprocal influence among the various
categories: for example, it would be interesting to know to
what degree the "Indian Gothic" novels influence the serious
literature that follows them. A Passage to India, for in-
stance, is a highly regarded work of literature that contains
the stock materials of the more or less sensational novel
about India--a violent confrontation between East and West,
a presumed sexual assault, a mystery and a crime, even
a central and pervasive encounter with the supernatural,
the irrational forces of mysticism and visionary religion.
A fruitful inquiry could be conducted into the relationship of
the masterpiece to the sensational or the domestic novel of
India. Further comparisons between Indian and English
versions of the same experience suggest themselves; here,
again, not only the colonial experience but particular human
experiences may be enlightening. Why do Indian writers
also employ the detective story, the juvenile story, the

historical novel, the forms that have so frequently engaged their English counterparts? Do they imitate available English models, do they influence English fiction, do they find popular forms useful to their purpose?

Another, possibly more rewarding, study evolves from analysis of the thematic similarities of Indian and English fiction. A great many novels of India treat the subject of nostalgia, an obvious consequence of isolation and alienation. The displaced Englishman quite naturally looked back to the land he called "Home" (always, it seems, with a capital letter), yearning for his past, his native land, his family, all that he had left behind. Forster and others treat this subject by turns sympathetically and satirically: that notion of the Englishman dressing for dinner in the middle of some foreign jungle or some otherwise alien and inhospitable place turns out to be quite close to the truth. Hence, English literature about India presents those pathetic enclaves, those recreations of dear old Blighty amid the strangest surroundings; the pretense that everywhere was England is a staple of much of this fiction. As history progresses, so does the quality of the nostalgia: it begins to be a yearning for the good old days, when the Raj ruled with benevolent despotism and kept the Wogs in their place, when things were bolder, simpler, clearer, truer. And, of course, after Independence, this nostalgia is both intensified and generalized, a yearning for anything but the turmoil and vexation of the present. Curiously, the Indian novels, too, exemplify this nostalgia, frequently for the same objects: the pre-English past, the rule of the Raj, when everyone knew his place, the comparative serenity of almost any time but the present. Whether this nostalgia is a quality borrowed from English literature, a manifestation of the native Indian tradition, or simply a normal human expression of dissatisfaction with one's condition, as a subject it invites, like so many others, a serious and scholarly investigation.

One of the most common figures in all the varieties of fiction represented in this study is the true Anglo-Indian, the Eurasian; he appears in one form or another in countless works about India. This character, his life, his peculiar problems, his divided loyalties and conflicts, his tragic search for some sense of his own identity is continually shown in these novels; clearly the Eurasian is worth a study in himself. If India has not yet produced a William Faulkner to deal with the inevitable crisis of mixed blood or interracial love, it has produced scores of lesser writers who perceive the special and compelling problems of the Anglo-Indian. If interracial love can express the persistent hope for brotherhood in these novels, then the problem of mixed blood can imply the terrible complexities such love can create. Again, Kipling has in Kim provided a background for the special problems of mixed blood; John Masters deals with it sympathetically from a more mature standpoint in Bhowani Junction. The subject, a hackneyed one for both Indian and English novelists, nevertheless remains a worthwhile possibility for investigation.

Perhaps the most challenging study, which would require a learned and versatile scholar, would be an inquiry into the influence of native Indian forms on the English novel; whether the incorporation of Indian tradition in novels written in English is profound and informative is an important and fruitful question. The degree to which such forms influence the English novel itself is a corollary question that this bibliography can help to answer.

These subjects certainly do not exhaust the possibilities of Mr. Gupta's work; there are many more to be explored and investigated. This monumental bibliography introduces us to the richness of a largely neglected body of literature. It serves scholarship in several disciplines by adding to human knowledge, by providing a guide to particular areas of study, and by recording the existence of a substantial and fertile territory of the human imagination. It adds further to our knowledge by suggesting additional kinds of study. By enumerating the variety of works that India has inspired, this bibliography commemorates the thoughts, deeds, and aspirations of generations of men vastly different from one another. It is a kind of repository of the spirit, of the hopes and dreams of two great countries over a long and troubled span of years. Scholars should be most grateful for this work: it can be used imaginatively as a way of gaining what Whitman calls, "Passage . . . to primal thought," a "Passage to more than India!"

George Grella
University of Rochester

INTRODUCTION

The purpose of this bibliography is to list all, or nearly all, novels, tales and collections of short stories written by Indian or foreign writers and depicting some aspect of India. Most entries have been annotated.

Only those titles that were written after 1800 have been included. Fiction either originally written in English or translated into English has been included. Translations of classical or medieval Indian fiction written before 1800 have been excluded. However, new renderings or transcreations of traditional folk tales, short stories, and other fiction have been included on a selective basis. The same limitation applied to juvenile literature. It has not been possible to include those detective or mystery novels in which India appears merely in passing.

In the author index, entries of South Indian names have been made under the penultimate element of the compound name; for example, SIVASANKARA PILLAI, TAKAHAZI. For other Indian names the last element in the compound name has been used as the surname; for example, SINGH, KHUSH-WANT, unless no surname is clearly indicated; for example, PREMCHAND. Fiction published under a pseudonym has been entered under the pseudonym and not under the author's real name. In this respect I have followed the British Museum.

B. J. K.

AUTHOR INDEX

1 Anonymous. Adventurer in the Punjaub. Delhi: No publisher given, 1842.
   Exhibits excellent knowledge of the Sikh states.

2 _____. As the clock struck twenty. By S. M. C. Bombay: Miranda, 196-.

3 _____. Autobiography of an Indian army surgeon, or leaves turned down from a journal. London: Bentley, 1854.

4 _____. The brahmin's prophecy. By a lady. Bombay: No publisher given, 1875.

5 _____. Carnee, or the victim of Khodistan; a scene from military life in India. By A. R. M. London: Hamilton and Adams, 1861.
   Two army officers discover the Khonds and the rite of human sacrifice.

6 _____. Chandrahasa; an ancient Indian monarch. Madras: Foster, 1881.
   Describes the ideals of polity in ancient India.

7 _____. Character sketches. By C. P. S. N. Madras: Gopaul Naidu, 1898.
   From the collector to the peon.

8 _____. Childhood in India, or English children in the east. London: No publisher given, 1890.
   Mutiny.

9 _____. The confessions of Meajahn, darogah of police. By a Moffussilite. Calcutta: Wyman, 1869.
   Affrays between planters and zamindars.

10 _____. The disinterested nabob. London: No publisher given, 1785.

16

11   _____ . Durga-Das, the Rahtore. Bombay: Mac-
Millan, 1932.
    Rajput romance set in Aurangzeb's era.

12   _____ . The English in India and other sketches.
By a traveller. 2 vols. London: Longmans, 1828.
    Accomplice to murder falls in love with a gentle
inexperienced Indian girl, and escapes his enemies
by going to the Himalayas.

13   _____ . The flight of the arrow and other stories.
By the author of 'Lal Singh'. London: No publisher given, 1909.

14   _____ . Harrison of Pomabari, a tale of Assam.
By J. E. G. Calcutta: Newman, 1903.

15   _____ . Harry Fortescue, or the grave in India:
a story founded on facts. London: Griffith and
Farran, 1858.

16   _____ . How will it end. By the author of 'Willy
Morgan'. 2 vols. London: Charing Cross Co.,
1878.

17   _____ . In the Company's service. London:
W. H. Allen, 1883.
    Mutiny.

18   _____ . The Indian adventurer or history of Mr.
Vanneck. London: W. Lane, 1780.

19   _____ . The Indian heroine, being some incidents
of the sepoy revolt of 1857. Bombay: No publisher given, 1877.

20   _____ . The indigo planters. London: No publisher given, 1840.
    Two greedy whites in search of indigo destroy a
temple and rob a Hindu merchant.

21   _____ . Janardana. London: P. Welby, 1906.

22   _____ . Lotus: a psychological romance. By the
author of 'A New Marguerite'. London: Redway,
1888.

23   . Marriage mart or society in India. By an Indian officer. London: No publisher given, 1841.

24   . Maurice Dering, or the quadrilateral. London: Tinsley, 1869.
Mutiny. Fiancé of a girl murdered during the revolt comes to India and executes every Indian he meets.

25   . The Morlands: a tale of the Anglo-Indian life. By the author of 'Sleepy Sketches'. London: Low, 1888.

26   . The nabob at home. 3 vols. London: Colburn, 1842.

27   . The nabob's wife. 3 vols. London: Bentley, 1838.

28   . The orphan of Nepaul; a title of Hindustan. London: Saunders, 1840.

29   . Our picnic at Chordi. By B. C. A. A. Bombay: No publisher given, 1926.

30   . The perilous adventures of the knight Sir Tommy and his following: a true tale. By our domestic novelist. Bangalore: Columbian Press, 1871.

31   . Ramji: a tragedy of the Indian famine. London: Fisher Unwin, 1897.

32   . A romance of bureaucracy. By Alpha Beta. Allahabad: Wheller, 1893.

33   . A romance of Indian crime. By an Indian detective. London: No publisher given, 1885.

34   . Rose Clarendon: or the trials of true love. By a young Indian author. London: Bell, 1934.

35   . The Scribbleton papers: confessions of a Eurasian. London: No publisher given, 1840.

36   . The secret of the lamas. London: Cassell, 1889.

37   . Some Indian stories. By P. V. N.
     Madras: No publisher given, 1896.

38   . The timely retreat. By two sisters.
     London: Bentley, 1858.

39   . The true history of Zoa. London: S.
     Fisher, 1801.

40   . Two stories or mysteries of government
     service. By the author of 'My Autobiography by
     Juju'. Calcutta: No publisher given, 1921.

41   . Yadnamuh: a chapter of oriental life.
     London: Hatchard, 1850.

42   . Zohar, a tale of zennana life. By Taj.
     London: Methuen, 1912.

43 Abbas, Khwaja Ahmad. Ajanta. Bombay: Jaico,
    1962.

44   . The black sun and other stories. Bombay:
     Jaico, 1963.

45   . Blood and stones. Bombay: Hind Kitabs,
     1947.
        Communal riots in Bombay.

46   . Cages of freedom and other stories.
     Bombay: Hind Kitabs, 1952.

47   . Defeat for death: a story without names.
     Baroda: Padamja, 1944.

48   . Divided heart. New Delhi: Paradise,
     1968.

49   . Inqilab. Bombay: Jaico, 1955.
     A young Muslim through the nationalist move-
    ment; excellent picture of life at Aligarh, 1919-32.

50   . Maria. Delhi: Hind Pocket Books, 1970.
     Six men and a woman in nationalist struggle in
    Goa.

51 _____. Mera nam Joker. Delhi: Hind Pocket
Books, 1970.

52 _____. The most beautiful woman in the world.
New Delhi: Paradise, 1968.

53 _____. Not all lies. Delhi: Rajkamal, 1945.

54 _____. One thousand nights on a bed of stones and
other stories. Bombay: Jaico, 1957.

55 _____. Rice and other stories. Bombay: Kutub,
1947.
Outstanding stories of the author; cross section
of urban and rural society.

56 _____. Tomorrow is ours. Delhi: Rajkamal,
1946.
Love between two westernized Indians, World
War II.

57 _____. When night falls. Delhi: Hind Pocket
Books, 1968.

58 Abbott, Anstice. A girl widow's romance. London:
Religious Tract Society, 1920.
Written to interest English women in Indian affairs, and to ask them to encourage men for military
service in India.

59 _____. Indian idylls. London: Elliott Stock,
1911.
Marathi women under the influence of Christian
missionary activities. Collection of tales.

60 Abbott, Mary. The Beverlys: a story of Calcutta.
Chicago: McClurg, 1890.
Love and separation; army officer on various
missions while his girl lives in Calcutta.

61 _____. Officer's children. London: No publisher
given. c. 1890.

62 Abdullah, Achmed. My nine lives. London: Hurst
and Blackett, 1934.
Adventures of a half-Russian and half-Indian spy
in various parts of the world.

63   Ackerley, J. R. <u>Hindoo holiday.</u> London: Chatto
      and Windus, 1963.
             A masterpiece; gay satire on Indian princely
      order.

64   Acott, J. H.   <u>The tower of purity; a fictitious love</u>
      <u>story.</u> Bombay: C. Murphy, 1943.

65   Afghan, pseud. <u>Bahadur Khan, warrior.</u> London:
      Herbert Jenkins, 1928.

66   .   <u>The best Indian chutney--sweetened.</u>
      London: Herbert Jenkins, 1925.
             Collection of short stories.   Pathan life.

67   .   <u>Exploits of Asaf Khan.</u> London: Herbert
      Jenkins, 1922.
             Afghan leader who is both a paladin and a
      monster.

68   .   <u>The wanderings of Asaf.</u> London: Herbert
      Jenkins, 1923.

69   Agyeya (pseud. of S. H. Vatsyayna).   <u>To each his</u>
      <u>stranger.</u>   Trans. by author and Gordon C. Roader-
      mel. Delhi: Hind Pocket Books, 1967.
             Hindi novel in the existentialist tradition.

70   Ahmad, Q. Kazi.   <u>Random short stories.</u> Calcutta:
      Khyber, 1951.

71   Ainsworth, Oliver (pseud. of Henry Sharp).   <u>The</u>
      <u>devil's tower.</u> London: Faber and Gwyer, 1927.

72   Aiyar, R. P. <u>In the crimelight.</u> Bombay: Pearl, 1967.

73   Ali, Aamir. <u>Via Geneva.</u> Bombay: Pearl, 1967.

74   Ali, Ahmed. <u>Ocean of night.</u> London: Peter Owen,
      1964.
             Muslim life in Lucknow; superbly told.

75   .   <u>Twilight in Delhi.</u> London: Hogarth, 1940.
             Life and death in an upper class old Muslim
      family; superbly told.

76   Ali, Hassan (pseud. of Ranjee Shahani).   <u>The change-</u>
      <u>ling.</u> London: H. Joseph, 1933.

A boy loses his life looking for the message of
love and hope, away from traditional Hinduism.

77   Alington, Cyril Argentine. The nabob's jewel. London:
      Faber, 1953. Mystery.

78   Allard, Hafiz. Nigris: a tale of the Indian Mutiny;
      and Bismillah, or happy days in Cashmere. London:
      Allen, 1869.
      Two dusky Muslim women in love with white
      soldiers.

79   Allardyce, Alexander. The city of sunshine. 3 vols.
      London: Blackwood, 1877.
      Above average picture of Hindu life in upcountry
      Bengal.

80   Alroy, Lionel. Shut out the sun. London: Longmans,
      1955.
      A number of unhappy people in espionage in
      Calcutta.

81   Altaf, David. Khem Karan and other war stories.
      New Delhi: Army Educational Services, 1967.

82   Alvares, Eulalia. Short stories. Bombay: The Author,
      1965.

83   Amma, N. Balamani. Mother. Translated by Moor-
      koth Kumhappa and the author. Bombay: Interna-
      tional Book House, 1950.

84   Anand, Bolwant Singh. Cruel interlude. Bombay: Asia
      Publishing, 1961.
      Based on the massacre of the ill-fated Sargodha
      Kafla following India's partition.

85   Anand, Mulk Raj. Across the black waters. London:
      Cape, 1940.
      Tale of an Indian infantry battalion that goes to
      fight in Europe during the first world war; superb
      attention to details. Second part of a trilogy that
      begins with The village.

86   _____. All men are brothers. Same as The
      sword and the sickle.

87   _____. The barber's trade union and other stories.
          London: Cape, 1944.

88   _____. The big heart. London: Hutchinson, 1945.
          Community of coppersmiths in Amritsar.

89   _____. Coolie. London: Lawrence and Wishart,
          1936.
              Anand's first successful novel. Poignant story
          of a coolie from the Panjab Hills who works at
          various jobs in northern India.

90   _____. Death of a hero: epitaph for Moqbool
          Sherwani. Bombay: Kutub, 1963.
              Pakistani tribesmen capture a Kashmiri during
          the Kashmir war, 1947.

91   _____. Lajwanti and other stories. Bombay:
          Jaico, 1966.

92   _____. Lament on the death of a master of arts.
          Lucknow: Naya Sansar, 1939.
              White collar unemployment; the hero dies of con-
          sumption.

93   _____. Lost child and other stories. London:
          Allen, 1934.

94   _____. Morning face. Bombay: Kutub, 1968.
              Autobiographical novel continues Seven summers.

95   _____. The old man and the cow. Bombay: Kutub,
          1960.

96   _____. Power and darkness and other stories.
          Bombay: Jaico, 1959.

97   _____. Private life of an Indian prince. London:
          Hutchinson, 1953.
              A powerful diatribe against the princely order
          and its wasteful ways.

98   _____. Reflections on the golden bed and other
          stories. Bombay: Current Book House, 1953.

99   _____. The road. Bombay: Kutub Popular, 1961.
              Set in rural Panjab of the 1930's. A young un-
          touchable watches the landlord's son destroy his
          village.

100 _____. Seven summers: the story of an Indian
        childhood. London: Hutchinson, 1951.
            Autobiographical; memories of childhood in
        western Panjab prior to World War I; valuable for
        its picture of domestic life.

101 _____. The sword and the sickle. London: Jona-
        than Cape, 1942.
            Third in the trilogy that begins with The village.
        The hero has become involved in peasant struggles
        in present day Uttar Pradesh.

102 _____. Tractor and the corn goddess and other
        stories. Bombay: Thacker, 1947.

103 _____. Two leaves and a bud. London: Lawrence
        and Wishart, 1937.
            Lives of sahibs and coolies on an Assam tea
        plantation. There is no cruelty or indignity which
        the coolies do not suffer. Anand's second success-
        ful novel.

104 _____. The untouchable. London: Lawrence and
        Wishart, 1935.
            A day in the life of a sweeper in a north Indian
        city.

105 _____. The village. London: Jonathan Cape, 1939.
            Vivid picture of Panjab rural life prior to World
        War I. See comments on Across the black waters,
        and The sword and the sickle.

106 Anantanarayanan, Madaiayya. The silver pilgrimage.
        New York: Criterion Books, 1961.
            Picaresque romance set in ancient India.

107 Anderson, Ethel Louisa. Indian tales. Sydney:
        Australasian Publishing Company, 1948.
            Several stories dealing with various periods,
        sensitively written.

108 _____. Little ghosts. London: Angus and Robert-
        son, 1959.
            Stories; some taken from Indian tales.

109 Anderson, Kenneth. Fires of passion. Bombay: Jaico,
        1969.

110 _____. Tales of Man Singh, king of Indian dacoits.
Bombay: Jaico, 1961.
Based on the life of famous Indian dacoit who
died in 1955.

111 Andrews, M. Henniker. An Indian mystery. London:
Lynwood, 1913.
Mystery dealing with super magical Brahmins
and their secret temple.

112 Anstey, F. (pseud. of Thomas Anstey Guthrie). Baboo
Hari Bungasho Jabberjee, B. A. London: Dent,
1897.
The Bengali is shown to take perverse pride in
his lack of courage.

113 _____. A bayard from Bengal, being some account
of the career of Chunder Bindabun Bhosh. London,
Methuen, 1902.
Ridiculous picture of Bengali babu; Bengalis are
shown as childish and effeminate.

114 _____. A fallen idol. London: Elder, 1886.
The first part deals with Hinduism and Jainism.

115 Anthon, Rosa Reinhardt. Stories of India. London:
Heinemann, 1906.
Spiritual and romantic stories, gathered "in out-
line from an authoritative teacher of Hindu wisdom."

116 Anthony, J. (pseud. of R. B. Beckett). The story of
Hassan. London: Nisbet, 1928.
Good descriptions of Muslim life, and how
Muslims observe the English.

117 _____. The story of Maryam: a continuation of
the story of Hasan told by Hasan. London: Nisbet,
1930.
Good descriptions of the zennana.

118 Arnold, William Delafield. Oakfield, or fellowship in
the East. 2 vols. London: Longmans, 1854.
A significant novel of the mid-nineteenth century.
The hero, a young Oxford graduate, brought up in
strict ideas of duty, is revolted by the dissipation
of English military and civilian officials in India.
Includes an excellent account of the battle of Chil-
lianwallah, 1849.

119   Arora, Shirley L.   What then, Raman?   London:
       Blackie, n. d.
             Sensitive story of a schoolboy.   For young adults.

120   Asha.   Promotion.   Secundrabad: Good New Literature
       Center, 1956.

121   Ashby, Philip.   The mad rani and other sketches of
       Indian life and thought.   London: . Routledge, 1923.
             Sketches drawn from the author's twenty-five
       years residence in India designed to show that the
       Indian mind is different from that of the West.

122   Askew, Alice and Claude.   The Englishwoman.   Lon-
       don: Cassell, 1912.
             English girl marries an Indian barbarian prince
       and is later united to her true lover.

123   Atkinson, George Franklin.   Curry and rice.   London:
       Day, 1859.
             Sketches of English life in Bengal.

124   Atkinson, Hugh.   The pink and the brown.   London:
       Gollancz, 1957.
             Race relations in independent India; story of a
       tragic love between a European man and an Indian
       girl in Bombay; excellent picture of Indian mob
       violence.

125   Aurora, Jagdish.   Senorita said.   Banaras: Swati
       Publications, 1964? 65.

126   Austin, Herbert Henry.   Gun running in the Gulf and
       other adventures.   London: John Murray, 1926.

127   _____.   Some rambles of a sapper (chiefly in
       India).   London: John Murray, 1928.

128   Ayscough, J.   (pseud. of F. B. D. Bickerstaffe-
       Drew)   On Kali's shoulder.   London: Devonport, 1897.
             Indian temple gems and English greed.

       Ayyar, C. Subramania.   See Guru-Kumara.

129   Ayyar, H. R.   Sringaramanjari, the courtesan who in-
       flamed love.   Bombay: Jaico, 1961.
             Based on Bhoja's famous story; set in ancient
       India.

Bahadur, Umrao. See Umrao Bahadur.

130   Baig, Tara Ali. The moon in Rahu. Bombay: Asia
      Publishing, 1969.
      Fictionalised account of the Bhowal Sanaysi case,
      1930-40.

131   Baillie, Peter. Chindwin's mission. London: Brown,
      Watson, 1960.
      Chin hills; Japanese invasion.

132   Bain, Francis William. The Indian stories of F. W.
      Bain. 13 vols. London: Riccardi Press, 1913-20.
      Traditional Indian stories and folk-tales retold;
      Hindu attitude towards life and death; romantic ap-
      preciation of Hindu femininity.

133   Baker, Amy Josephine. The good man's wife. London:
      John Long, 1927.

134   _____. Leaf in the wind. London: John Long,
      1935.
      An English girl's happiness is destroyed when
      she goes to India with her husband.

135   _____. Six merry summers. London: John Long,
      1930.
      A child-like novel about six cheery people; Indian
      background is weak.

136   Baker, Olaf. Shasta of the wolves. London: Harrap,
      1921.
      Graphic tale of a little Indian boy lost in the
      forest who makes his home among the wolves.

137   Bala, Krishna. The love of Kusuma, an eastern love
      story. London: Werner Laurie, 1910.
      Unconvincing minutiae of Indian life.

138   Balakrishna Mudaliyar, A. The reminiscences of a
      retired Hindu official containing short hints on Hindu
      philosophy. Madras: No publisher given, 1905.

139   Balakrishnan, Purasu. The gold bangle and other
      stories. Bombay: Bharatiya Vidya Bhavan, 1966.
      28 stories; mostly translated from Tamil.

140   Baldwin, J. R.   Indian gup: untold stories of the In-
      dian Mutiny.   London: Beeman, 1896.

141   Baldwin, Olivia A.   Sita, a story of child-marriage
      fetters.   New York: Revell, 1911.
      Well told story of the zennana activities of a
      memsahib in an orphanage; girl converts to Chris-
      tianity to evade child marriage.

142   Bali, Amar Nath.   Laughs at life.   Delhi: Indian Book
      Depot, 1967.

143   Ballinger, Bill S.   The forty-nine days of death.   New
      York: Sherbourne, 1969.
      A Buddhist swami instructs a wounded white man
      in meeting death; a novel of mysticism.

144   Balu, V.   Day dreams.   Mysore: Nanumal, c. 1964.

145   Bambi, R. P.   The crusaders of Tibet.   Dalhousie:
      Khampa Pocket Books, 1960.

146   Bamburg, Lilian.   Beads of silence.   London: Selwyn
      and Blount, 1926.
      A sacred string of Indian amulets disappears.

147   _____.   The riddle of the dead.   London: Wells
      Gardner, 1930.
      Detective story.

148   Banaji, M. M.   Sublime though blind: a tale of Parsi
      life.   Bombay: No publisher given, 1922.

149   Banerjea, S. B.   The adventure of Mrs. Russell.
      London: Stockwell, 1909.
      Five mystery stories.

150   _____.   Indian detective stories.   London: Gay and
      Hancock, 1911.

151   _____.   Indian tales, etc.   London: Humphrey
      Milford, 1926.

152   _____.   Misunderstood and other sketches of Indian
      life.   Calcutta: S. Bandyapadya, 1907.

153   _____.   Tales of Bengal.   London: Longmans, 1910.

17 sketches with solid ethnographic details.

154   Banerjee, Manik. Boatman of the Padma. Bombay:
      Kutub, 1948.
      East Bengal river village life by a Marxist.

155   _____. The primeval and other stories. New
      Delhi: Peoples Publishing, 1958.

156   Banerjee, Samarendra Nath. Step mother. New Delhi:
      Hind Pocket Books, 196-.

157   Banerjee, Tarasankar. Epoch's end. Translated
      from Bengali by Hirendranath Mookherjee. Calcutta:
      Mitralaya, 1945.
      Calcutta during 1942-43; city under air raids,
      famine and pestilence; disintegration of the old
      social order. Sensitive.

158   _____. The eternal lotus. Translated from Ben-
      gali. Calcutta: Purvasa Ltd., 1945.

159   _____. The judge. Translated by Sudhansu Mohan
      Banerjee. Delhi: Hind Pocket Books, 1947.

160   _____. The Temple Pavilion. Translation of
      Ganadevata by Lila Ray. Bombay: Pearl, 1969.

161   Banerji, Bibhutibhushan. Pather panchali. Trans-
      lated by T. W. Clark and Tarapada Mukherji.
      Bloomington: Indiana University Press, 1970.
      Immortalised by Satyajit Ray in the movie of the
      same title.

162   Banks, Polan. Maharajah. New York: Dodd Mead,
      1962.
      An absentee Indian ruler; his westernised bride;
      her American lover; his French mistress; and his
      mother who refuses accession to India and causes a
      bloody strife. Excellent portrait of the gaudy
      Indian durbar.

163   Bannisdale, Vane Erskine (pseud. of Portal Vane
      Erskine). Quest and conquest. London: Longmans,
      1929.
      Romance of an Irish sailor in eighteenth-century
      India.

164   Bareh, Hamlet.   Khasi fables and folk tales.   Calcutta:
      K. L.   Mukhopadhyay, 1970.

165   Barkataki, Satyendranath.   The grand Panjandrum and
      other stories.   Translated from the Assamese.   Cal-
      cutta: Modern Press, 1961.

166   _____.   Tribal folk tales of Assam.   Gauhati:
      Publications Board, 1970.

167   Barker, Dalgairns Arundel.   The great leviathan.
      London: John Lane, 1920.
      Contains "The glory of God" with an excellent
      description of Hardwar.

168   _____.   The rani's dominion.   London: Hutchinson,
      1926.
      Life in less pleasant parts of Bombay, and in-
      trigues in a Central Indian state are superbly drawn.

169   Barnby, Adeline.   A tropical romance.   London: Mur-
      ray and Evenden, 1920.
      An English girl goes to India to join her be-
      trothed and finds herself involved in court intrigues
      in an Indian state.

170   Barrass, Godfrey.   The elephant.   A satirical work on
      Indian political life.   Bombay: C. Murphy, 1946.

171   Barret, George.   Far away from home.   Bombay:
      Thacker, 1942.
      Impressions of life and misery in Bombay. Poor.

172   _____.   Fortythree years: Jayant and Tara.   Bom-
      bay: Thacker, 1944.
      First four decades of the twentieth century in the
      life of an Indian.

173   Basil, Martin.   Goodbye India.   London: Jackson, 1964.

174   Basu, Baren.   The recruit.   Bombay: Peoples Pub-
      lishing, 1954.
      Translation of Rangrut.   A Bengali in Indian
      army during World War II.

175   Basu, Manoje.   The beauty.   Translated by Sachindra
      Lal Ghosh from the Bengali novel Rupavati.   Bom-
      bay: Jaico, 1969.

176 _____. The forest goddess. Translated by
      Barindra Nath Das from the Bengali novel Jalajanga.
      Bombay: Asia Publishing, 1961.
      Bengal river country.

177 _____. Trappings of gold. Delhi: Hind Pocket
      Books, 1968.

178 Basu, Romen. A house full of people. Calcutta:
      Navana, 1968.
      Three generations of joint family in Bengal.

179 Basu, Subodh. The city of new moghuls. Calcutta:
      S. C. Bose, 1947.
      The city is New Delhi; the characters are trans-
      planted Bengalis; the heroine is a student in a
      fashionable school for girls.

180 Bates, Herbert Ernest. The jacaranda tree. London:
      M. Joseph, 1949.
      Japanese invasion of Burma brings into close
      proximity a number of people who normally had
      little contact with each other.

181 _____. The purple plain. London: M. Joseph,
      1947.
      War-time experiences of R. A. F. on the India-
      Burma theater.

182 _____. The scarlet sword. London: M. Joseph,
      1950.
      A refugee from East Pakistan and an Indian
      swami meet.

183 Batley, Dorothy Sibella. Bengali schooldays: a tale.
      London: Society for the Propagation of Christian
      Knowledge, n. d.

184 _____. The bridegroom secret. London: Zenith
      Press, 1949.

185 _____. Chand's little sisters. London: Central
      Board of Missions, 1920.

186 _____. David's bond. London: Zenith Press, 1935.

187 _____. Gems from the mine. London: Church of
      England Zennana Mission Society, 1929.

188 _____. The grey squirrel: a story founded on Indian myth. London: Zenith Press, 1947.

189 _____. The kamini bush: a story of Bengal. London: Church Missionary Society, 1925.

190 _____. The priceless jewel. London: Church of England Zennana Mission Society, 1925.

191 _____. Romoni's daughter: a story of India. London: Zenith Press, 1933.

192 _____. Shorna's day: the story of a Bengali child. London: Zenith Press, 1947.

193 _____. The taming of Ambo. London: Society for the Propagation of Christian Knowledge, 1924.

194 _____. Topsy's day: the story of a Bengali child. London: Society for the Propagation of Christian Knowledge, 1922.

195 _____. The two shilling baby. London: Zenith Press, 1936.

196 Bax, Arthur Nesham. The story of Joan Greencroft. London: Mills and Boon, 1912.
     Early 19th century Anglo-Indian life.

197 Baxter, Gregory (pseud. of John Sillar Matheson Ressich and Eric Debonzie). Death strikes at six bells. London: E. Benn, 1930.
     Theft of jewels in Kohatistan resolved after several murders. The authors may have written other mysteries with Indian setting.

198 Baxter, Walter. The image and the search. London: Heinemann, 1953.
     Moral collapse of a highly sensual girl after the death of her husband during the war.

199 _____. Look down in mercy. London: Heinemann, 1951.
     Slow degradation of a young British officer who betrays all his beliefs.

200 Bayley, Victor. City of fear. London: R. Hale, 1939.

201 _____. Dangerous derelict.   London: R. Hale,
      1941.

202 _____. Dynamite.   London: R. Hale, 1940.

203 _____. Frontier fires.   London: R. Hale, 1937.

204 _____. House of hatred.   London: R. Hale, 1939.

205 _____. Indian artifex.   London: R. Hale, 1939.

206 _____. Khyber contraband.   London: R. Hale,
      1938.

207 _____. Liquid fury.   London: Jarrolds, 1936.

208 _____. Northwest mail.   London: R. Hale, 1939.

209 _____. Pathan treasure.   London: R. Hale, 1938.

210 _____. Underground treasure.   London: R. Hale,
      1944.
      Secret service novels.

211 Beal, H. E. Indian ink. London: Harrap, 1954.
      Charming story of an Indian clerk who manages
      to earn a fortune on the side.

212 Beaman, Ardern Arthur Hulme. At government house.
      London: Mills and Boon, 1926.
      Kiplingesque account of upcountry club life.

213 Bechhofer, Carl Eric. The brahmin's treasure.
      London: Mills and Boon, 1923.
      Englishman caught between oriental occultism and
      western love.

    Beck, Eliza Louise Moresby. See Lily Adams Beck.

214 Beck, Lily Adams (pseud. of Eliza Louise Moresby
      Beck). Dreams and delights. London: E. Benn,
      1932.
      Indian spirituality.

215 _____. The house of fulfilment. London: Fisher
      Unwin, 1927.
      Chinese traveller in search of Hindu yoga and
      Buddhism.

216   _____.   The ninth vibration and other stories.
         London: Fisher Unwin, 1928.

217   _____.   The openers of the gate.   New York: Cos-
         mopolitan, 1930.

218   _____.   Perfume of the rainbow and other stories.
         London: E. Benn, 1931.

219   _____.   The splendour of Asia.   London: Collins,
         1927.
              Buddha and Buddhism.

220   _____.   The way of stars.   London: Collins, 1926.
         Mysticism of the east and Bolshevik influence.

         Beckett, R. B.   See J. Anthony.

221   Beckett, Ursula A.   In extenuation of Sybella.   London:
         Stanley Paul, 1910.
              Extravagant English girl goes to India with her
         widowed aunt.

222   Beckford, William.   Vathek.   London: P. Allan, 1930.
              Vague and ludicrous descriptions of India.

223   Bedi, Kishan Singh.   The fear of retribution.   Chandi-
         garh: No publisher given, 1970.

224   Bedi, Rajinder Singh.   I take this woman.   Translated
         by Khushwant Singh.   Delhi: Hind Pocket Books, 1967.
              A prizewinning novel of poverty, widowhood, and
         half-sensuous half-spiritual love between a girl and
         her brother-in-law.

225   Beercroft, Eric C.   Indian interlude.   Bombay:
         Thacker, 1944.
              English lieutenant adrift in India.

226   Begbie, Arundel.   The real India.   London: Lincoln
         William, 1934.
              Virtues of British rule.

227   Bell, Eva Mary.   The foreigner.   London: Hodder and
         Stoughton, 1928.
              An Irish adventurer and his affair with Begum
         Sumroo.

228 _____. Happiness. London: Hodder and Stoughton,
     1916.
        Captain turns into clergyman.

229 _____. Hot water. London: Hodder and Stoughton,
     1929.
        A parliamentry commission goes into India and
     learns more about her than the civil servants on the
     spot.

230 _____. Jean, a halo and some circles. London:
     Hodder and Stoughton, 1926.
        Life in Quetta; the empire, says Mrs. Bell, owes
     a deep gratitude to suffering and infrivolous
     Englishwomen in India.

231 _____. Safe conduct. London: Hodder and
     Stoughton, 1927.
        Simla; powerful men and influential women at work.

232 _____. Those young married people. London:
     Hodder and Stoughton, 1926.

     Also see John Travers.

233 Bellew, Francis John. Memoirs of a griffin: or a
     cadet's first year in India. 2 vols. London: W. H.
     Allen, 1843.

234 Benophul (pseud. of Balaichand Mukherji). Betwixt
     dream and reality. Translated from Bengali.
     Calcutta: Alpha Beta, 1965.
        Partition of Bengal and its tragic effect on a
     Hindu family.

235 _____. Bhuvan Shome. Translated from Bengali by
     Lila Ray. Delhi: Hind Pocket Books, 1970.

236 Beresford, Leslie. The second rising. London: Hurst
     and Blackett, 1910.
        Anarchist and socialist movements in Bengal dur-
     ing Bengal's partition, 1905.

237 Berry, John. Flight of the white crows. New York:
     Macmillan, 1962.
        Short stories mainly concerning western charac-
     ters coming to grips with Indian mysticism and cul-
     ture.

238 _____. Krishna fluting. New York: Macmillan,
        1959.
        Half-Indian half-Philadelphia-Quaker, half-poet,
        half-man of action must rid a Himalayan village of
        a man-eating python which has terrorised the Quaker
        school.

239 Beschi, Constanzo Guiseppe. The adventures of the
        Gooroo Noodle. Translated by Benjamin Babington.
        Allahabad: Panini Office, 1915.
        Story written about 1730 by an Italian friar.

240 Besemeres, John Daly. No actress: a stage door
        keeper's story. London: Effingham, Wilson. 1870.
        English girl in India.

241 Best, James William. The marked man eater, a
        jungle romance founded on fact. London: Witherby,
        1934.
        Excellent ethnological descriptions of the Bagais
        of Central India.

242 Betham, G. K. The story of a dacoity and the Lolapur
        week: an upcountry sketch. London: W. H. Allen,
        1893.

        Bethell, Leonard Arthur. See Pousse Cailloux.

243 Bevan, C. Elnith. A collection of ghosts: eleven In-
        dian fantasies. Amersham: Morland, 1920.

244 Bezbaroa, Lakshmi Nath. Tales of a grandfather from
        Assam. Bangalore: Indian Institute of Culture,
        1955.

245 Bhadur, K. P. The story of Rama. Allahabad: Indian
        Press, 1962. Ramayana retold for the small fry.

246 Bhaduri, Satinath. The vigil. Translated from Bengali
        by Lila Ray. Bombay: Asia Publishing, 1965.
        Impact of the Quit India movement of 1942 upon a
        Bengali family of stern Gandhian father, his tradi-
        tionalist wife; and their idealistic and courageous
        son.

247 Bhagwat, Durga Nath. Romance in sacred lore: twenty-
        two stories. Allahabad: Kitab Mahal, 1946.

248   Bharadwaj, Ravuri. Phantomy Quintette and other
      stories. Translated by Purush. Hyderabad: India
      Grandha Mala, 1970.

249   Bharucha, Perin. The fire worshippers. Bombay:
      Strand, 1968.
      Parsi life.

250   Bhaskara Rao, K. Candle against the wind. Banga-
      lore: No publisher given, 1963.

251   _____. Yachts, hamburgers and a Hindu: a sum-
      mer escapade. Bangalore: The Author, 1962.

252   Bhattacharjee, Jyotsma. Shadows in the sunshine.
      Calcutta: Alpha Beta, 1965.

253   Bhattacharya, Basudeb. The saffron veil. Nyack:
      Prana Press, 1953.

254   Bhattacharya, Bhabani. A goddess named gold. New
      York: Crown, 1960.
      Tragicomic novel of a village girl who can turn
      copper into gold, and the enterpreneurs who seek to
      manufacture good deeds for the miracle to take
      place.

255   _____. He who rides a tiger. New York: Crown,
      1954.
      A Bengali blacksmith caught up in the era of
      famine becomes a Brahmin and the lord of a temple.

256   _____. Music for Mohini. New York: Crown, 1952.
      Calcutta bred girl marries an unrefined village
      boy.

257   _____. Shadow from Ladakh. New York: Crown,
      1966.
      American trained engineer seeks to dispossess a
      Gandhian colony which believes in nonviolence and
      cottage industry. The colony stands firm in the
      face of Chinese invasion.

258   _____. So many hungers. London: Gollancz, 1947.
      Bengal famine during World War II.

259   _____. Steel hawk and other stories. Delhi: Hind

Pocket Books, 1968.

260   Bhondi, O. S. Man and God. Bombay: Raj Ratan
        Press, 1970.

        Bickerstaffe-Drew, F. B. D. See J. Ayscough.

261   Birla, Lashmi Niwas. Folk tales from Rajasthan.
        Bombay: Asia Publishing, 1964.

262   _____. Sultan and Nihalde. Calcutta: Grantham,
        1964.
        Historical romance set in the time of Partihar
        rule.

263   Bishop, Constance E. The moon slave. London:
        Heath Cranton, 1920.

264   _____. The seventh wave and other stories. Lon-
        don: Washbourne, 1913.

265   _____. A vision splendid. London: Heath Cranton,
        1917.

266   _____. The wine of sorrow. London: Heath
        Cranton, 1921.
        Disparaging sketch of Anglican missionary life in
        India.

267   Biswas, Anil Chandra. Stories of Indian life. New
        Delhi: Amrit, 1964.

268   _____. Through sunlight and gloom. New Delhi:
        Amrit, 1964.

269   _____. Trials of glory. New Delhi: Amrit, 1966.
        Indian freedom struggle, 1942.

270   Biswas, Karali Kanta. Stories of Bengal. Calcutta:
        Purvasa, 1944.

271   Biswas, Subodh. Glare in gloom. Calcutta: Bhowani-
        pore Press, 1962.

272   Blair, Hamish. Governor Hardy. London: Blackwood,
        1931.
        Hero of the Mutiny turns his attention to malad-
        ministration in Bengal.

273   _____. Nineteen fiftyseven. London: Blackwood,
       1930.
           The centenary of the Mutiny brings collapse of the
       Raj and its rescue by an English hero.

274   Blaker, Richard. Geoffery Castleton, passenger.
       London: Cape, 1923.
           A tourist clerk escorts a lady to Russia. The
       novel has flashbacks on India.

275   _____. Scabby Dichson. London: Hodder and
       Stoughton, 1927.
           A lonely English boy at a boarding school in
       northern India.

276   Blanch, Lesley. Nine tiger man: a tale of a low be-
       haviour in high places. New York: Atheneum, 1965.
           Titled English lady and her maid fall in love with
       a visiting Rajput prince and end up in his harem.
       Entertaining.

277   Bond, Ruskin. My first love and other stories. Bom-
       bay: Pearl, 1968.

278   _____. The neighbour's wife and other stories.
       Madras: Higginbothams, 1967.

279   _____. The room on the roof. London: Deutsch,
       1956.
           An English boy runs away from home to indulge
       in low level Indian life.

280   _____. Strange men, strange places. Bombay:
       Pearl, 1969.

281   Bonnell, Dorothy. She wore a star. New York:
       Messner, 1964.
           A Quaker girl in service to India. For young
       adults.

282   Booz, Elisabeth Benson. The seal of Jai. New York:
       Macmillan, 1968.
           Children's story.

283   Boozer, Celina Luzanne (pseud.) Heritage of Buddha:
       the story of Siddhartha Gautama. New York: Philo-
       sophical Library, 1953.

284   Bose, B. An acre of green grass. London: Long-
      mans, n. d.

285   Bose, Irene. Totaram, the story of a village boy in
      India. New York: Macmillan, 1933.
          For young adults.

286   Bothwell, Jean. Dancing princess. New York: Har-
      court, Brace, 1965.
          Temple theft solved by an Indian princess.

287   _____. Defiant bride. New York: Harcourt, Brace,
      1969.
          16th-century India; girl resists arranged marriage.

288   _____. The emerald clue. New York: Harcourt,
      Brace, 1961.
          A young girl rebels against traditional way of life.

289   _____. Little boat boy: a story of Kashmir. New
      York: Harcourt, Brace, 1956.

290   _____. Men and monsoon. London: Chatto and
      Windus, 1962.

291   _____. American title: Cobras, cows and courage.

292   _____. The missing violin. New York: Harcourt,
      Brace, 1959.

293   _____. Mystery at the house of the fish. New
      York: Harcourt, Brace, 1968.

294   _____. Omen for a princess. New York: Abelard-
      Schuman, 1963.
          Story of Princess Jahanara, seventeenth century.

295   _____. The promise of the rose. New York: Har-
      court, Brace, 1958.

296   _____. The red scarf. New York: Harcourt,
      Brace, 1962.

297   _____. Ride, Zarina, ride. New York: Harcourt,
      Brace, 1966.
          Eighteen-year-old Zarina meets with adventure in
      sixteenth-century India.

298 _____. Ring of fate. New York: Harcourt, Brace,
      1957.
      Young Muslim girl in Panjab is in love.

299 _____. Romany girl. London: Harcourt, Brace,
      1964.
      Novel of modern India, and of a gypsy girl.

300 _____. Search for a golden bird. New York:
      Harcourt, Brace, 1956.
      Search for a kidnapped cousin in India of 1946.

301 _____. The silver mango tree. New York: Har-
      court, Brace, 1960.
      An American girl in India must choose between
      an Indian prince and an American teacher.

302 _____. White fawn of Phalera. New York: Har-
      court, Brace, 1963.
      An American becomes a nurse in a missionary
      hospital in Rajasthan.
      Miss Bothwell's novels are for young adults, ages
      14 and up.

303 Bowlong, Colonel (pseud.) Black prince and other
      stories. London: Lawrence, 189-.

304 _____. Bluff. Allahabad: Wheeler, 1922.
      The fort of Simghur is held during the Mutiny by
      Bowlong against Indian onslaught.

305 _____. Told in the den. Allahabad: Wheeler,
      1922.
      Superhuman military adventures of the British.

306 _____. Told in the verandah. Allahabad: Pioneer,
      1922.
      Military adventures; autobiographical musings.

307 Boxwallah (pseud.) The leopard's leap. London: A.
      Melrose, 1919.
      A married woman is seduced by an Indian army
      officer who is also a murderer.

308 Bradley, Shelland. The adventures of an A. D. C.
      London: John Lane, 1910.
      The A. D. C. of a lieutenant governor at a hill

station sketches the lives of those who frequent the
Government House.

309   _____. An American girl at the durbar.   London:
       John Lane, 1912.
       The Delhi durbar of 1911.

310   _____. An American girl in India.   English edition
       of the above.

311   _____. The doings of Berengaria.   Allahabad:
       Pioneer, 1902.
       Station life.

312   _____. Fifty.   London: John Lane, 1927.
       European spiritedness, Indian spinelessness, and
       Eurasian chicanery. An English knight goes to
       India to break up the engagement of his blue-blood
       nephew to a Eurasian girl.

313   _____. More adventures of an A. D. C.   London:
       John Lane, 1915.

314   _____. The sacred crocodile.   London: John
       Murray, 1927.
       Tales of India.

315   Bray, Claude Arthur. Randall Devenant: a tale of the
       Mahrattas.   London: F. Warne, 1892.
       Battle of Panipat, 1761.

316   Brayne, Frank Lugard. Socrates in an Indian village.
       London: Oxford University Press, 1929.
       Socratic arguments with Indian villagers about the
       social evils which prey upon them. A superb novel.

317   _____. Socrates persists in India.   London: Oxford
       University Press, 1932.
       Likewise.

318   Brereton, Frederick Sadlier. A hero of Lucknow: a
       tale of the Indian Mutiny.   London: Blackie, 1905.

319   _____. Jones of the 64th: a tale of the battles of
       Assaye and Laswarie.   London: Blackie, 1907.
       Wellesley crushes the Marathas.

320   _____. With Roberts to Candahar: a tale of the
       third Afghan war. London: Blackie, 1906.
           All these novels are for children.

321 Broker, Gulabdas Harjivandas. Of life and love: short
       stories. Bombay: Bharatiya Vidya Bhavan, 1966.

322 Bromfield, Louis. Night in Bombay. London: Cassell,
       1940.
           A reformed playboy arrives in Bombay and meets
       his former wife and a college friend doing social
       work in India. Excellent portrait of Indian poverty
       and degradation.

323   _____. The rains came: a novel of modern India.
       London: Cassell, 1937.
           The efforts to improve the level of life in an In-
       dian state. Most characters are two dimensional
       and flat.

324 Brown, Andrew Cassels. Dark dealing. London:
       Methuen, 1930.
           An old English country house in an eerie atmos-
       phere created by an Indian fakir. World wide con-
       spiracy to liberate India from the British yoke is
       also thrown in.

325 Brown, Charles Hilton. Dictators limited. London:
       Allen and Unwin, 1923.
           Life of a civil servant in a lonely station of
       South India.

326   _____. Dismiss. London: Methuen, 1923.
           Race relations and nationalism through the eyes of
       a British official stationed in South India.

327   _____. Glory's children. New York: Knopf, 1937.
           A novel of striking craftsmanship depicting the
       history of three generations of a Scotch family.

328   _____. Locust flood. London: G. Bles, 1937.
           Romance set in South India.

329   _____. Maya: some more South Indian stories.
       Calcutta: Art Press, 1937.

330   _____. One virginity: a novel set in India. Bombay:
       Jaico, 1960.

331   _____. Potter's clay. London: Simpkin Marshall,
       1927.
       Very convincing stories; South India.

332   _____. Susanna. London: Allen and Unwin, 1926.
       An English girl rebels against her provincial
       background and marries a planter in South India.

333   _____. Torteval. London: G. Bles, 1938.
       An orphan in India and in Scotland.

334   Brown, Joel David. Glimpse of a stranger. New
       York: Morrow, 1968.
       American playwright, resident in London, goes to
       India to overcome his spiritual malaise, and be-
       comes an acolyte to a lovely and mysterious French-
       woman and her husband turned Hindu swami.

335   Brown, John (pseud.) Mr. and Mrs. John Brown at
       home. Allahabad: Wheeler, 1893.

336   Brown, John Cave. Incidents of Indian life. London:
       Dickinson, 1895.
       Stories of various Indo-British wars, including the
       Mutiny.

337   Brown, Michael. Tales of the trader. Bombay:
       Thacker Spink, 1943.

338   Bruce, Henry. The bride of Shiva. London: John
       Long, 1920.
       An English doctor falls in love with a Eurasian
       girl who is a devadasi to Shiva. Race riot.

339   _____. The Eurasians. London: John Long, 1913.
       Discrimination of Eurasians by the pucca sahibs.

340   _____. The native wife, or Indian love and
       anarchism. London: John Long, 1909.
       The influence of Asian elements on European life
       style.

341   _____. The residency, an Indian novel. London:
       John Long, 1914.
       An Englishwoman, later found out to be a Eura-
       sian, has passion for a raja.

342 _____. The song of surrender. London: John
Long, 1915.
Another Eurasian girl in love with a Hindu raja.

343 _____. The temple girl. London: John Long, 1919.
A missionary saves a Eurasian girl from becom-
ing a devadasi.

344 _____. The wonder mist. London: John Long,
1917.
A Eurasian girl must be rescued from a rock
bound castle fortress where she is being kept by a
Maratha prince.

345 Buchan, John. The half hearted. London: Houghton,
1900.
A few superficial sections on Kashmir and Afghan
frontier.

346 Buchan, William de L'Aigle. Kumari. London: Duckworth, 1955.
India of the 1930's through the eyes of a detached,
liberal English traveller, and his two great loves:
the first a sophisticated English girl in Calcutta, the
other a shy Indian girl in Assam hills. A book of
great beauty.

347 Buck, Pearl Sydenstricker. Come, my beloved. New
York: John Day, 1953.
Three generations of an American family in India.
The grandson goes to India to prevent his daughter
from marrying an Indian doctor.

348 _____. Mandala. New York: John Day, 1970.
Beliefs of a maharaja and his maharani affect
their marriage and the Americans and the English
surrounding them: the maharaja is infatuated with
a foot-loose American girl, the maharani with an
English priest. The climax is the death of the
maharaja's son during the Sino-Indian war.

349 Budden, John Austin. The further adventures of Jungle
John. London: Longmans, 1929.
Hero gets pneumonia in England and is hurried
back to India where his strength is restored.

350 _____. Jungle John. London: Longmans, 1927.

Both these are children's stories set in north
Indian jungles.

351   Burn, Irene.   The border line.   London: Chapman and
      Hall, 1916.
      Dangers of mixed marriage between English and
      Eurasians.

352   _____.   The unforgiving mute.   London: Fisher
      Unwin, 1913.

353   _____.   The unknown steersman.   London: Fisher
      Unwin, 1912.
      An English girl in India to find love goes through
      Indian glare, dust and strain.   Excellent sketch of a
      purdah party.

354   Burt, Michael.   The case of the laughing Jesuit.
      London: Ward, Lock, 1948.
      Mystery.

355   _____.   Catch 'em alive.   London: Chambers, 1938.
      Murder mystery.

356   _____.   Hill quest.   London: Ward, Lock, 1937.
      The northwest frontier.

357   _____.   The house of sleep.   London: Ward, Lock,
      1945.
      Mystery; a good one.

358   _____.   Lean brown men.   London: Ward, Lock,
      1940.
      Soldiering in the Panjab frontier force.

359   _____.   Road to roundabout.   London: Ward, Lock,
      1937.
      Indian nationalist unrest.

360   _____.   Secret orchards.   London: Ward, Lock,
      1938.
      Secret service stories.

361   _____.   We'll soldier no more.   London: Ward,
      Lock, 1939.
      Conflict with the Pathans.

362   Butenschen, Andrea.   The life of a Mogul princess.

London: Routledge, 1937.
The great empire of Akbar disintegrates as seen through the eyes of "Princess Jahanara".

363   Butt, K. M.   Ptahlith: some Indian and other stories.
Calcutta: Newman, 1897.

364   Butt, Mary Martha (later Mary Martha Sherwood). The history of George Desmond. London: No publisher given, 1821.
A young man going to India is warned by a missionary to avoid Indian girls and nabobery.

365   _____ .   The lady and her ayah.   London: No publisher given, 1816.
The degenerating influence of oriental life.

366   _____ .   The lady of the manor.   7 vols.   Wellington: Houlston, 1825-29.
Story of Olivia and her degeneration in her uncle's orientalised household.

367   Cadell, Elizabeth.   Sun in the morning.   New York: Morrow, 1950.
Three English girls in Calcutta and the beautiful and sensitive memories of their childhood in Bengal.

368   Cadell, Mrs. H. M. (Jessie Ellen).   Ida Craven.
2 vols. London: H. S. King, 1876.
Military adventures and romance in the post-Mutiny period on the Frontier.

Caffyn, Kathleen Mannington.   See Iota.

369   Cailloux, Pousse (pseud. of Leonard Arthur Bethell).
His majesty's shirtsleeves.   London: Blackwood, 1930.
Eleven stories of the Frontier.

370   Cameron, Charlotte.   A durbar bride.   London: Stanley Paul, 1912.
Tragic story set during George Vth's imperial durbar in Delhi.

371   Campbell, H. M. F.   The star of destiny.   London: Oldhams, 1920.

English girl falls in love with a westernised Indian, and later discovers that her lover was married
and that the East is a fraud.

372   Campbell, Hazel. The burqa: a detective story.
London: John Long, 1930.
An Indian nationalist is murdered on the voyage
from London to Bombay.

373   _____. The Makara mystery. London: John Long,
1930.
Indian eeriness combined with anti-British senti-
ment.

374   _____. The secret brotherhood. London: John
Long, 1930.
Mystery set in the Panjab.

375   _____. The servants of the goddess. London: John
Long, 1928.
Thriller set in Indian hills. Good portrait of
Hindu landowners.

376   Campions, Evelyn Russell. Daughter of the Dahl.
London: Butterworth, 1939.
Kashmir.

377   Candler, Edmund. Abdication. London: Constable,
1922.
Critical of Montagu-Chelmsford Reforms. India
is no longer a proper place for the British, who
should get out.

378   _____. The emergency man. London: Cape, 1926.
Short stories, some deal with India.

379   _____. The general plan. Edinburgh: Blackwood,
1911.
Nine stories, contemptuous of Indians and things
Indian.

380   _____. Siri Ram, revolutionist: a transcript from
life, 1907-1910. London: Constable, 1912.
Critical of Arya Samaj's role in Indian nationalist
politics. Despite its pro-British bias, it is an excellent political novel.

381   Carew, T. Man for man. London: Constable, 1955.
       Indian army in the Burma campaign of World War
       II.

382   Carlene, Victor. Tales from here and there. Madras:
       Higginbotham, 1902.

383   Carlyle, Thomas. Sartor resartus. London: Chapman
       and Hall, 1841.
       The daughter of the British resident in Hyderabad
       and his Indian princely wife are immortalised.

384   Carnoy, Emile Henry. The fiddler and the elves and
       other stories. Translated by A. M. Westwood.
       London: Blackie, 1937.

       Carter, Thomas. See J. Claverdon Wood.

385   Carstairs, R. Harma's village. Manbhum: Santal
       Mission Press, 1935.
       Excellent ethnographical description of Santal life.

386   Carus, Paul. Amitabha: a story of Buddhist theology.
       Chicago: Open court, 1906.
       An Indian noble prevented from attaining nirvana
       in a Buddhist monastery falls in love and discusses
       the problem of celibacy, renunciation, differences
       between Hinduism and Buddhism with a Buddhist
       philosopher.

387   _____. Karma: a story of early Buddhism.
       Chicago: Open Court, 1896.

388   _____. Nirvana: a story of Buddhist philosophy.
       Chicago: Open Court, 1896.

389   Casserly, Gordon. Dwellers in the jungle. London:
       Ward and Lock, 1925.
       Eight stories told in the Kipling style.

390   _____. The elephant god. London: P. Allan, 1920.
       The adventures of Major Dermont with a sacred
       elephant.

391   _____. In the green jungle. Melbourne: Ward and
       Lock, 1927.

392 _____. The jungle girl. London: P. Allan, 1921.
     An English huntress in Rajputana.

393 _____. Life in an Indian outpost. London: Werner
     Laurie, 1914.

394 _____. Monkey god. London: P. Allan, 1933.
     A hunter's friendship and adventures with the grey
     apes of Central India.

395 _____. Tiger girl. London: P. Allan, 1934.
     Set in Terai forests; crude descriptions of a
     gypsy tribe.

396 Caunter, Robert. Nur Jahan and Jahangir. Calcutta:
     Susil Gupta, 1950.

397 Cavalier, Z. L. The soul of the orient. London:
     Murray and Evenden, 1913.
     Astrology, eastern mysticism.

398 Chakravarti, Kedar Nath. The liberation. Calcutta:
     B. G. Chakravarti, 1924.
     Moral tales illustrating Hindu virtues.

399 Chakravarti, Khetrapal. Sarala and Hinjana. Cal-
     cutta: Basu, Mitra, 1895.

400 Chaman Lal, editor. Spiritual stories from India.
     Tokyo: Tuttle, 1964.

401 Chander, Krishan. Virgin and the well. Dehra Dun:
     English Book Depot, 1968.
     Short stories.

402 Chandu Menon, O. Indulekha: a Malayalam novel.
     Madras: Addison, 1890.
     Nayar family life.

403 Channing, Mark. Indian village. London: Hutchinson,
     1939.
     Muslim youth and a Hindu girl in love.

404 _____. King cobra. London: Hutchinson, 1933.
     Set in northwest of India. An outlaw kidnaps an
     English girl; and a secret service agent is trapped
     in a temple of snakes.

405 _____. Nine lives. London: Harrap, 1937.
       Mystery set in northwest India.

406 _____. The poisoned mountain. London: Hutchin-
       son, 1935.
       Mystery and eerie mysticism.

407 _____. The sacred falls. Philadelphia: Lippincott,
       1939.
       Same as Indian village.

408 _____. White python. London: Hutchinson, 1939.
       Supernatural happenings.

409 Chatterjee, Promode Kumar. Whom God protects.
       Translated from Bengali by Kalyan Chaudhuri.
       Pondicherry: Sri Aurobindo Ashram, 1969.
       Hindu religious fiction.

410 Chatterjee, Sita. The cage of gold. Calcutta: R.
       Chaterjee, 1923.
       Calcutta domestic life.

411 Chatterjee, Sita Devi and Santa Devi Chatterjee. The
       garden creeper. Translation of Udayana Lata.
       Calcutta: No publisher given, 1931.

412 _____. The knight errant. Calcutta: Modern Re-
       view Office, no date.

413 _____. The tales of Bengal. London: Oxford Uni-
       versity Press, 1922.

414 Chatterji, Bankim Chander. The abbey of bliss.
       Translation of Anandmath by Nares Chander Sengupta.
       Calcutta: P. M. Neogi, 1906.
       Sanyasi rebellion of 1773. (Another edition Dawn
       over India, 1941, omits all anti-Muslim references.)

415 _____. Chandrashekhar. Translated from Bengali
       by D. C. Mullick. Calcutta: Thacker Spink, 1905.
       Mir Qasim's struggle against the British.

416 _____. Devi Chaudhurani. Rendered into English
       by Subodh Chunder Mitter. Calcutta: Chuckervertty,
       Chatterjee, 1946.
       Poor and neglected wife of a well-to-do Brahmin,

victim of an unfounded scandal, becomes a female
Robin Hood.

417   . Durgesh Nandini: a Bengali romance.
Translated by Charu Chandra Mookerjee. Calcutta:
H. M. Mookerjee, 1880.
The tragedy of inter-communal love in Bengal
during Akbar's reign.

418   . Indira and other stories. Translated by
J. D. Anderson. Calcutta: Modern Review, 1918.
A wife on way to her husband's home is abducted.

419   . Kapal Kundala. Translated by D. N. Ghose.
Calcutta: K. M. Bagchi, 1919.
Tragic tale of a young Bengali caught between the
love of his wife and a Tantric worshipper.

420   . Krishna Kanta's will. Translated by J. C.
Ghosh. New York: New Directions, 1962.
The tragic ruin of a married man in love with a
pretty young widow is portrayed against the sacri-
ficial love of a devoted wife.

421   . The poison tree. Translation of Bisabriksa
by Miriam S. Knight. London: T. Fisher Unwin,
1884.
Domestic tragedy brought about through a widow's
remarriage.

422   . Radharani. Translated by R. C. Maulik.
Calcutta: Metcalfe Press, 1910.
A new Bengali woman chooses her own husband.

423   . Rajani. Translated by P. Majumdar. Calcutta: The Book Co., 1928.
The romance of a blind flower girl.

424   . Rajmohan's wife. Calcutta: R. Chatterjee,
1935.
Originally written in English; a novel of domestic
life in Bengal.

425   . Sitaram. Translated by Sib Chandra
Mukerji. Calcutta: Cambray, 1943.
Insurgency of a Bengali Hindu chief against im-
potent Muslim rule in seventeenth-century Bengal.

426 _____. Tales from Bankim. Translated and edited
      by Gopal Chandra Mukherji and Chandra Kumar
      Ghosh. Calcutta: Auddy, n. d.

427 _____. The two rings. Translation of Bengali
      novel Yugalanguria by R. C. Cannerjee. Calcutta:
      Bengal Medical Library, 1897.
      A king helps patch up a broken romance.

428 Chatterji, Sarat Chandra. The betrothed. Translated
      by Sachindralal Ghosh. Calcutta: Silpee Sangstha,
      1964.

429 _____. Chandranath or the queen's gambit. Trans-
      lated by Sachindralal Ghosh. Bombay: Jaico, 1969.

430 _____. Chitraheen. Translated from Bengali by
      Benoy Lal Chatterjee. Bombay: Jaico, 1962.
      Manners and morals of upper class Bengali
      brahmins.

431 _____. The deliverance. Translated by Dilip
      Kumar Roy. Revised by Sri Sri Aurobindo. Bombay:
      Nalanda Publications, 1944.
      Excellent description of Bengali joint family life.

432 _____. The drought and other stories. Translated
      from Bengali by Sasadhar Sinha. New Delhi:
      Sahitya Akademi, 1970.

433 _____. The eldest sister and other stories. Alla-
      habad: Central Book Depot, 1950.
      Three stories; the first is the translation of
      Baradidi, the love story of a Hindu widow; the
      second attacks conventional morality; and the third
      is set in Burma.

434 _____. The fire. Translated by Sachindralah Ghosh.
      Calcutta: Silpee Sangstha, 1964.
      Bengali girls rebel against tradition.

435 _____. Mothers and sons; two novelettes. Trans-
      lated by Dilip Kumar Roy. Bombay: Pearl, 1968.
      One of them is The deliverance, the other is The
      compliant prodigal.

436 _____. Srikanta. The autobiography of a wanderer.

Translated by Kshitis Chandra Sen.   Banaras: Indian
Publishers, 1945.

437   _____.   Vijaya.   New Delhi: Verma Bros. , 1963.

438 Chattopadhyaya, Harindranath.   The queen's parrot and
the king's ape.   Bombay: India Book House, 1968.
For children.

439 Chattopadhyaya, Romesh Chandra.   Punishment: the
life history of an R. M. S. sorter.   Calcutta: B. C.
Ghose, 1928.

440   _____.   The sorrows of a subpostmaster.   Calcutta:
The Book Company, 1927.
Both of these novels deal with the poverty of
postal clerks.

441 Chaudhuri, Bhabes Chandra.   Rural ghost.   Calcutta:
Alpha Beta, 1966.
India of the 1930's.

442 Chaudhuri, Pramatha.   Tales of four friends.   Trans-
lated by Indira Devi Chaudhurani.   Calcutta: Visva
Bharati Book Shop, n. d.
Romantic episodes involving Indian men and
European women.

443 Chauvelot, R.   Parvati.   New York: Century, 1919.
A French painter falls in love with a maharani
whose portrait he is commissioned to paint.

444 Chesney, George Tomkyns.   The dilemma.   3 vols.
London: Blackwood, 1876.
The first full fledged novel of the Mutiny by a
person who himself took part in it.   Deals with the
defence of a country station by a dedicated and
small group of Englishmen.

445   _____.   A true reformer.   3 vols.   London: Blackwood, 1873.
Life in Simla during the viceroyalty of Lord Mayo
(1869-72), and the effort of an India-hand to become
member of Parliament in order to reform the army.

446 Chetter, Govinda Krishna.   The ghost city.   Mangalore:
Basel Mission, 1932.

447   Chettur, S. K. <u>Bombay murder.</u> Madras: Higgin-
      botham, 1940.
            Detective story which throws light on the ultra-
      modern life of people living in Bombay's luxurious
      apartments.

448   _____ . <u>The cobras of Dharmashevi and other</u>
      <u>stories.</u> Madras: Higginbotham, 1937.

449   _____ . <u>Muffled drums and other stories.</u> Madras:
      No publisher given, 1927.

450   _____ . <u>The spell of Aphrodite and other stories.</u>
      Bombay: Jaico, 1950.

451   Chevalier, P. J. <u>Tower of silence.</u> Bombay: The
      Author, 1928.
            Detective story set in the background of Poona's
      Tower of Silence.

452   Chew, Gertrude. <u>Nellie's vows, a romance.</u> Cal-
      cutta: The Author, 1888.

453   Chillington, J. C. <u>Dual lives.</u> 3 vols. London:
      R. Bentley, 1893.
            Romance and mystery set in Assam hills.

454   Chinna Durai, J. <u>Sughirta.</u> London: Hulbert, 1929.
            Missionary propaganda against child marriage
      and the state of Hindu widows; set in Madras.

455   Chintamani, V. V. <u>Vedantam, the clash of traditions.</u>
      London: Heath Cranton, 1938.
            An Indian student in South India, and later in
      England, discovers that east and west are irrecon-
      cilable.

456   Chitale, Venu (<u>pseud.</u> of Leelabai Khare). <u>In transit.</u>
      Bombay: Hind Kitabs, 1950.
            A chitpavan family of Poona during the nationalist
      movement, 1915-35.

457   Chitera, Piya. <u>After the knock.</u> English version by
      S. C. Chitrey. Saharanpur: Arman Publications,
      194-.

458   Chitrabhanu. <u>Fountain of inspiration.</u> Bombay: Jaico,
      n. d.

459   Chitty, Helen Mary.   The black Buddha.   London:
      H. Jenkins, 1926.
          Talismans, human sacrifices, sinister idols, and
      lavish use of coincidences.

460   Christie, Douglas.   The rajah's casket.   London: Hurst
      and Blackett, 1933.
          White man penetrates forbidden north Indian hill
      territory.

461   _____.   The striking force.   London: Rich and
      Cowan, 1934.
          Northwest frontier.

462   _____.   Tender observation.   London: Hurst and
      Blackett, 1931.
          Secret service agent thwarts Afghan tribal plans
      for a jehad.

463   _____.   Terry of Tangistan: a story of the north-
      west frontier.   London: Hurst and Blackett, 1933.

464   _____.   Trouble on the frontier.   London: Rich
      and Cowan, 1935.

465   Christlieb, Marie Luise.   Golden tales for all.   Man-
      chester: Religious Tract Society, 1927.

466   _____.   How can I bear suffering.   London: Richard
      and Cowan, 1944.

467   _____.   If I lived in India.   London: Edinburgh
      House Press, 1930.

468   _____.   Indian neighbors.   London: Student Christian
      Movement Press, 1930.

469   _____.   Lalappa: an Indian story.   London: Mis-
      sionary Society, 1928.

470   _____.   Old stories.   London: Student Christian
      Movement Press, 1929.

471   _____.   They found God, an account of some little
      known holy lives.   London: Allen and Unwin, 1937.

472   _____.   An uphill road in India. London: Allen and
      Unwin, 1927.

473 _____. Uphill steps in India.   London: Allen and
        Unwin, 1930.

474 _____. Winniamma.   London: Missionary Society,
        1926.
        All these are missionary stories for children.

475 Clark, Laurence Walter.   Kingdom come.   London:
        Centaur, 1958.
        Delightfully absurd story of a nurse's romance in
        Calcutta.   Clark may have written other novels with
        Indian setting.

476 Clark, William.   Special relationship.   Boston:
        Houghton Mifflin, 1969.
        Rednecked American administration wants to keep
        India out of the Peking bloc in 1977.

477 Clarke, Laurence Ayscough.   A prince of India.   Lon-
        don: Hodder and Stoughton, 1915.
        Secret service protects an Indian prince.

478 Cleary, Jon.   The pulse of danger.   New York:
        Morrow, 1966.
        An Australian scientist and his wife in Bhutan
        during the Sino-Indian war trying to endure and sur-
        vive the Himalayas.

479 Cleeve, Roger.   The last long journey.   New York:
        Scribners, 1969.
        Anglo-Indian life.

480 Cocharan, Peter Gregory.   Now I can see: stories of
        Christians in South India.   London: Cargate Press,
        1967.

481 Cocks, S. W.   Tales and legends of ancient India.
        Bombay: Cooper, 1947.

482 Cole, Margaret A.   Love for a doctor.   London:
        R. Hale, 1960.
        English doctor and Indian cholera epidemic.

483 Collier, Richard.   The lovely and the damned.   Lon-
        don: Pilot Press, 1948.
        Secret agents in action during World War II.

484 _____. Pay off in Calcutta. London: Pilot Press,
      1948.

484a _____. In the United States: The solitary witness.
      Mystery that captures the mood of Calcutta in 1940.

Collins, R. S. Harper. See Snilloc.

485 Collins, William Wilkie. The moonstone. 3 vols.
      London: Tinsley, 1868.
      A perfect mystery in which the object of mystery
      is a rare precious stone.

486 Collis, Maurice Stewart. Quest for Sita. London:
      Faber and Faber, 1946.
      Sita's abduction; the Ramayana story.

487 Coloquhoun, M. J. (pseud. of Mrs. C. Scott). Every
      inch a soldier. 3 vols. London: Chatto and
      Windus, 1888.
      Mutiny; good description of the Hodson's Horse.

488 _____. Primers in India. 2 vols. London:
      Chapman and Hall, 1885.
      Part of the second volume deals with the era of
      Sirajuddaullah, 1756.

489 Combe, Mrs. Kenneth. Cecilia Kirkham's son. Lon-
      don: Blackwood, 1909.
      A heedless Englishman runs away with the English
      wife of a disloyal raja.

490 _____. The upward flight. London: Skeffington,
      1919.
      Army life.

491 Comfort, Will Levington. Samadhi. Boston: Houghton
      Mifflin, 1927.
      An American falls in love with an elephant, his
      reverent mahout, and an Indian girl.

492 Comfort, Will Levington and Z. K. Dost. Son of
      power. London: Butterworth, 1922.
      A Chicago boy, interested in circus, runs away
      to India.

493 Compton, Herbert Eastrick. The dead man's gift.
      London: W. H. Allen, 1890.

Romance; Indian tea plantation.

494 _____. A free lance in a far land. London:
Cassell, 1895.
A run away English lad becomes raja of a
princely state in India.

495 _____. A fury in white velvet: a princely tale of
intrigue and romance. London: W. H. Allen, 1901.

Conber, Elizabeth. See Suyin Han.

496 Conquest, Joan. Leonie of the jungle. London:
T. Werner Laurie, 1921.
Warns against Indian sycophancy.

497 Contemporary Indian short stories. 2 vols.
New Delhi: Sahitya Akademi, 1959.

498 Cooper, Brian. A mission for Betty Smith. London:
Heinemann, 1967.
Murder and brutality during the first days of
India's independence, 1947.

499 _____. Monsoon murder. New York: Vanguard,
1968.
India of mid-1940's. Detective.

500 _____. A time to retreat. New York: Vanguard,
1963.
A retired English general wants to vindicate his
strategy that he adopted in the India-Burma theater.

501 _____. A touch of thunder. New York: Vanguard,
1962.
A German Jew, a Chinese prostitute, a Hindu
merchant, and a beautiful girl in Himalayan foothills
expecting war time sabotage. Comical.

502 _____. The Van Langeren girl. New York: Van-
guard, 1960.
A Eurasian girl in Assam suspected of being a
Japanese agent vindicates herself.

503 Cooper, Elizabeth. My lady of the Indian purdah.
New York: Stokes, 1927.
A princess wants to marry for love.

504   Cooper, Frank. The scar of remembrance. London:
      John Long, 1930.
          An English planter marries a Nepali girl and
      falls afoul of his English fiancee.

505   Cooper, Parr. Ayah. London: Allen and Unwin, 1942.
          A South Indian ayah in service to two English
      sisters of diverse temperament.

506   _____. Not at home. London: Allen and Unwin,
      1939.

507   _____. Time is so short. London: Peter Davies,
      1949.
          Panjab during the last days of British rule.

508   _____. Uninvited guests. London: Peter Davies,
      1946.
          English jitters about Nazi influence in India.

      Cory, Vivian. See Victoria Crosse.

509   Cotes, Mrs. Everard (Sara J. Duncan). The burnt
      offering. London: Methuen, 1909.
          Excellent sketch of life in Bengal.

510   _____. His honour and a lady. London: Rose and
      Sons, 1896.
          Light satire on English life in India: the victims
      are two governors, one a martyr to his honesty, the
      other is successful through his hypocrisy.

511   _____. The path of a star. London: Methuen,
      1899.
          Anglo-Indian romance set in Calcutta.

512   _____. Pool in the desert. London: Methuen, 1903.
          Good description of memsahib.

513   _____. Set in authority. London: Constable, 1906.
          Memsahib's zennana and missionary activities are
      well described.

514   _____. The simple adventures of a memsahib.
      London: Chatto and Windus, 1893.
          How memsahibs are made: they teach Bible, sew
      in zennana homes; stay with married sisters; keep
      house for older brothers.

515   . Story of Sony sahib. London: Macmillan,
     1894.
     A boy is rescued from the Cawnpore massacre
     during the Mutiny and is brought up at a native
     court.

516   . Vernon's aunt: experiences of Miss
     Livonia Moffat. London: Chatto and Windus, 1894.
     For young adults.

517 Couldrey, Oswald Jennings. The phantom waterfall
     and other illusions. Abingdon: Abbey Press, 1949.

518 Cowasjee, Saros. Stories and sketches. Calcutta:
     Writers Workshop, 1970.

519 Cox, Edmund. The achievements of John Carruthers.
     London: Constable, 1911.
     An Indian police official writes about crime.

520   . The exploits of Kesho Naik, dacoit. Lon-
     don: Constable, 1912.

521   . John Carruthers, Indian policeman. Lon-
     don: Cassell, 1905.
     Crime detection.

522 Craig, A. Elsie Rundall. The beloved rajah. New
     York: Minton, Balch, 1926.
     Son of a British official in hopeless passion for
     the daughter of degenerate Rajput prince.

523   . Palace of intrigue. New York: Minton,
     Balch, 1932.
     Indian maharani steals a Scottish lad and raises
     him as her own son.

524 Crawford, Francis Marion. Dr. Claudius. London:
     Macmillan, 1883.
     Romantic tale of the Second Anglo-Afghan war.

525   . Mr. Isaacs: a tale of modern India.
     London: Macmillan, 1882.
     Mystery; an esoteric Buddhist captivates an
     English girl.

526 Cress, Charles. Above what he could bear. London:
     Stockwell, 1916.

Two cousins, one English the other Eurasian, run a coffee plantation.

527   Croft-Cooke, Rupert. Another sun, another home. New York: Holt, 1949.
A retired English colonel with nostalgia for India.

528   Croker, Bithia Mary. Angel, a sketch in Indian ink. London: Methuen, 1901.
Romance, set in northern India. Good descriptions of Lucknow.

529   _____. Babes in the wood. London: Methuen, 1910.
Indian forest officer and his extremely good looking sister depicted through well conceived incidents.

530   _____. A bird of passage. 3 vols. London: Sampson Low, 1886.
Partly laid in the Andamans. Excellent sketches of the Irish working class.

531   _____. The cat's paw. London: Chatto and Windus, 1902.
Club life in South India.

532   _____. The company's servant, a romance of South India. London: Hurst and Blackett, 1907.

533   _____. Diana Barrington, a romance of Central India. 3 vols. London: Ward, Downey, 1888.
Experiences of a young girl brought up in Indian jungles.

534   _____. A family likeness: a sketch in the Himalayas. 3 vols. London: Chatto and Windus, 1892.

535   _____. Given in marriage. London: Hutchinson, 1916.
Partially laid in South India. A penniless girl is "given in marriage" to satisfy her father's dying wish; her loathing turns to love.

536   _____. Her own people. London: Hurst and Blackett, 1903.
An English girl, orphaned, goes to India to find love.

537 _____ . In the kingdom of Kerry and other stories.
London: Chatto and Windus, 1896.

538 _____ . In old Madras. 3 vols. London: Hutchinson, 1913.
An English captain goes to Madras to search a
long lost relative.

539 _____ . Interference. 3 vols. London: F. V.
White, 1891.
Excellent knowledge of horsemanship and hunting;
good messroom scenes.

540 _____ . Jason and other stories. London: Chatto
and Windus, 1899.

541 _____ . Jungle tales. London: Holden Hardingham,
1919.

542 _____ . Mr. Jervis: a romance of the Indian hills.
London: Chatto and Windus, 1894.
Jervis delays his marriage because he thinks
insanity runs in his family.

543 _____ . A nine day's wonder. London: Methuen,
1905.

544 _____ . Odds and ends. London: Hutchinson, 1919.

545 _____ . The old cantonment and other stories of
India and elsewhere. London: Methuen, 1905.

546 _____ . The pagoda tree. London: Cassell, 1919.
Princes, residencies and high life.

547 _____ . Pretty Miss Neville. 3 vols. London:
Tinsley, 1883.
Cousins estranged in Ireland are united in India.

548 _____ . Proper pride. London: Chatto and Windus,
1882.
Domestic unhappiness caused by the young wife of
an older man, led astray by a Eurasian.

549 _____ . Quicksands. London: Cassell, 1915.
Two orphans fall in quicksand.

550 _____. A rolling stone. London: F. V. White,
        1911.

551 _____. A state secret and other stories. London:
        Methuen, 1901.

552 _____. "To let" etc., stories. London: Chatto
        and Windus, 1893.

553 _____. Village tales and jungle tragedies. London:
        Chatto and Windus, 1895.

554 Crommelin, Maria Henrietta. Pink lotus: a comedy
        in Kashmir. London: Hurst and Blackett, 1914.
        Outstanding descriptions of Kashmir.

555 Crooke, William. Religion and folklore of northern
        India. Edited by R. E. Enthoven. London: Oxford
        University Press, 1926.

556 _____. The talking thrush and other tales from
        India. Edited by W. H. D. Rouse. London: Dent,
        1899.

557 Crosby, J. Never let her go. New York: McCall
        Publishing Co., 1970.
        Mystery stories.

558 Crosse, Victoria (pseud. of Vivian Cory). Life of my
        heart. London: John Long, 1914.
        Pathan country.

559 Crosthwaite, Charles Hankes Tod. Thakur Pertab
        Singh and other tales. Edinburgh: Blackwood, 1913.
        India as a land of misery and disease.

560 Cunningham, Henry Stewart. Chronicles of Dustypore.
        A tale of modern Anglo-Indian society. 2 vols.
        London: No publisher given, 1875.
            Satirical account of the "competitionwallahs" who
        are contrasted to the "old blockheads" of the pre-
        Mutiny period.

561 _____. The Coeruleans. 2 vols. London: Mac-
        millan, 1887.
            India is depicted as a lovely intellectual wasteland
        for British civil servants; marvellously humorous.

562 _____. The Heriots. 3 vols. London: Macmillan,
        1890.

563 _____. Wheats and tares. London: Macmillan,
        1861.

564 Currie, Fendal. Below the surface. London: Con-
        stable, 1900.

565 _____. The land of regrets. London: Constable,
        1903.
        Both are novels of Indian manners.

566 Currimbhoy, Asif. Thorns on a canvas and the cap-
        tives. Bombay: Soraya Publications, 1964.

567 Curwen, Henry. Dr. Hermoine. Edinburgh: Black-
        wood, 1890.
        Cumberland, Egypt and India.

568 _____. Lady bluebeard. 2 vols. Edinburgh:
        Blackwood, 1888.
        Experiences of a girl in India; luxuriant descrip-
        tions of the tropics.

569 _____. Zit and Xoe: their early experiences.
        Edinburgh: Blackwood, 1886.
        Story of Adam and Eve from the Darwinian point
        of view; exquisite prose.

570 Cuthell, Edith E. By a Himalayan lake. London:
        Ward and Downey, 1893.

571 _____. Comrades in camp and bungalow. London:
        Wells, Gardner, 1907.

572 _____. In tent and bungalow. London: Methuen,
        1892.

573 _____. Indian idylls. Calcutta: Thacker Spink,
        1890.

574 Dalal, Nergis. Minari. Bombay: Pearl, 1967.

575 Dale, Darley (pseud. of Francesca Maria Steele). The
        master of the house. London: Heath Cranton, 1923.

English judge in India of autocratic tendencies
becomes a tyrannical parent.   Miss Dale may have
written other novels with Indian background.

576   Dalton, William.   The next hunters: or adventures in
       the Indian archipelago.   London: Arthur Hall, 1863.

577   _____.   Phaulcon: the adventurer.   London: Breton,
       1881.
       Both are stories for children.

578   Daly, Tim (pseud.) Mess stories.   Edited by F. E.
       W. Bombay: Thacker, 187-.

579   Daniel, P. H.   Red tea.   Madras: Higginbothams,
       1969.
       Social novel depicting the life of plantation workers
       in South India of the 'twenties.

580   Daniell, William.   Eastern legendary tales and oriental
       tales and oriental romance.   London: No publisher
       given, 1838.

581   Daryani, K. S.   Sharavan Kumar: A Hindu mythological
       story of a youth's devotion to parents.   Bombay:
       Mahimker, 1945.

582   Das, Frieda Mathilda Hauswirth.   Into the sun.   Lon-
       don: Dent, 1933.
       First half of the book dealing with an Indian
       household and its social system is excellent.

583   Das, Manoj.   Short stories.   Madras: Triveni, 1969.

584   _____.   Song for Sunday and other stories.   Madras:
       Higginbothams, 1967.

585   Dass, Trilokya Nath.   Hirimba's wedding.   Midnapore:
       No publisher given, 1884.

586   Dastur, D. N.   Rajput rani, being a booklet containing
       the story of Rani Rajba of Rajputana.   Bombay:
       Ahura Printing, 1939.

587   Datta, H.   Lieut. Suresh Biswas, his life and adven-
       tures.   Calcutta: P. C. Dass, 1900.

588 _____. Profoulla: a tale of today. Calcutta:
        C. Dutt, 1891.
        Intercaste relations destroy a person's reputation.

589 Datta, Sasi Chandra. The young zemindar. 3 vols.
        London: No publisher given, 1883.

590 David, Wilfrid. Monsoon. London: Hamish Hamilton,
        1933.
        A stinging indictment of the English man's rule
        in India. First rate.

Davies, John Evan Weston. See Berkely Mather.

591 Day, Lal Behari. Bengal peasant life. Calcutta: No
        publisher given, 1847. Reprinted, Calcutta: K. L.
        Mukhopadhyay, 1969.
        There is no better ethnological novel on Bengal
        than this one.

592 _____. Folk tales of Bengal. London: Macmillan,
        1883.

593 _____. Govinda Samanta: or the history of a
        Bengal raiyat. London: Macmillan, 1874.
        Prize-winning novel of Bengali rural life.

594 De, R. P. Mother and daughter, or a true picture of
        Hindu life of Bengal. Calcutta: Oriental Publishing,
        1906.
        A Bengali widow's life in the mid-nineteenth
        century.

595 Dean, M. P. (pseud. of M. K. and G. Svoronos-
        Gigantes). Childish brides. New York: Double-
        day, 1960.
        An adulterous husband agrees to a penance: to
        take an Indian family to a religious festival to ob-
        tain cure for a baby's ailment. Instead of a miracle,
        a disaster follows.

Debonzie, Eric and John Sellar Matheson Ressich.
See Gregory Baxter.

596 Dehan, Richard (pseud. of Clotilda Inez Mary Graves).
        The lovers of the market place. London: Butter-
        worth, 1928.
        Some stories deal with India.

597   Dekobra, Maurice (pseud. of Ernest Maurice Tessier).
       The sphinx has spoken.   Translated by Metcalfe
       Wood.   London: Werner Laurie, 1930.
       Life on Indian outposts.

598   Dell, Ethel Mary.   By request.   Same as Peggy by
       request.

599   _____ .   Lamp in the desert.   New York: Putnams,
       1919.
       Triangular romance involving a subaltern's
       sister and his superior officer, rather unrealistic.

600   _____ .   Peggy by request.   New York: Putnams,
       1928.
       Girl goes to India to attend her father whose
       mind has begun to fail, and finds romance with her
       childhood friend spoiled by unfounded gossip.

601   _____ .   The safety curtain and other stories.   Lon-
       don: Fisher Unwin, 1917.
       Two of the five stories deal with military life in
       India.

602   _____ .   Way of an eagle.   London: Fisher Unwin,
       1912.
       Ugly little hero with a heart of gold rescues his
       lady love on the Frontier.   Miss Dell may have
       written other novels with Indian background.

603   Dellbridge, John.   The days of separation.   London:
       John Long, 1929.
       Modernized Muslims and Pathans and their social
       relations with Europeans.

604   _____ .   The moles of death.   London: Diamond
       Press, 1927.
       Frontier mystery.

605   _____ .   Sons of tumult.   London: John Long, 1928.
       An Englishman escapes the Karachi jail with a
       mixed gang of non-European convicts; a Muslim con-
       federation threatens the peace of India.

606   [Denning, J. R.]   In a dark bungalow.   A collection of
       short stories.   By J. A. N.   Madras: Addison &
       Co., 1895.

607   De Noronha. <u>Stories.</u> Calcutta: Writers Workshop,
      1966.

608   Deobhanker, N. R. <u>Hemakumari and other stories.</u>
      Bombay: Nalanda, 1940.

609   Desai, Anita. <u>Cry the peacock.</u> London: Peter Owen,
      1963.
          Difficulties experienced by a sensitive young girl
      married to a much older but sensible and pedestrian
      husband.

610   _____. <u>Voices in the city.</u> London: Peter Owen,
      1965.
          Calcutta, old and new.

611   Desani, G. V. <u>All about H. Hatterr.</u> London:
      F. Aldor, 1948.
          Mr. Hatterr is mishandled by his wife, his club,
      his employer and a delightful procession of swamis.

612   Deshpande, Nirmala. <u>Chingling.</u> Translated by N. R.
      Deobhanker. Varanasi: Sarva Seva Sangh, 1966.
          A Chinese girl through Vinoba's <u>bhoodan</u> move-
      ment.

613   Despard, Charlotte. <u>The rajah's heir.</u> London:
      Smith, Elder, 1890.
          Good description of princely states involved
      against and in support of the British during the
      Mutiny.

614   Devasher, P. G. <u>The otto of roses; a romance of Nur
      Jahan's times.</u> Bombay: Orient Longmans, 1969.

615   Devereaux, Charles. <u>Venus in India.</u> Brussels: No
      publisher given, 1899.
          Pornography.

616   De Verteuil, Charles. <u>White memasahib.</u> London:
      Redman, 1958.
          An Anglo-Indian girl fights the handicap of her
      ancestry during the partition of India.

617   Devi, Raj Lakshmi. <u>The Hindu wife or the enchanted
      fruit.</u> Calcutta: No publisher given, 1876.

Devi, Swarna Kumari. See Mrs. Ghosal.

618 De Viri, Anne. Indrani and I. New York: Red Dust,
     1965.

619 De Wohl, Louis. The last thug. London: Methuen,
     1939.
        American animal collector and his relationship
     to an Indian yogi.

620 Dhar, Triloki Nath. Tale of a Soviet biologist. Cal-
     cutta: Alpha Beta, 1965.

621 Dick, G. Fitch and his fortunes; an Anglo-Indian
     novel. London: Elliot Stock, 1898.
        English civil servant loves his Indian landlady
     and plans to develop a hybrid race equal to Anglo-
     Saxons. Tragedy.

622 Dickson, F. Thorold and M. L. Pechill. A ruler of
     Ind. London: No publisher given, 189-.

623 Dikshit, Sudhakar. The republic of Pompapaur.
     Bombay: Chetana, 1962.
        Political satire on the Indian princely order.

624 Dilip, Hiro. A triangular view. London: Dobson,
     1969.

625 Dimmitt, Marjorie A., editor. When the tom tom
     beats and other stories. By students of Isabella
     Thorburn College. Lucknow: Methodist Publishing
     House, 1932.
        Contains "When love was young" by Attia Husain.

626 Dimock, Edward C. Thief of love, Bengal tales from
     court and village. Chicago: University of Chicago
     Press, 1963.

627 Diver, Katherine Helen Maud. Awakening: a study in
     possibilities. Same as Lilamani.

628 _____. Candles in the wind. London: Blackwood,
     1909.

629 _____. Captain Desmond, V. C. London: Black-
     wood, 1907.

With Candles in the wind and Great amulet con-
stitutes a trilogy dealing with life on the northwest
frontier.   Fine ideals of duty and strenuous devotion
are contrasted with the fickle Indian life style.

630 _____. Desmond's daughter. London: Blackwood, 1916.
Tirah campaign of 1897-98 is the background for
this Frontier romance.

631 _____. The dream prevails. London: John
Murray, 1938.
Sequel to The singer passes; story of interracial
love.

632 _____. Far to seek. A romance of England and
India. London: Blackwood, 1921.
Son of a happily married English baron and his
Rajput wife goes to India in search of love and
adventure.

633 _____. The great amulet. London: Blackwood,
1908.
Love, separation, and reconciliation on the
Frontier. Frontier warfare, Himalayan explorations,
cholera camps, and family tensions are deftly depicted.

634 _____. The hero of Herat: a frontier biography in
romantic form. London: Constable, 1912.
Siege of Herat, 1942; biography of Major Eldred
Pottinger.

635 _____. The judgment of the sword: a tale of the
Kabul tragedy and of the part played therein by
Major E. Pottinger. London: Constable, 1913.

636 _____. Lilamani, a study of possibilities. London:
Hutchinson, 1910.
An Englishman of a proud old family marries the
daughter a high caste Brahmin.

637 _____. Lonely furrow. London: Grosset and Dun-
lap, 1923.
Wife does not share her husband's love for India
and chooses to live in England.

638 _____. Ships of youth. London: Blackwood, 1931.

A tempestuous yet beautiful marriage in the Himalayan shadow.

639 _____. Siege perilous and other stories. London: John Murray, 1924.

640 _____. The singer passes: an Indian tapestry. London: Blackwood, 1934.
A distinguished writer goes to India and develops hostility to the Gandhian movement.

641 _____. Strange roads. London: Constable, 1918.

642 _____. Sunia and other stories. London: Blackwood, 1913.

643 _____. A wild bird. London: John Murray, 1929.
A girl who spent her childhood in India can't get India out of her mind.

644 Douglas, O. Olivia in England: the adventures of a chota mis sahib. London: Hodder and Stoughton, 1913.

645 _____. Olivia in India: the adventures of a chota mis sahib. London: Hodder and Stoughton, 1913.

646 Douie, Marjorie. The man who tried everything. London: Hutchinson, 1919.
Plot against British rule is foiled.

647 Douthwaite, L. C. Scorpion's realm: a detective novel. Bombay: Hamilton, 1933.

648 Doyle, Arthur Conan. The adventures of Sherlock Holmes. London: Newnes, 1892.

649 _____. The return of Sherlock Holmes. London: Newnes, 1905.

650 _____. The sign of four. London: Spencer, Blackett, 1890.

651 _____. A study in scarlet. London: Ward, Lock, 1888.
Several stories contain Indian characters. India is depicted as a land of immense wealth, whose

Muslims are athletic heroes whereas the Hindus are conniving.

652   Drago, George. John Hobbs: a tale of British India.
      London: Partridge, 1862.
          Missionary story; alcoholic becomes a teetotaler.

653   Drury, W. P. The incendiaries. London: Mills and
      Boon, 1922.
          A well meaning British M. P. allows himself to
      be used in a German intrigue to end the British raj.

654   Duggal, Kartar Singh. Banked fires and other stories.
      Bombay: Pearl, 1969.

655   _____. Nails and flesh, stories. Bombay: Pearl,
      1969.

656   _____. Stories from India and abroad. Delhi:
      Sahitya Sangham, 196-.

657   Dunbar, George Duff Sutherland. Jungbir, secret
      agent. London: Burns, Oates, 1934.
          Set in Ladakh and Tibet, a story for children.

658   _____. Poisoned arrow. London: Burns, Oates,
      1934.
          A children's story with accuracy of detail about
      the Frontier.

659   Duncan, Margaret. The faces of courage. New Delhi:
      N. C. E. R. T. , 1967.
          Stories depicting the courage of Indian sepoys.

660   Duncan, Ronald Aver. So is life. Bombay: Thacker,
      1937.

661   _____. Some like the hills. A romance of the
      northwest frontier of India. London: Methuen,
      1939.

      Duncan, Sara Jeanette. See Mrs. Everard Cotes.

662   Durand, Henry Mortimer. Helen Trevenyan, or the
      ruling race. London: Macmillan, 1892.
          Deals with the Second Afghan War, 1878-79, and
      is one of the best descriptions in fiction of the
      northwest frontier.

663   _____ . Nadir Shah, a romance. London: Con-
         stable, 1904.
         Good historical novel on Nadir Shah.

         Also see John Roy.

664   Dutt, H. Bijoy Chand. Calcutta: H. C. Dutt, 1888.
         Santal life.

665   _____ . The library of anecdote. Calcutta: H. C.
         Dutt, 1888.

666   Dutt, Ram Kindoo. A genial anecdote. Chittagong:
         No publisher given, 1884.

667   Dutt, Romesh Chandra. The lake of palms: a story
         of Indian domestic life. London: Fisher Unwin,
         1902.
         Bengal village and city life in the late nineteenth
         century; excellent description of a pilgrimage to
         Puri; discusses the question of widow remarriage.

668   _____ . Pratap Singh, the last of the Rajputs: a
         tale of Rajput courage and chivalry. Translated
         from Bengali by Ajoy C. Dutt. Allahabad: Kita-
         bistan, 1943.

669   _____ . Sivaji: a historical tale of the great
         Mahratta hero and patriot. Allahabad: Kitabistan,
         1944.
         Translation of Maharashtra Jivan Prabhat, it
         mingles an account of Sivaji's life with story of a
         Rajput in his service.

670   _____ . The slave girl of Agra: an Indian his-
         torical novel. London: Fisher Unwin, 1909.
         Based on the traditional story Madhavi Kankan,
         it portrays social life under Mughul rule in the
         sixteenth and seventeenth centuries.

671   _____ . Todar Mull, the conqueror of Bengal; an
         historical novel. Allahabad: Kitabistan, 1947.
         Akbar's revenue minister and Hindu zamindars
         of Bengal.

672   Dutt, S. Stories from Bengal. Bombay: Jaico, 1957.

673 Easton, John. Ferrol Bond. London: Putnam's, 1933.
    Bengali revolutionaries are foiled.

674 _____. Matheson fever. London: Allan, 1928.
    Thriller; Matheson loses his life in the attempt to possess a sacred temple emerald.

675 _____. Red sap. London: Eyre and Spottiswoode, 1938.
    Mystery; inner Himalayas.

676 Eaubonne, Francoise d'. A flight of falcons. Translated by Naomi Walford. London: R. Hale, 1952.
    Love, hates and struggles of four men travelling in India; excellent descriptions of late sixteenth century.

677 Edge, Kathleen Mary. The after cost. London: E. Nash, 1904.
    Ordinary romance.

678 _____. Ahana. London: Chapman and Hall, 1902.
    Romance and adventure, with religious overtones, set in the 1850's. Race relations with Eurasians.

679 _____. The shuttles of the loom. London: John Murray, 1909.
    Moral grandeur of the life of a white housewife in India, a land of passion, stress and sorrow.

680 Edgeworth, Miss. Tales, the stories of Englishmen going to India to make fortunes. London: No publisher given, 1825.

681 Edwood, May. Autobiography of a spinster: a story of Anglo-Indian life. Calcutta: Thacker, 1893.
    Flirtations of an English girl.

682 _____. Elsie Ellerton: a novelette of Anglo-Indian life. Calcutta: Thacker, 1892.

683 Elder, R. After my own fashion. London: Longmans, 1949.
    Friendship between two Sikhs is broken up on the issue of support or opposition to British rule.

684   Eliade, Mircea. Two tales of the occult. New York:
        Herder and Herder, 1970.
            Two mysteries that explore the themes of karma,
        maya, and samsara.

685   Elliot, Robert Henry. Written on their foreheads.
        2 vols. London: No publisher given, 1879.
            Mysore plantation life.

686   Elwin, Harry Verrier Holman. A new book of tribal
        fiction. Shillong: NEFA, 1970.

687   _____. Phulmat of the hills: a tale of the Gonds.
        London: John Murray, 1937.
            Thoroughly reliable novel of Gond life.

688   Emery, J. Inman. The Luck Udaipur: a romance of
        old Devon, Hindostan, and the fringe of the blue
        Pacific. London: Jarrolds, 1925.
            A Rajput diamond is stolen by an English ad-
        venturer.

689   _____. The tiger of Bargunga. London: Jarrolds,
        1924.
            The tiger is a famous emerald which is stolen
        from a maharaja.

690   Endrikar, Y. Gamblers in happiness. London: Heath
        Cranton, 1930.
            An English governor causes crisis in the Euro-
        pean community in India by insisting that Indians be
        admitted to a whites-only club.

691   Enriquez, Colin Metcalfe Dellas. Khyberie: the story
        of a pony on the Indian frontier. London: A. C.
        Black, 1934.
            For the younger set.

692   Enthoven, R. Edward. The folklore of Bombay.
        London: Clarendon, 1924.

        Erskin, Portal Vane. See Vane Erskine Bannisdale.

693   Eustace, Alice. Diamonds and jasmine. London:
        Mills and Boon, 1929.
            Romance set in princely India.

694   _____. Flame in the forest. London: Mills and
           Boon, 1927.
           Fine appreciation of Rajput life.

695   _____. A girl from the jungle. London: Mills and
           Boon, 1928.
           Karin the heroine is a female Kim; she escapes
           from the zennana of a nawab, finds a mendicant cum
           secret agent and marries him.

696   _____. He'll love me yet. London: Mills and
           Boon, 1932.
           Of princely life with clichés about the 'good'
           princes; opposed to nationalist sentiment.

697   _____. My purdah lady. London: Mills and Boon,
           1933.
           Marriage through the usual difficulties.

698   Evarts, Hal George. The secret of the Himalayas.
           New York: Scribner, 1962.
           Search for the Snowman, for young adults.

699   Evelyn, Charles. I am a smuggler. London: Cas-
           sell, 1952.
           The Indian underworld, 1920-44; smuggling
           through Portuguese and French enclaves.

700   Eyre, Donald Cuthbert. Foxes have holes. London:
           R. Hale, 1949.
           India-Burma theater during World War II.

701   _____. John Sikander. London: R. Hale, 1954.
           Search for an heir who is busy scaling the Him-
           alayas.

702   Eyton, John Seymour. Bulbulla. London: Arrow-
           smith, 1928.
           A true artistic story of a Eurasian boy who runs
           away from school and shares all kinds of adventures
           with an Indian friend.

703   _____. The dancing fakir and other stories. Lon-
           don: Longmans, 1922.
           Vivid stories of life in nothern India.

704   _____. Diffidence. London: Arrowsmith, 1925.
           Wild-life charming story of a new Mowgli.

705   _____. Expectancy. London: Arrowsmith, 1924.
        Sensitive motherless child's impression of India;
        shows intimate knowledge of the Himalayas.

706   _____. Jungle born. London: Arrowsmith, 1924.
        Beauty and cruelty of Indian jungle life; boy is
        raised by apes.

707   _____. Kullu of the carts. London: Arrowsmith,
        1926.
        Eurasian boy runs away from school.

708   _____. Mr. Ram. London: Arrowsmith, 1929.
        Indian boy marries the landlady's daughter at
        Oxford; effect of environment on the mind. A first
        rate story.

709   Fairley, Helen M. Bharosa. London: Hutchinson,
        1932.
        Poor, confused novel.

710   _____. A heritage of the dust. London: Hutchin-
        son, 1924.
        Racial prejudices and antagonisms tragically
        developed through the fortunes of a Eurasian girl.

711   _____. The holders of the gate. London: Hutch-
        inson, 1923.
        German spy; a faithful raja; love and intrigue on
        the Indian frontier.

712   _____. The justice of the white sahibs. London:
        Hutchinson, 1925.
        Frontier story.

713   _____. Kali's jewels. London: Hutchinson, 1926.
        Criminal instincts, says the story, are trans-
        mitted through heredity. Abdullah is the name
        given to a Hindu.

714   Fakhruddin, M. Rapture. Bangalore: Murthy and
        Son, 1969.

715   Fanthorne, J. F. Miriam: a story of the Indian
        mutiny of 1857. Benares: Chandraprabha Press,
        1896.

Supposedly based on the real experiences of a
Christian family, the story appears unauthentic.

716   Faure, M. Bharamganj: a tale of India before inde-
      pendence. Ilfracombe: Stockwell, 1960.
            India 1938; mystery involving a dacoit, an Aus-
      trian, a police officer and the Gestapo.

717   Fazli, Fazl Ahmad Karim. The jamadar. Trans-
      lated from Urdu by Rafiq Khawar. London: Cas-
      sell, 1961.

718   Fenn, Clive Robert. For the old flag. London:
      Sampson Low, 1899.
            English hero in the Mutiny. For young adults.

719   Fenn, George Manville. The bag of diamonds and
      three bits of paste. London: Chatto and Windus,
      1900.

720   _____. Begumbagh: a tale of the Indian mutiny.
      London: Chambers, 1893.

721   _____. Bent not broken. 3 vols. London:
      Tinsley, 1867.

722   _____. Black shadow. London: Chatto and
      Windus, 1902.

723   _____. Gil the gunner. London: Christian
      Knowledge Society, 1892.
            All these five books are for young adults.

724   Ferguson, John Alexander. Secret road. London:
      John Lane, 1925.

725   Ferguson, Margaret. Broken grain. London: John
      Long, 1933.
            Mystery; artful handling of miscegenation.

726   _____. Crooked corner. London: Robert Hale,
      1963.
            An illegitimate girl happy in India becomes an
      heiress to an English estate, but struggle with the
      contestants in England embitters her.

727   _____. Dust upon wind. London: Hutchinson, 1935.
            Terrorism in Bengal and its effect upon the life style.

728   _____. Green afternoon. London: John Long,
       1932.
       An English girl's life enriched by India.

729   _____. Immortal garland. London: Robert Hale,
       1946.
       Frontier expedition.

730   _____. Inconstant moon. London: John Long,
       1933.
       India's northwest; anti-Eurasian in tone.

731   _____. Sugar in spice. London: Robert Hale,
       1952.
       English girl on her last pennies goes to India
       and becomes governess to an Indian princess, but
       her two past lovers follow her. Good mystery with
       beautiful local color.

732   _____. Thorn harvest. London: Hutchinson, 1936.
       English girl's adventures in Persian Gulf, India
       and Dalmatia.

733   _____. Vain bondage. London: Hutchinson, 1938.
       A ballet dancer's marriage and the effect of
       India upon her.
       Miss Ferguson, a prolific writer, probably wrote
       other mysteries with Indian setting.

734   Fernandez, G. Arnold. The romance of a zennana.
       Bombay: Advocate of India Press, 1900.

735   Feuchtwanger, Lion. Marianne in India and seven
       other tales. New York: Viking, 1935.

736   Fforde, Arthur Barlow. The maid and the idol: a
       tangled story of Poona. Allahabad: Wheeler, 1891.

737   _____. The phantoms of the dome. Allahabad:
       Wheeler, 1895.
       English life in India, especially with their Indian
       servants.

738   _____. The sign of the snake. Calcutta: Wheeler,
       1895.

739   _____. The subaltern, the policeman and the little

girl. London: Sampson Low, 1890.
A girl must choose between the two.

740 _____. That little owl: a tale of a lunatic, a
loafer, and a lover. Allahabad: Wheeler, 1893.

741 _____. The trotter: a Poona mystery. London:
Sampson Low, 1890.
Gentleman burglar in action in Poona.

742 Field, E. M. Bryda: a story of the Indian mutiny.
London: Wells, Gardner, 1888.
A girl through the Mutiny and the thugs.

743 Fielding, Henry (pseud. of Henry Fielding Hall).
Love's legend. London: Constable, 1914.
An English girl comes to India to marry a pucca
sahib, who turns out to be thoroughly Indianized.

744 _____. One immortality. London: Macmillan,
1909.
A group of English travellers in India interested
in Indian life. No plot, no action.

745 _____. Palace tales. London: Harper, 1900.

746 Fisher, Richard. Indian police. London: Selwyn and
Blount, 1939.
Socially ostracised low cadre English officer in
Bihar resolves a dacoity.

747 Fitzgerald, Ena. Patcola: a tale of a dead city.
London: Greening, 1908.
Rise and fall of the Vijayanagar empire.

748 Fletcher, A. H. Here's rue for you. Calcutta:
Thacker, 1883.
Stories.

749 _____. Poppied sleep. Calcutta: Thacker, 1887.
Christmas story in an upcountry station.

750 Foran, Bedford. The border of blades. London:
Hodder and Stoughton, 1916.
Russian agent makes trouble in Peshawar district.

751 Foran, W. Robert. Roshanara of the seven cities.
London: Hutchinson, 1933.

752   Forbes, H. D. E.   Brought to bay.   Allahabad:
       Wheeler, 1894.
              Two educated Indians incite a riot.

       Ford, William.   See William St. Clair.

753   Forrest, R. E.   The bond of blood.   London: Smith
       Elder, 1896.
              Vivid romance against the background of Rajput
       customs.

754   _____.   Eight days.   3 vols.   London: Smith
       Elder, 1891.
              Historically accurate descriptions of Delhi during
       the Mutiny.

755   _____.   The ruby of Rajasthan.   London: East and
       West, 1914.
              Akbar and Rajasthan.   Ain-i-Akbari and Tod
       followed conscientiously.

756   _____.   The sword of Azrael: a chronicle of the
       great mutiny by John Hayman, Major General.
       London: Methuen, 1903.
              Escape of an officer from the sepoys.

757   Forster, Daphne Kathleen.   Hidden cities.   London:
       Hammond and Hammond, 1950.
              Station and club life.

758   _____.   Horse leeche's daughter.   London: Ham-
       mond and Hammond, 1955.

759   _____.   Sandalwood gate.   London: Hurst and
       Blackett, 1947.
              Nautch girls of Allahabad and their influence on
       Indian nobles.   Very sensitive portrait.

760   _____.   Twin giants.   London: Hammond and Ham-
       mond, 1952.

761   Forster, Edward Morgan.   A passage to India.   Lon-
       don: E. Arnold, 1924.
              A striking novel with literary distinction, but the
       portrait of India is not accurate.

762   Forster, Roy.   Diamond harbour.   London: Joseph,
       1959.

Calcutta 1909. An English boy comes to India
trailing family clouds of glory. Weak story but
with superb sketches.

763 _____. The flute of Asoka. London: Eyre and
Spottiswoode, 1955.
Indian nationalism, World War II.

764 Foster, George (pseud. of Chetwynd John Drake Haswell). Indian file. London: M. Joseph, 1960.
Straight faced satire on soldiering in India in
1930's.

765 Fraser, F. J. Little number three. Lahore: Civil
and Military Gazette, 189-.

766 Fraser, George Macdonald. Flashman: from the
Flashman papers. New York: World, 1969.
Splendidly entertaining spoof of British army
anti-hero; liar, lecher, bully, coward and survivor
of all wars in India from the siege of Lucknow to
the battle of Little Big Horn.

767 _____. Royal Flash. New York: Knopf, 1970.
More of the above.

768 Fraser, William Alexander. Caste. London: Hodder
and Stoughton, 1922.
An English officer marries an Indian and becomes
an outcaste. Anglo-Maratha hostilities.

769 _____. The Sa'zada tales. London: David Nitt,
1905.
For children.

770 _____. Thirteen men. New York: Appleton, 1902.
Three stories, Pathan frontier.

771 Frazer, Robert Watson. Silent gods and sun steeped
lands. London: Fisher Unwin, 1895.
Seven realistic stories.

772 Frere, Mary Eliza Isabella. Old Deccan days.
London: John Murray, 1869.
Stories and legends from South India.

773 Futehally, Zeenuth. Zohra. Bombay: Hind Kitabs, 1951.

Domestic life of upper class Muslim families of
Hyderabad portrayed in wealth of detail.

774   Fyzee-Rahamin, S.   Gilded India.   London: Herbert
         Joseph, 1937.
         Intrigues, chaos, luxury and sordidness in Indian
         palaces.

775   Gamon, Richard B.   The strange thirteen.   London:
         Drane's, 1926.
         Thirteen stories, some dealing with the tragedy
         of Eurasian life.

776   _____.   Warren of Oudh.   London: Macdonald,
         1926.
         Set in the times of Warren Hastings, it deals
         with the life of Col. Jack Warren of the Oudh State
         Army.

777   Ganga Vardhan.   The memoirs of a maharajah's mis-
         tress.   Rajkot: Kitabghar, 1943.

778   Ganguli, Jatindra Mohan.   Bond of blood.   Calcutta:
         East and West Publishers, 1967.
         Commercial strife in Calcutta, 1967.

779   _____.   Fire on the snows of Himalayas.   Cal-
         cutta: Ganguli, 1965.
         Sino-Indian confrontation.

780   _____.   The fisherman of Kerala.   Calcutta: East
         and West Publishers, 1968.
         Influence of communist ideology on Kerala poli-
         tics.

781   _____.   So the world goes.   Calcutta: East and
         West, 1969.

782   _____.   Son of Jesus, Sister Pauline at the cross-
         road, the lean lamb and other stories.   Calcutta:
         East and West Publishers, 1967.

783   _____.   Three women had made him a saint and
         'I'm polluted' she told him.   Calcutta: East and
         West Publishers, 1967.

784 _____. Two mothers. Calcutta: Ganguli, 1964.

785 Ganguli, Taraknath. The brothers. Translated from
    the Bengali novel Svarnlata by Edward Thompson.
    London: India Society, 1928.
    Faithful picture of Bengali domestic life.

786 _____. A glimpse into the Indian inner home.
    Calcutta: Lahiri, 1903. Same as The brothers.

787 Ganpat (pseud. of Martin Louis Gompertz). High
    snow. London: Hodder and Stoughton, 1927.
    Very good stuff on Tibet and Ladakh.

788 _____. Mirror of dreams. London: Hodder and
    Stoughton, 1928.
    Dream of a young princess, a journey to find
    her, a smuggled treasure and Tibetan lama's plot
    against the peace of India.

789 _____. The one eyed knave. London: Hodder and
    Stoughton, 1936.
    Indo-Afghan border mystery.

790 _____. Out of evil. London: Hodder and Stough-
    ton, 1933.
    Mystery set in Kashmir and on the Indo-Afghan
    border.

791 _____. Roads of place. London: Hodder and
    Stoughton, 1931.
    Indian frontier, 1919-20. The effect of tribes-
    men on Indian life, their relations with the British,
    Waziri politics.

792 _____. Seven times proven. London: Hodder and
    Stoughton, 1934.
    A necklace is lost in the Himalayan foothills.

793 _____. The snow falcon. London: Hodder and
    Stoughton, 1935.
    Mystery, Ladakh.

794 _____. Snow rubies. London: Blackwood, 1925.
    Romance and adventure: Panjab, Kashmir and
    the 'frontier'.

795 _____. The speakers in silence. London: Hodder
     and Stoughton, 1929.
         Suspense; an old race mentioned in the Old Test-
     ament is presumed to be alive and well possessing
     ultra-audible sounds.

796 _____. Stella Nash. London: Blackwood, 1924.
         Three boys and one girl go north of Kashmir to
     find the source of snow rubies.

797 _____. The three R's. London: Hodder and
     Stoughton, 1930.
         Mystery in the Himalayas and beyond.

798 _____. A voice of Dashin. London: Hodder and
     Stoughton, 1926.
         Brother and niece are rescued from Himalayan
     captivity.

799 _____. Wrexham's romance. London: Hodder and
     Stoughton, 1935.
         Himalayas and behond; suspense.

800 Garbe, Richard. The redemption of the Brahmin.
     Chicago: Open Court, 1894.
         A 'new' Hindu saves a widow with British help;
     excellent information on 19th-century life of Indian
     women.

801 Gaskell, Mrs. North and South. Edited by G. H.
     Kelkar. Poona: N. T. Bhide, 1932.

802 Gasper, D. M. Prisoner for libel. Calcutta: Sunday
     Times, 1894.

803 Gay, Thomas. Androcles, the tiger, and other short
     stories. Bombay: Somaiya Publications, 1967.

804 Gazdar, Manek. Adventures of a fair girl. Allaha-
     bad: Kitabmahal, n. d.

805 Ghosal, Mrs. (same as Swarna Kumari Devi). The
     fatal garland. London: T. W. Laurie, 1915.
         Historical romance, fifteenth-century Bengal.

806 _____. Short stories: social and historical.
     Madras: Ganesh, 1930.

807 _____. An unfinished song. London: T. W.
Laurie, 1913.
Members of the Reformed Party of Bengal adopt
some western manners.

808 Ghose, Aurobindo. The phantom hour. Pondicherry:
Sri Aurobindo Ashram, 1951.
Occult.

809 Ghose, Barindra Kumar. The tale of my exile.
Pondicherry: Arya Office, 1922.
Prison experiences, autobiographical, of a
terrorist.

810 Ghose, Lotika. White dawns of awakening. Calcutta:
Thacker, 1950.

811 Ghose, Sarath Kumar. 1001 Indian nights: the trials
of Narayan Lal. London: Heinemann, 1904.

812 _____. The prince of destiny. London: Rebman,
1909.
A Rajput refuses to oppose the British.

813 _____. Verdict of the gods. New York: Dodd
Mead, 1905.
A fairy tale, almost. The prince after numerous
ordeals wins the princess.

814 Ghose, Sudhin N. And gazelles leaping. London:
Michael Joseph, 1949.
Near autobiographical account of growing up in
Calcutta.

815 _____. Cradle of the clouds. London: Michael
Joseph, 1951.
Continues the preceding, but the scene shifts to
Santal life.

816 _____. The flame of the forest. London: Michael
Joseph, 1955.
Experiences of a youth from the Parganas.

817 _____. The vermillion boat. London: Michael
Joseph, 1953.
Life and love in the Burdwan district.

818   Ghose, Zulfikar.   The contradictions.   London: Mac-
        millan, 1966.
             British civil servants in Delhi on the eve of
        India's independence.

819   _____. The murder of Aziz Khan.   London: Mac-
        millan, 1967.
             The brutal and immoral destruction of ancient
        and intuitive cultures by the demands of western
        technology.   Both Pakistan and India.

820   Ghosh, Ooron, tr.   Dance of Shiva and other folk
        tales from India.   New York: New American Li-
        brary, n. d.
        Ghosh, Sarath Kumar.   See Sarath Kumar Ghose.

821   Gibbon, Frederick P.   The disputed V. C.   London:
        Blackie, 1903.
             Indian Mutiny for the young.

822   _____. Prisoner of the Gurkhas.   London: Rout-
        ledge, 1903.
             Ochterlony's campaign retold for the young.

823   _____. With rifle and kukri.   London: Religious
        Tract Society, 1910.
             Short stories.

        Gibbs, Henry.   See Simon Harvester.

824   Gibney, Robert Dwarris.   My escape from the muti-
        nies in Oudh.   2 vols.   London: R. Bentley, 1858.

825   Gidvani, M. M.   A counterfeit coin.   Hyderabad:
        Sind Art Publications, 192-.

826   Giles, A. R.   Whilom raiders, or winnowings from
        the Lushai hills.   Allahabad: Pioneer Press, 1907.

827   Gillespie, Leslie.   The man from Madura.   London:
        Boardman, 1952.
             Eurasian, successful in Burma, wants to become
        English and hates India: his friend loves India.
        Sufferings of war.

828   Gillespie, Susan.   Cantonment.   London: G. Bles, 1936.
             Military cantonment in India.

829 _____ . Clash by night. London: G. Blex, 1950.
Young Englishman comes to India during her
partition and finds the peace he is seeking in his
cousin's home. An Indian politician is swept away
by intrigue in the princely state.

830 _____ . The day the soldier died. London: G.
Bles, 1960.
India of the 1920's; wife of an army officer in
love with another man.

831 _____ . Diamond in the night. London: G. Bles,
1962.
Two army officers of the Nicholson's Horse
meet and re-live life in a princely state in the
1930's and 1940's. Tiger hunt.

832 _____ . Frozen lake. London: G. Bles, 1964.
Infidelity of an English woman during her husband's absence to war; agony of parents over their
delinquent son; mostly set in Himalayan hills.

833 _____ . Government House. London: G. Bles,
1937.
An English girl visits a governor's house, and
falls in love.

834 _____ . Himalayan view. London: G. Bles, 1947.
Last days of an English family in India; with
their faithful Indian servants.

835 _____ . Janet Firbright. London: Hutchinson,
1953.
An English girl in India falls in love with a
widower.

836 _____ . North from Bombay. London: G. Bles,
1944.
Romance with excellent portrait of the Sikhs.

837 _____ . The promotion of fools. London: G. Bles,
1942.
Prince married to an American girl is forced to
abdicate; Anglo-American rivalries.

838 _____ . The rajah's guests. London: G. Bles, 1935.
Set in a princely state. Anglo-American rivalries.

839   Gilson, Charles.   The lost empire: a tale of many
      lands.   London: Frowde, 1909.

840   Gjellerup, Karl Adolf.   The pilgrim Kamanita: a
      legendary romance.   Translated by J. E. Logie.
      London: Heinemann, 1911.
            Moving tribute to the Buddha.

841   Glasgow, Geraldine.   Black and white.   Lucknow:
      Methodist Publishing, 1889.
            The author wrote several other missionary tales
      for children.

842   Goddard, Richard E.   Obsession.   London: Hurst and
      Blackett, 1925.
            If Britain stopped policing Bengal there wouldn't
      be a virgin or a rupee left there.

843   _____.   Peterkin Sahib, and other sketches.   Bom-
      bay: Thacker, 190-.

844   Godden, John.   The city and the wave.   London: M.
      Joseph, 1954.
            Eurasian living alone in a crowded city near the
      Bay of Bengal befriends a homeless girl, finds
      love, and achieves paternity.

845   _____.   The peacock.   New York: Rinehart, 1950.
            An English couple with two friends on a hunting
      trip to India.

846   _____.   The seven islands.   New York: Knopf,
      1956.
            Peace of some sacred islands in the Ganges is
      disturbed by an Indian who sets up a religious es-
      tablishment.

847   Godden, Rumer.   Black narcissus.   London: Peter
      Davies, 1939.
            Anglican nuns come to India to set up a school
      and a hospital in remote Himalayan region.   Master-
      piece.

848   _____.   Breakfast with Nikolides.   London: Peter
      Davies, 1942.
            Exotic, poetic and morbid novel of lopsided and
      tormented characters in Bengal watching a dog die.

849 _____. Gone: a thread of stories. New York:
Viking, 1968.
Included is a magnificant story 'Whither the
swans and the turtles go' set in the Himalayas,
where a lonely mother teaches her children to take
care of a cheetah fawn.

850 _____. Kingfishers catch fire. London: Macmillan, 1953.
An English widow with two small children and
very little money seeks to settle in Kashmir and to
make people like her.

851 _____. Lady and the unicorn. London: Peter
Davies, 1937.
Sentimental portrayal of life in Bengal.

852 _____. Mooltiki: stories and poems from India.
London: Macmillan, 1957.

853 _____. The river. London: Michael Joseph, 1946.
Two adolescent Anglo-Indian girls grow up in
Bengal.

854 Godinho, J. Abdul Aziz. Bombay: Nicol's, 1892.
A short story set in the time of Nur Jahan.

855 Gokhale, Arvind Vishnu. Kamalna. Bombay: Popular,
1952.

856 _____. The unmarried widow and other stories.
Translated by Snehprabha Pradhan, Bombay: Jaico,
1957.

857 Goldsack, William. Ghulam Jabbar's renunciation.
Madras: Christian Literature Society, 1913.
East Bengal: conversion to Christianity.

Gompertz, M. L. A. See Ganpat.

858 Gopal, Haldar. Ekada. New Delhi: Peoples Publish-
House, 1969.

859 Gopala-Panikkar, T. K. Storm and sunshine. Cali-
cut: No publisher given, 1916.
Malayalee life.

860   Gopalan, S. Old Tanjore: an historical novel. Madras: Rama Iyer, 1937.
      Eighteenth-century Tanjore facing European intrusion.

861   Gordon, H. K. (pseud.) Prem. London: Arnold, 1926.
      Agrarian problems of northern India sympathetically described, but nationalism is considered a tool of Bolshevism and anarchism.

862   _____. The shadow of Abdul. London: Arnold, 1928.
      College friendship between an Indian and an Englishman put to severe strain in India by different approaches to politics.

863   Gore, Catherine Grace Francis. Banker's wife. 3 vols. London: No publisher given, 1843.
      A satirical representation of an Old Indian.

864   Gouldsbury, Charles Elphinstone. Dulall the forest guard. London: Gibbings, 1909.
      Forests of Bengal.

865   Gour, Hari Singh. His only love. London: Walker, 1930.
      Alliance of east and west is advocated, but modern Indians cut from ancient moorings are considered adrift.

866   Gowry (pseud.) An Indian village girl. Madras: C. Foster, 1876.

867   Gracias, Louis. Eastern clay. Calcutta: No publisher given, 1948.
      Fourteen stories.

868   Grange, Beatrice. The heart of a maid. Allahabad: Wheeler, 1890.
      An English girl marries in India to escape her mother in England.

      Granger, Francis Edward. See Headon Hill.

869   Grant, Colquhoun. Their heart's desire. London: J. Long, 1910.
      A magistrate in India in love with a countess.

870   Grant, James. <u>Did she love him</u>? 3 vols. London:
      Tinsley, 1876.
          Covers a number of countries under the British
      flag.

871   _____ . <u>Duke of Albany's own highlanders.</u> 3 vols.
      London: Routledge, 1880.
          Scottish highlanders, their adventures and ro-
      mances in India.   For young adults.

872   _____ . <u>Fairer than a fairy.</u> 3 vols. London:
      Tinsley, 1874.
          Army adventures in India.

873   _____ . <u>First love and last love: a tale of the</u>
      <u>Indian Mutiny.</u> 3 vols. London: Routledge, 1868.

874   _____ . <u>Only an ensign.</u> 3 vols. London: No
      publisher given, 1871.
          Retreat from Kabul.

      Graves, Clotilda Inez Mary. <u>See</u> Richard Dehan.

875   Gray, Maxwell (<u>pseud.</u> of Mary Gleed Tutiet). <u>In the</u>
      <u>heart of the storm.</u> London: Kegan Paul, 1891.
          English girl is moved by the plight of Indian
      women during the Mutiny.   Miss Gray may have
      written other novels with Indian setting.

876   Greave, Peter. <u>The painted leopard.</u> London: Eyre
      and Spottiswoode, 1960.
          Poor Englishman living in a slum in riot-torn
      Calcutta of 1946 thinks more of his girl than his
      creeping leprosy and the riot.   Very good.

877   _____ . <u>Young man in the sun.</u> London: Eyre and
      Spottiswoode, 1958.
          Poor and unsuccessful English salesman in Cal-
      cutta falls hopelessly in live with a Eurasian girl.

878   Green, Evelyn Everett. <u>The double house.</u> London:
      Stanley Paul, 1914.
          In one half of the house lives an attractive Eng-
      lish widow, in the other half a gallant colonel under
      the suspicion of murder.   Miss Green may have
      written other novels with Indian setting.

879   Greenhow, Harry M. <u>Amy Vivian.</u> London: Skeffing-
      ton, 1897.
             Romance and intrigue on the Indo-Afghan border.

880   _____. <u>The bow of fate.</u> London: Allen, 1893.
             'Frontier' cantonment story.

881   _____. <u>Brenda's experiment.</u> London: Jarrolds,
      1896.
             English girl marries a Muslim and lives through
      the Mutiny and thereafter. Excellent ethnographical
      details.

882   _____. <u>The emperor's design.</u> London: Digby
      Long, 1901.
             Sir Thomas Roe and Jahangir.

883   _____. <u>The tower of Ghilzan.</u> London: R.
      Bentley, 1896.
             Infatuation of an Afghan wife for a British officer.

884   Greening, Arthur. <u>The curse of Kali.</u> London:
      Jarrolds, 1922.
             A simple and elegant tale of the abduction of an
      English girl by the Indian thugs.

      Gregg, Hilda. <u>See</u> Sydney Carolyn Grier.

885   Grier, Sydney Carolyn (<u>pseud.</u> of Hilda Gregg). <u>The</u>
      <u>advanced guard.</u> London: Blackwood, 1903.
             Northwest frontier before the Mutiny, with an
      account of native dungeons and torture practices,
      1849.

886   _____. <u>Berringer of Bandeir.</u> London: Black-
      wood, 1919.

887   _____. <u>England hath need of thee.</u> London: Black-
      wood, 1916.
             Diplomatic mission to Afghan tribesmen.

888   _____. <u>The great proconsul: the memoirs of Mrs.</u>
      <u>Hester Ward, formerly in the family of Hon'ble</u>
      <u>Warren Hastings.</u> London: Blackwood, 1904.
             Warren Hastings and other chief characters of
      his time.

889 _____. The heir. London: Blackwood, 1906.
      Two rival claimants for the throne of the Eastern
   empire.

890 _____. In furthest Ind: the narrative of Edward
   Carolyn of the Hon'ble East India Company's service. London: Blackwood, 1894.
      Imaginary autobiography of a Company servant
   who visited the court of Aurangzib; good descriptions of Surat, and Portuguese inquisitions at Goa
   in the 17th century.

891 _____. The keepers of the gate. London: Blackwood, 1911.
      Indian northwest frontier at the time of the
   Mutiny.

892 _____. Like another Helen. London: Blackwood,
   1899.
      Black Hole; Clive; Battle of Plassey.

893 _____. The path to honour. London: Blackwood,
   1909.
      Sequel to The keepers of the gate; revolt of
   Granthi Regiment, 1850.

894 _____. Peace with honour. London: Blackwood,
   1897.
      Frontier romance.

895 _____. The power of the keys. London: Blackwood, 1907.
      'Modern' invasion of India by the Scythians.

896 _____. Two strong men. London: Blackwood,
   1923.
      Official life in India about the beginning of Vic-
   toria's reign. Romance and military episodes.

897 _____. The warden of the marches. London:
   Blackwood, 1901.
      Defence of the 'forward' policy on the Frontier.

898 Griffith, Arthur. Before the British raj: a story of
   military adventures in India. London: Everett,
   1903.
      Set in the reign of Shah Alum when race relations
   were good.

899   _____. A royal rascal: episodes in the career of
           Col. Sir Theophilius St. Clair, K. C. B.   London:
           Fisher Unwin, 1905.
                Gentleman-soldier in action against Tippoo.

900   Groves, John Percy.   The duke's own.   London:
           Griffith, 1887.
                Siege of Seringapatam for school children.   The
           author may have written other stories on India.

901   _____. Soldier born, or the adventures of a subal-
           tern of the 95th in the Crimea and Indian Mutiny.
           London: Griffith, 1886.

902   Guisborough, John.   A song of Araby.   London: Mills
           and Boon, 1921.
                Love and laughter spiced with adventures.

903   Gulvadi (pseud. of S. V. Shiva Rao).   The optimist and
           other stories.   Bombay: Popular, 1925.

904   Gupta, Dilip Kumar (editor).   Best stories of modern
           Bengal.   2 vols.   Calcutta: Signet, 1944-45.
                Contains autobiographical notes on the authors.

905   Gupta, Yogesh.   A city without she.   Delhi: Writers
           Forum, 1966.

906   Gurudatta.   Desire.   New Delhi: Paradise, 1969.

907   Guru-Kumara (pseud. of C. Subramania Ayyar).   A
           daughter's shadow.   Madras: The author, 1943.

908   _____. Life's shadows. Bombay: Taraporevala, 1938.
                Relations of a man with his brother, wife, son
           and friend.   Daughter's shadow deals with his rela-
           tions with his daughter.   The sketches are a mild
           protest against westernization.

909   Guthrie, Mrs.   My year in an Indian fort.   2 vols.
           London: Hurst and Blackett, 1878.
                Quite accurate picture of life in the Belgaum fort.

       Guthrie, Thomas Anstey.   See F. Anstey.

910   Habib, Muhammad.   The desecrated bones and other
           stories.   London: Luzac, 1926.

Two supernatural stories set in contemporary
Uttar Pradesh; the third is set in the fourteenth
century and is historical.

911   Hainsselin, Montagu Thomas.   Markham of Mohistan.
       London: Greening, 1909.
              Love, war and mystery set in Bombay and be-
       yond.

912   Hales, Alfred Greenwood.   The Glusky in India.   Lon-
       don: John Long, 1930.
              Treasure hunt; for children.   Mr. Hales may
       have written other children's stories set in India.

913   Hall, G. P.   Bar sinister.   Bombay: C. Murphy,
       1944.
              A gripping story of love and adventure in the
       Indian jungles.

       Hall, Henry Fielding.   See Henry Fielding.

914   Halls, Geraldine.   Cats of Benares.   London: Harper,
       1967.
              A UNESCO instructor's marriage breaks up in
       Benares due to the effect of Indian culture.

915   Hamilton, John.   In a Bengal backwater.   Calcutta:
       Thacker, 1920.
              Excellent internal description of the home life of
       a Bengali family; east versus west.

916   Hamilton, Lillias.   A vizier's daughter: a tale of the
       Hazara war.   London: John Murray, 1900.
              Afghan life and manners.

917   Hamilton, M.   (pseud. of Mary Churchill Luck).   The
       general's wife.   London: Stanley Paul, 1916.
              Sensitive portrait of two boys affected by an in-
       compatible marriage in a military station of India.

918   _____.   Mrs. Brett.   London: Stanley Paul, 1913.
              Srinagar.   Domestic situation of the whites in a
       hill station.

919   _____.   Poor Elisabeth.   London: Hurst and
       Blackett, 1901.

920   Hampden, Ernest Miles Hobart.   The price of empire.
      London: Blackwood, 1911.
          Sedition; treachery of an Indian in British ad-
      ministration.   Tragic love drama of east and west.

921   _____. The taming of Tarm.   London: Nisbet,
      1914.
          Young adult story set in the jungles of India with
      some princely local color.

922   Hampden, Helene.   Billy and the boy.   London: Hum-
      phrey Milford, 1920.

923   _____.   The cave of Hanuman.   London: Sheldon
      Press, 1929.

924   _____.   Chinna etc.   London: Wells Gardner, 1924.

925   _____.   Little prince Tota.   London: Sheldon
      Press, 1930.

926   _____.   The little rajah.   London: T. Nelson,
      1922.

927   _____.   Louisa.   London: Wells Gardner, 1927.

928   _____.   The sleeping city.   London: Wells Gard-
      ner, 1932.

929   _____.   Two little wanderers.   London: Humphrey
      Milford, 1924.
          All these are children's stories.

930   Han Suyin (pseud. of Elizabeth Conber).   The moun-
      tain is young.   London: Cape, 1958.
          Frigid and devitalized white married woman
      thaws magically under the influence of an Indian
      in the Khatmandu valley.

931   Handa, Rajendra Lal.   Lengthening shadows.   Delhi:
      Sterling Publishers, 1969.

932   Hanley, Gerald.   The journey homeward.   London:
      Collins, 1961.

933   Hanley, M. P.   Tales and songs of an Assam tea
      garden.   Calcutta: Thacker, 1928.

934   Hanli, Sheela. Potpourri: a series of short tales.
      Calcutta: Thacker, 1912.

935   Hanshew, Thomas W. and Mary W. The riddle of the
      purple emperor. London: Simpkin and Marshall,
      1918.
          A big diamond is looted from an Indian temple.
      Charming.

936   Harcourt, Alfred Frederic Pollock. Jenetha's venture:
      a tale of the siege of Delhi. London: Cassell,
      1899.
          An Englishwoman in Delhi during the Mutiny,
      1857.

937   _____. The last of the peshwas: a tale of the
      third Maratha war. London: Blackie, 1906.
          Elphinstone and Baji Rao, 1817-18.

938   _____. On the knees of the gods. 2 vols. London:
      Bentley, 1897.
          An Indian noble wants to abduct a Eurasian girl
      but is double crossed by her cousin. Anti-Eura-
      sian, anti-Indian.

939   _____. The peril of the sword. London: Skeffing-
      ton, 1903.
          Havelock's relief of Lucknow during the Mutiny.

940   _____. The prince of Balkh: a tale of the wars
      of Aurangzeb. London: Blackie, 1904.
          A Scot in Central Asia during Aurangzeb's wars,
      1660-85.

941   Harding, Dan. Venus in India: or adventures of love
      in Hindostan. Paris, Oceanic Press, 1959.

942   Harding, Robert. Firebrand fakir: tales of adventure
      in India and Afghanistan. London: Latimer House,
      1952.

943   _____. The keys of freedom: stories of the east.
      London: Boys Own Paper, 1933.

944   _____. Pioneer Jack and other stories. London:
      Boys Own Paper, 1935.

945 _____. The poison mountain: a tale of the Indian
       secret service.   London: C. A. Pearson, 1931.

946 _____. Poison of Kali.   London: Lutterworth
       Press, 1939.

947 _____. The riddle of the frontier.   London: Boys
       Own Paper, 1932.

948 _____. Tales of the frontier.   London: Boys Own
       Paper, 1938.

949 _____. Timber Sahib: tales of the Indian secret
       service.   London: Boys Own Paper, 1937.
             All the above titles are for young adults; mostly
       detective.

950 Harman, John.   Northwest frontier.   London: Trans-
       world, 1959.
             June 1907; Prince Kishan's death is demanded by
       Muslim nobles but he is whisked away by a British
       army officer.

951 Harrison, Mary St. Leger.   Damaris.   London:
       Hutchinson, 1916.
             A widower's romance, and its ups and downs,
       with an alluring married woman; his five-year-old
       daughter Damaris helps resolve the dilemma.

952 Hartigan, Henry.   Stray leaves from a military man's
       notebook.   Calcutta: T. S. Smith, 1877.

953 Hartley, James.   Indian life: a tale of the Carnatic.
       3 vols.   London: Saunders, 1840.

954 Harvester, Simon (pseud. of Henry Gibbs).   Tiger in
       the north.   New York: Walker, 1963.
             Intrigue in an Indian border state where British
       oilmen are prospecting.   Harvester may have
       written other mysteries with India as setting.

955 Harvey, G.   On the march: a tale of the Deccan.
       Madras: No publisher given, 1867.

956 Harvey, G. T. B.   Duet in Kerath.   London: Hutch-
       inson, 1936.
             Restless young European works in an Indian state

where he is befriended by an American missionary
and his niece; witnesses the rivalry between two
Hindu princes; one a product of Oxford, the other
of Hindu temples.   Notable; much originality.

Haswell, Chetwynd John Drake. See George Foster.

957   Haynes, Herbert. Clevely Sahib: a tale of the Khyber
Pass. London: T. Nelson, 1897.
British expedition into Afghanistan; murder of
Macnaughten; retreat through the Khyber and mas-
sacre; and revenge upon Kabul under Pollock. One
of the best Afghan horse operas.

958   Hazari (pseud. of Marcus Abraham Malik). An Indian
outcaste: the autobiography of an untouchable.
London: Bannisdale, 1951.
Superb ethonological document. A Moradabadi
untouchable works in hills stations and for various
European families; converts to Islam and acquires
education.

959   Heller, Frank (pseud. of Gunnar Serner). The marriage of Yussuf Khan. Translated by Robert E.
Lee. New York: Crowell, 1923.
An Indian maharaja with a hundred weight of
jewels, guarded by an escort of black scimitars
encounters Mirza, the jewel thief.

960   Hemingway, Kenneth. Chi-chi. London: Quality
Press, 1947.
Indo-Burma theatre during the second world war.
Low quality.

961   Henderson, H. B. The Bengales or sketches of society and manners in the east. London: Smith
Elder, 1829.
Rough humor; the victims are Bengalis and some
non-Bengalis.

962   Henty, George Alfred. Bears and the dacoits: a tale
of the ghauts. London: Blackie, 1896.

963   _____. The Brahmin's treasure or Colonel Thorndyke's secret. London: Hurst and Blackett, 1898.

964   _____. For name and fame. London: Blackie, 1886.

965   _____ . In the days of the Mutiny. New York:
           Ogilvie, 1893.

966   _____ . In times of peril. London: Griffith and
           Farran, 1881.

967   _____ . On the Irrawaddy: a story of the first
           Burmese war. London: Blackie, 1897.

968   _____ . The point of the bayonet: a tale of the
           Maratha war. London: Blackie, 1902.

969   _____ . The queen's cup. 3 vols. London: Chatto
           and Windus, 1897.

970   _____ . Rujeeb the juggler. 3 vols. London:
           Chatto and Windus, 1893.

971   _____ . Through the Sikh war. London: Blackie,
           1893.

972   _____ . Through three campaigns. London: Blackie,
           1904.

973   _____ . The tiger of Mysore: a story of the war
           with Tippoo Sahib. London: Blackie, 1896.

974   _____ . To Herat and Cabul. London: Blackie,
           1902.

975   _____ . With Clive in India, or the beginnings of
           an empire. London: Blackie, 1884.
               Tales of British adventures in India read widely
           in British schools for generations, and dedicated to
           the proposition that courage is more important than
           book learning for the British Raj.

976   Hervey, Harry. Caravans by night. New York:
           Century, 1922.
               Well written detective yarn about Indian jewels,
           a Hindu witch, a Mongol prince, and an American
           girl; set in Indore, Delhi, Calcutta, Bhutan and
           Sikkim.

977   Hervey, Harry Clay. Veiled fountain. London: W. H.
           Allen, 1949.
               An English musician in India falls in love with the
           former girl friend of his brother. Very readable.

978 Hervy, H. J. A. Through the furnace: a tale of the
     northwest frontier. Madras: Higginbothams, 1907.

979 _____. Weathered: a P. & O. story. Madras:
     Higginbothams, 1907.

980 Hesse, Hermann. Siddhartha. Translated by Hilda
     Rosner. London: Peter Owen, 1954.
        A magnificant novel dealing with the life of the
     Buddha and greatly in vogue in the 1950's.

981 Heston, Winifred. Bluestocking in India. London:
     Andrew Melrose, 1910.
        An American girl goes to India as a medical
     missionary.

982 Hill, Headon (pseud. of Francis Edward Grainger).
     Divinations of Kala Persad. London: Ward and
     Lock, 1895.

983 _____. The rajah's second wife. London: Ward
     and Lock, 1891.
        Missionary activities.

984 _____. A traitor's wooing. London: Ward and
     Lock, 1909.
        A maharaja kidnaps an English girl who refuses
     him marriage.

985 Hill, Keats. Bound in shallows. London: Richard
     and Cowan, 1950.
        An irresolute English lad in Bengal learns to
     make decisions in an upriver Bengal town.

986 _____. Rumor's daughter. London: Richard and
     Cowan, 1949.
        Mystery; Assam.

987 Hill, Samuel Woods. An avatar in Vishnu land.
     London: Scribners, 1928.
        Journey from the Red Sea to India; inter-racial
     conflict; good descriptions of Rajasthan and the west
     coast. Opium smuggling.

988 _____. Mahatma. London: Methuen, 1931.
        Racial animosities; fumbling administration; In-
     dian nationalism.

989   Hillary, Louise. A yak for Christmas: the story of
      a Himalayan holiday. London: Hodder and Stough-
      ton, 1968.

990   Hilliers, Ashton (pseud. of Henry M. Wallis). As it
      happened. London: Hutchinson, 1909.
          London to Madras to London to Gibraltar.

991   _____. An old score. London: Ward and Lock,
      1906.
          Lord Gough's Sikh campaign; wrong is righted
      after two generations.

992   Hilton, James. Lost horizon. London: Macmillan,
      1933.
          Peshawar, Afghanistan, Tibet and Shangri-la.

993   Hinkson, Pamela. Golden rose. London: Collins,
      1944.
          Colorful story of the loves of two women against
      the background of a model hospital in India.

994   Hitrec, Joseph George. Angel of gaiety. New York:
      Harper, 1951.
          A Eurasian widow in Bombay faces the identity
      crisis.

995   _____. Ruler's morning and other stories. New
      York: Harper, 1946.

996   _____. Son of the moon. London: Michael Joseph,
      1949.
          Kshattriya Hindu returns to Bombay after a stay
      in England and feels cross cultural influences.

997   Hockley, William Browne. The English in India.
      3 vols. London: No publisher given, 1828.

998   _____. The memoirs of a Brahmin or the fatal
      jewels. 3 vols. London: Newby, 1843.

999   _____. Pandurang Hari, or the memoirs of a
      Hindoo. 3 vols. London: No publisher given, 1826.
          Proto-type of Confessions of a thug; story of a
      Maratha warlord.

1000 _____. Tales of the zennana; or a nawab's leisure
      hours. 2 vols. London: No publisher given, 1874.

1001 _____ . The vizier's son, or the adventures of a
Mogul. 3 vols. London: No publisher given, 1831.

1002 Hofland, Barbara Hoole. Captives in India: a tale:
and a widow and a will. 3 vols. London: R.
Bentley, 1834.
Overland journey to India and the fortitude of
English women; heroism of the British in South
India.

1003 _____ . The young cadet or Henry Delamere's
voyage to India. London: John Harris, 1827.
Oudh and Ellora Caves, and well described.
Miss Hofland may have written other yarns dealing
with India.

1004 Holden, C. L. Videhi: a novel of Indian life. London: Macmillan, 1953.
An Indian girl of orthodox Hindu parents is im-
pressed by western ideas of romantic love, but is
given in an arranged marriage from which she flees.

1005 Hollis, Gertrude. The pearl fishers. London: Nelson,
1907.
Xavier's mission to India; for young adults.

1006 Holmes, Alec. Anglo-India. Allahabad: Pioneer
Press, 1904.

1007 _____ . Anglo-Indian life in the sixties. Allahabad:
Pioneer, 1910.

1008 _____ . The emporium. London: George Allen,
1912.

1009 _____ . The song of the stars. London: George
Allen, 1917.
Kidnapping and release of an English girl on the Afghan
frontier; superb pictures of Afghan life in Quetta.

1010 Home, Dhirendra Chandra. Floods along the Ganges.
Bombay: Peoples Publishing House, 1953.
Growth of political consciousness among Bengal
peasants in the twentieth century.

1011 _____ . Hungry hearts. Calcutta: Kathashilpa, 1965.
Lovers, writers, communists, Congresswallahs at
the time of India's partition.

1012 _____. Poison and passion. Bombay: Kanak
      Publishers, 1955.
      Movie stars at work and play.

1013 _____. So many, so gallant. Bombay: No pub-
      lisher given, 1951.
      Bombay in the 'thirties; and Marxist groups.

1014 Hook, Theodora Edward. Gilbert Gurney. London:
      No publisher given, 1836.

1015 _____. Gurney married. London: No publisher
      given, 1839.
      Exploits of a 'nabob'.

1016 _____. Sayings and doings. A series of sketches
      from life. Two series. London: H. Colburn, 1825.

1017 Horniman, Roy. The living Buddha. London: Fisher
      Unwin, 1903.
      Station society uprooted by the Mutiny finds itself
      in Tibet and Nepal; wretched description of Tibetan
      Buddhism.

1018 Horsman, Dorothy. Justine Gay. London: Werner
      Laurie, 1932.
      An English girl goes to India upon marriage and
      is made to feel a guest rather than a mistress in
      her house. Innocent affair in Kashmir.

1019 Hosain, Attia. Phoenix fled and other stories. Lon-
      don: Chatto and Windus, 1953.
      Outstanding stories of Muslim life, old and new.

1020 _____. Sunlight on a broken column. London:
      Chatto and Windus, 1961.
      An outstanding novel of Muslim life. An orphaned
      girl, raised in two different households, must choose
      between political nationalism and personal emanci-
      pation.

      Hosken, Alice Cecil Seymour. See Coralie Stanton.

1021 Howell, Constance. Married in India. London:
      Ousley, 1910.
      Attitude of post-Mutiny officials towards Indians
      in the 'sixties, and the rise of the attitude of racial
      superiority.

1022 Huddleston, George. A daughter of India. London:
      Stockwell, 1934.
             Some good scenes of Marwari life in eastern
      India, and the Home Rule movement.

1023 _____. Kissed by the sun. London: Stockwell,
      1934.
             Indigo fields and Calcutta society.

1024 _____. Tales for the train. Allahabad: Wheeler,
      1923.

1025 _____. The white fakir. London: Ocean Publish-
      ing, 1932.
             An Englishman marries his father's secretary;
      and lives in the mystical east, hoping to bring
      about reconciliation between east and west.

1026 Hukk, Jane. Abdullah and his two strings. London:
      Hurst and Blackett, 1927.
             A Muslim doctor marries a Scottish girl and
      brings her to India where his Muslim wife awaits
      him. The description of the Muslim household; the
      security that joint family and old servants provide,
      and the dilemma of the western educated Indian is
      superbly told. The soundest, most convincing novel
      written on India.

1027 _____. End of a marriage. London: Andrew
      Melrose, 1935.
             Handsome Indian and a Scot girl secretly marry
      and secretly depart. They meet again in India; she
      is the wife of a police officer, he an anarchist.
      Another capable story.

1028 Humphrey, E. J. Heerah: a story of the sepoy
      mutiny. Boston: Long and Putnam, 1878.

1029 Hunt, Gordon. The forgotten land. London: G. Bles,
      1967.

1030 Hunter, Hall (pseud.) Bengal tiger. London: R. Hale,
      1954.
             Calcutta; love and adventure.

1031 Hunter, William W. The old missionary. London:
      Frowde, 1896.

Idyllic picture of India in the early nineteenth
century; Baptist missionary is the hero of this
pathetic story.

1032 Hurst, Samuel Bertram Haworth. Coomer Ali: a story
of Arabia and India. New York: Harper, 1922.
An Arab leads an abortive revolution against the
British and is imprisoned in Calcutta. His adventures with a Scot.

1033 Hussain, Iqalunnisa. Purdah and polygamy: life in an
Indian Muslim household. Bangalore: Hosali Press,
1944.

1034 Hutheesingh, Krishna. Shadows on the wall. New
York: Day, 1948.
Twelve stories of prison and fellow prisoners.

1035 Ingrestone, Richard (pseud.) At bay: a book for king
and parliament. London: No publisher given, 1902.

1036 Iota (pseud. of Kathleen Mannington Caffyn). Mary
Mirrielies. London: Hurst and Blackett, 1916.
English sapper goes to India, his wife to Zurich,
and eventually they reconcile.

1037 Ireland, William Wotherspoon. Golden bullets: a
story in the days of Akbar and Elizabeth. Edinburgh: Bell and Bradfute, 1890.
English merchant becomes Mughal artillery
officer.

1038 _____. Randolph Methyl: a story of the Anglo-
Indian life. 2 vols. London: No publisher given,
1863.
Anglo-India, 1830-50.

1039 Irvine, Andrew Alexander. Damfool Smith Sahib.
Lahore: Civil and Military Gazette, 1899.
Contrived humor about a pucca sahib.

1040 _____. The devil's finger. London: John Murray,
1937.
Rajput states at the time of Akbar.

1041 _____. In a Simla season. Lahore: Civil and

Military Gazette, 1910.
Simla bureaucracy, of course.

1042 Irwin, Henry Crossley. <u>A man of honour.</u> London:
A. & C. Black, 1896.

1043 _____. <u>Love besieged: a romance of the residency
of Lucknow.</u> London: No publisher given, no date.
Siege of Delhi during the Mutiny.

1044 _____. <u>With sword and pen.</u> London: Fisher
Unwin, 1904.
Annexation of Oudh; life in a native court; relief
of Lucknow during the Mutiny.

1045 Isherwood, Christopher. <u>Meeting by the river.</u> New
York: Simon and Schuster, 1967.
Philosophical and psychological explorations on
conflicting temperaments of two brothers: one about
to become a Hindu monk, the other a Hollywood
producer.

1046 Ishvani. <u>Girl in Bombay.</u> London: Pilot Press, 1947.

1047 Isvaran, Manjeri S. <u>Angry dust.</u> Madras: Shakti
Karayalam, 1944.
Interpersonal relationships in South India.

1048 _____. <u>Fancy tales.</u> Madras: Shakti Karayalam,
1947.
Fourteen once-upon-a-time stories of gods and
goddesses, kings and queens.

1049 _____. <u>Immersion.</u> Madras: S. Viswanathan, 1951.
A married couple journey to Benares with his
father's ashes, and on the way the wife allows herself to be seduced.

1050 _____. <u>Naked shingles.</u> Madras: Shakti Karayalam, 1941.
South Indian life.

1051 _____. <u>No anklet bells for her.</u> Madras: Mitra,
1949.

1052 _____. <u>Painted tigers.</u> Madras: Dhanus, 1956.

1053 _____. Rickshawallah. Madras: Alliance Co.,
        1946.
        These four preceding titles are collections of
        South Indian stories mainly dealing with husband-
        wife relationships.

1054 _____. Siva ratri. Madras: Shakti Karayalam,
        n. d.

1055 Jackson, Alice F. Brave girl, true story of the
        Indian Mutiny. London: Christian Knowledge So-
        ciety, 1899.

1056 Jacob, Nirmal. Monsoon. Bombay: Higginbotham,
        1968.

1057 Jag, S. S. Vice and virtue. Delhi: Atmaram, 1964.

1058 Jagmohan, Sarla, translator. Selected stories from
        Gujarat. Bombay: Jaico, 1961.

1059 Jai Ratan. The angry goddess. Calcutta: Writers
        Workshop, 1963.

1060 _____. Contemporary Hindi short stories. Cal-
        cutta: Writters Workshop, 1962.
        Sixteen authors are represented.

1061 Jainendra Kumar. The resignation. Translated by
        S. H. Vatsyayana. Delhi: Siddharatha, 1947.
        Story of a fallen woman and her dharma. Po-
        tentialities of nonresistance to evil as a positive
        spiritual force.

1062 James, Lionel. A few Indian stories. Lahore: Civil
        and Military Gazette, 1895.

1063 _____. Shadows from the east. Lahore: Civil
        and Military Gazette, 1896.
        33 stories.

1064 Jarrett, T. The tale of Nala. Cambridge: Wareh,
        1875.

1065 Jay, Charlotte (pseud. of Geraldine Jay). The yellow
        turban. London: Collins, 1950.

An Englishman in Karachi pursued by a man in yellow turban.

Jay, Geraldine. See Charlotte Jay.

1066 Jayakar, Pupul. God is not a full stop and other stories. Bombay: Kutub, 1949.

1067 Jeffery, Jeffery C. James Vraille: the story of a life. 2 vols. London: Allen, 1890.
Life and love of an English family in India: Eurasian ayah well drawn.

1068 Jenkins, Robin. The tiger of gold. London: Macdonald, 1962.
Scottish girl falls in love with an Indian aristocrat in Southeast Asia and is ostracised by the European community. Goes to India and finds her lover engaged to his childhood sweetheart.

1069 Jesse, Fryniwyd Marsh Tennyson. The lacquer lady. London: Heinemann, 1929.
One of the best historical novels; expedition for the annexation of Upper Burma. Superb description of Mandalay.

1070 Jhabvala, Ruth Prawer. Amrita. New York: Norton, 1956.
Westernized girl rebels against her family in New Delhi.

1071 _____. A backward place. New York: Norton, 1965.
An English girl married to an Indian actor. Sharp satire on the organizers of culture who believe that the state can do everything.

1072 _____. Esmond in India. New York: Norton, 1958.
Two prominent Indian families and an Englishman who acts as a catalyst in their lives. Esmond, a colonial type, marries Gulab, profoundly eastern.

1073 _____. Get ready for battle. London: Norton, 1963.
Wealthy Delhi businessman and his marital difficulties.

1074 _____. The householder. New York: Norton, 1960.

Adjustment of two young people in an arranged marriage.

1075 _____. Like birds, like fishes. New York: Norton, 1964.
Short stories; all but one set in Delhi.

1076 _____. The nature of passion. London: Allen and Unwin, 1956.
Conflict between tradition and modernity in a Panjabi upper class family living in Delhi; and the moral bankruptcy of the younger generation.

1077 _____. A stronger climate. New York: Norton, 1969.
Nine stories.

1078 _____. To whom she will. Same as Amrita.

1079 Jhabvala, Shavaksha Hormusji. Tanoo: the leper child; a tale of leprosy in India. Bombay: Published by the author, n. d.

1080 John, Michael. The heir of the Malik. London: H. Jenkins, 1923.
Englishman crosses over the Afghan tribal area, engages in tribal politics and marries an Afghan girl.

1081 John, Usha. The unknown lover and other short stories. Bombay: Longmans, 1960.

1082 Johnston, G. H. Monsoon. New York: Dodd Mead, 1950.
A cashiered English officer in India, on the verge of revolution. Benares during the monsoon.

1083 Jose, Sebastian. The space, time, and I. Calcutta: Alpha Beta, 1966.

1084 Joshi, Arun. The foreigner. Bombay: Asia, 1968.
Indian, born in Kenya, educated in the west, returns to India and finds alienation all around him.

1085 Judah, Aaron. Clown of Bombay. London: Faber, 1963.
A Jewish boy in Bombay of 1939; an aggressive black sheep.

1086 _____ . Clown on fire. New York: Dial, 1967.
       Continuation of the earlier title. The hero
struggles with the enigmas of authority, adolescent
sex, western education and brotherhood of races.

1087 Julian, Mary. Where jasmines bloom. London:
       Hodder and Stoughton, 1917.
       Unhappy married life caused by environment--
Indian plains; love discovered in pleasant surround-
ings--Kashmir.

1088 Kabir, Humayun. Men and rivers. Bombay: Hind
       Kitabs, 1945.
       The river is Padma in Bengal; the men, Muslim
peasants.

1089 _____ . Of cabbages and kings. Bombay: Hind
       Kitabs, 1947.

1090 _____ . Three stories. Bombay: Hind Kitabs,
       1947.
       Muslim life.

1091 Kabir, Humayun (editor). Green and gold: stories
       and poems from Bengal. Bombay: Asia, 1957.

1092 Kaikini, R. R. The recruit. Bombay: New Book
       House, 1937.

1093 Kapur, Pushpa. Rajni. New Delhi: Ramkrishna, 19--
       Westernized Panjabis during World War II and
the problem of arranged marriage.

1094 Kapur, Vimla. Life goes on. Lahore: Associated
       Publications, 1946.

1095 Karaka, Dasoo Framjee. Just flesh. Bombay:
       Thacker, 1941.
       An Indian in London and Oxford during the
'thirties.

1096 _____ . There lay the city. Bombay: Thacker,
       1942.
       Indians and Eurasians in Bombay during World
War II.

1097 _____. We never die. Bombay: Thacker, 1944.
       Inter-communal love in a village.

1098 Karnath, Kota Shivarama. Back to the soil. Trans.
       by A. N. Murthy Rao. Puttur, Kerala: Harsha
       Printing, 1950.
       A solidly ethnographical novel of village life on
       the Kannada coast.

1099 Karney, Evelyn S. The dust of desire, or in the days
       of the Buddha. London: R. Scott, 1912.
       The insufficiency of domestic life; the influence
       of Buddhism.

1100 Karnik, Anant S. Kashmir princess. Bombay: Jaico,
       1958.

1101 Kaul, Narendra Nath. The heart's way. New Delhi:
       Hamsa, 1957.
       The course of hopeless love is reviewed in an
       epistle to a woman, now that she is married.

1102 Kaveri Bai, H. Meenakshi's memoirs: a novel of
       Christian life in South India. Madras: Natesan,
       1937.

1103 Kaye, John W. Long engagements: a tale of the
       Afghan rebellion. London: Chapman and Hall, 1846.
       Wife idly flirts in Calcutta while her husband
       fights for the Raj on the Afghan border.

1104 _____. Peregrine pultuney, or life in India.
       London: No publisher given, 1844.
       Life of a cadet in Bengal artillery.

1105 _____. The story of Basil Bouverie. Calcutta:
       Privately printed, 1842.

1106 Kaye, Mary Margaret. Death walked in Kashmir.
       London: Staples Press, 1953.
       An easy mystery surrounding the death of two
       European women in Kashmir.

1107 _____. Shadow of the moon. London: Longmans,
       1957.
       An excellent reconstruction of India on the eve of
       the Mutiny outbreak; the atmosphere of joy and ir-
       responsibility.

1108 Kaye, Mollie. Strange island. Bombay: Thacker, 1944.
Romance in the Andamans.

1109 Keating, Henry Raymond Fitzwater. Inspector Ghote caught in meshes. New York: Dutton, 1968.
Mystery set within an erotically decorated temple.

1110 _____. Inspector Ghote hunts the peacock. New York: Dutton, 1968.

1111 _____. Inspector Ghote plays a joker. New York: Dutton, 1969.

1112 _____. Inspector Ghote's good crusade. London: Collins, 1966.
An Indian detective at work in Bombay.

1113 _____. The perfect murder. New York: Dutton, 1965.

Kelly, Joan Collis. See Joan Sutherland.

1114 Kennedy, S. A. Spellbound: the story of Arthur Denniston Claire. Bombay: Thacker, 1943.

1115 Kennedy, Sara Mackenzie. St. Valentine's day. London: Burleigh, 1900.

1116 Kent, Louise Andrews. He went with Vasco da Gama. Boston: Houghton, 1938.
Two boys, one Irish, the other Portuguese, on voyage around Africa to India. For young adults.

1117 _____. The red rajah. New York: Houghton Mifflin, 1933.
A mystery story for older boys and girls.

1118 Kernahan, John Coulson. The woman who understood. London: Hodder and Stoughton, 1916.
Melancholy European existence in the East.

Kerr, O. C. See Robert Newell.

1119 Kerry, Stephen (pseud.) Doctor sahib. London: Cassell, 1967.

1120 Kershaw, Isabel Blanche. Tarnished virtue. London:
Hutchinson, 1927.
Army officer suffers amnesia and suspects his
wife of infidelity.

Khare, Leelabai. See Venu Chitale.

1121 Khosla, Gopal Das. Grim fairy tales and other facts
and fancies. Bombay: Asia, 1967.

1122 _____. The horoscope cannot lie and other stories.
Bombay: Asia, 1961.

1123 _____. The last Mughal. Delhi: Hind Pocket,
1969.
Historical; based on the life of the last Mughal
ruler, Bahadur Shah Zafar.

1124 _____. The price of a wife. Bombay: Jaico,
1958.
Collection of short stories.

1125 Kincaid, Charles Augustus. The anchorite and other
stories. London: Oxford University Press, 1922.

1126 _____. An anthology of Indian tales. London:
Humphrey Milford, 1924.

1127 _____. Deccan nursery tales or fairy tales from
the south. London: Macmillan, 1914.

1128 _____. Folk tales of Sind and Guzarat. Karachi:
Daily Gazette Press, 1925.

1129 _____. The Indian heroes. London: Humphrey
Milford, 1915.

1130 _____. Shri Krishna of Dwaraka and other stories.
Bombay: Taraporevala, 1920.

1131 _____. The tale of Tulsi plant and other stories.
Bombay: Times of India, 1908.

1132 _____. Tales from the Indian drama. Bombay:
Oxford University Press, 1923.

1133 _____. Tales from the Indian epics. Bombay:
Humphrey Milford, 1918.

1134 _____ . Tales of Indian cavaliers. London: Macmillan, 1937.

1135 _____ . Tales of old Ind. Bombay: Times of India Press, 1938.

1136 _____ . Tales of old Sind. London: Humphrey Milford, 1922.

1137 Kincaid, Dennis Charles Alexander. Cactus land. Same as Moonrise on the Indus.

1138 _____ . Durbar. London: Chatto and Windus, 1937. Story of an opium addicted Indian prince.

1139 _____ . The final image. London: Routledge, 1939. Excellent depiction of Maratha life.

1140 _____ . The grand rebel: an impression of Sivaji, founder of the Maratha empire. London: Collins, 1937. Outstanding historical novel.

1141 _____ . Moonrise on the Indus. London: Chatto and Windus, 1934. A Eurasian girl becomes a dancer and a courtesan. Outstanding description of Indian manners and folkways.

1142 _____ . Their ways divide. London: Chatto and Windus, 1936. Another good one on Anglo-Maratha relations.

1143 King, E. Theodore. Ajanta: a historical novel. New Delhi: Delhi Press, 1962. On Ajanta caves.

1144 King, Percy J. Fool's delight. London: Hurst and Blackett, 1925. Club life in India; triangular romance.

1145 _____ . Forasmuch. London: Selwyn and Blount, 1927. British officials; Afghan frontier and club life.

1146 King, R. Raleigh. Coffee coloured honeymoon. London: Cecil Palmer, 1930.

A newly-married couple settle in India as
coffee planters; good description of coolie life.

1147 Kingsley, Henry. Stretton. 3 vols. London: Tinsley
Brothers, 1869.
1857 and all that; excellent characterisation; but
many absurd descriptions and quaint language.

1148 Kingston, William Henry. Adventures in India. London: Routledge, 1883.
For children.

1149 _____ . The young rajah: a story of Indian life
and adventures. London: No publisher given, 1876.
Brave and handsome English hero; treacherous
Indian ministers and a foolish young raja.

1150 Kipling, Rudyard. The complete works of. Sussex
edition. London: Macmillan, 1937-39.

1151 _____ . V. 1: Plain tales from the hills (1888);
forty stories.

1152 _____ . V. 2: Soldiers three; Story of the Gadsbys;
In black and white (1888-92); 23 stories.

1153 _____ . V. 3: Wee Willie Winkle; Under the
deodars; The phantom rickshaw; And other stories
(1888-92); 20 stories.

1154 _____ . V. 4: Life's handicap (1888-90); 28 stories.

1155 _____ . V. 5: Many inventions (1892); 14 stories.

1156 _____ . V. 6: The day's work (1898); 12 stories.

1157 _____ . V. 12: The jungle book; The second jungle
book (1894-95); 15 stories.

1158 _____ . V. 19: The Naulakha (written with Wolcott
Balestier) (1892); novel.

1159 _____ . V. 21: Kim (1901); novel.

1160 Kirby, Charles. The adventures of an Arcot rupee.
London: No publisher given, 1867.
Wellesley and Tipu Sultan, and the Pagoda Tree in
full luxuriance.

1161 Kirby, Margaret. <u>An English girl in the east.</u>   London: Andrew Melrose, 1913.
Tragedy of Eurasian marriages.

1162 Klass, Sheila Solomon. <u>Bahadur means hero.</u> Boston: Gambit, 1969.
Clash of Nepali and American cultures brings a young man's downfall.

1163 Knight, Francis A. <u>The Rajpoot's rings.</u>   London: Dent, 1911.
Of the Mutiny period.

1164 Knight, W. Kobold. <u>Monsoon bird.</u>   London: Cassell, 1927.
A young Englishman in love with his employer's wife; and a Tamilian in love with an Indian girl sold to a cruel old man.   Happiness forever to both couples.

Krishan, Bal. <u>See</u> Bal Krishna.

1165 Krishan Chander. <u>The dreamer.</u>   Tr. by Jai Ratan. Delhi: Hind Pocket Books, 1970.

1166 _____. <u>Flame and the flower.</u>   Bombay: Current Book House, 1951.
Fifteen stories translated from Urdu.

1167 _____. <u>I cannot die; a story of Bengal.</u>   Translated from Urdu by K. A. Abbas.   Poona: Kutub, 1943.
Bengal famine seen through the eyes of a foreign diplomat, an upper class Bengali, and a victim.

1168 _____. <u>Mr. Ass comes to town.</u>   Delhi: Hind Pocket Books, 1970.

1169 _____. <u>Seven faces of London.</u>   Delhi: Paradise, 1969.

<u>Also see</u> Chandra, Krishan

1170 Krishnan, O. U. <u>A little laugh.</u>   Bombay: Karnatak Press, 1927.
Short stories.

1171 Krishnan Kutty, G. Anguish. Trivandrum: Mitranike-
     than, 1965.

1172 Krishnaswami, T. B. The queen of the coral-reefs.
     Madras: Maga Subramanya Row Brothers, n. d.

1173 _____. Selma, a tale of the times old. Madras:
     Naga Subramanya Row Brothers, n. d.

1174 Krishnaswamy, Sucheendrum Yegnanarayana. Kalyani's
     husband. Madras: Higginbothams, 1967.

1175 Kulkarni, G. V. Heritage of murder. Bombay:
     Kutub Popular, 1963.

1176 Kumar, Paramjit. Till God wakes; immortal story of
     Sino-Indian war in NEFA. Chandigarh: People's
     Guardian, 1964.
        1962 Sino-Indian conflict in Kameng division.

1177 Lahiri, Kali Krishna. Roshinara, a historical ro-
     mance. Chittagong: R. R. Sen, 1912.
        Based on a Bengali novel by Nobo Chandra Sen,
     published in 1869. It deals with the love of Roshi-
     nara, daughter of Aurangzib, for Sivaji.

1178 Laksmana Suri, M. Sri Bhishma vijaya. Madras:
     No publisher listed, 1909.
        From the Mahabharata.

1179 Lall, Anand (pseud. of Arthur Lall). The house at
     Adampur. New York: Knopf, 1956.
        Family life of a wealthy Hindu in and around
     Delhi at the height of Indian nationalist struggle,
     1930-44.

1180 _____. Seasons of Jupiter. New York: Harper,
     1958.
        A wealthy family of Amritsar searches for a fully
     satisfying way of life.

     Lall, Arthur. See Anand Lall.

1181 Lambert, Derek. The kites of war. New York:
     Coward-McCann, 1969.
        During the Chinese invasion of India in 1962, a

British ex-newspaperman seeks to persuade a
peace loving Buddhist abbot to organize resistance
to Chinese.

1182 _____. For infamous conduct. New York: Coward-
McCann, 1970.

1183 Lang, John. My friend's wife or you are wanted.
London: Ward and Lock, 1859.
Misfortunes of a young officer on ship from India
to England.

1184 _____. Wanderings in India and other sketches of
Indian life. London: Ward and Lock, 1859.

1185 _____. The Wetherbys: father and son; or sundry
chapters of Indian experience. London: Chapman
and Hall, 1853.
Bitter and caustic satire on the social life of
Bengal army officers and 'half castes.'

1186 _____. Will he marry her? London: Routledge,
1858.
Amusing burlesque of military life in India and
battles against the Sikhs.

Also see Mofussilite.

1187 Lang, Monica. Invitation to tea. Chicago: People's
Book Club, 1952.
London girl leaves her comfortable home to
marry the manager of a tea plantation in Assam.

1188 Langton, Jarvis. A foster son, a tale of the Indian
Mutiny. London: Simpkin, Marshall, 1896.

1189 Larneuil, Michel. The short march in Telangana.
Translated by June P. Wilson and Walter B.
Michaels. New York: Morrow, 1969.
An English journalist goes to interview a com-
munist guerrilla leader; good comments on Indian
metaphysical and political subtleties.

1190 Lawrence, James Henry. The empire of the Nairs, or
the rights of women: an utopian romance. 4 vols.
London: No publisher given, 1811.
Kerala.

Lawrence, Rosamund. See Rosamund Lawrence Napier.

1191 Laxman, R. K. Sorry: no room. Bombay: Pearl,
       1969.

1192 Lee Tung. The wind obeys Lama Toru. Bombay:
       Kutub Popular, 1967.
              Inner Himalayas; lamas and lamaseries. Science
       fiction.

1193 Leighton, Margaret. Voyage to Coromandel. New
       York: Farrar Straus, 1965.
              King Alfred in 888 sends messengers with rich
       gifts to the shrine of St. Thomas; adventure story.

1194 Leslie, Cecile. The blue devils. London: Cassell,
       1951.
              Civil servants cause disasters to the indigo in-
       dustry in Bihar in the mid-nineteenth century.

1195 _____. Goat to Kali. London: Cassell, 1948.
              Terrorism in Bengal during 1941-42; good in-
       sights into the use of Bhagvad Gita for revolutionary
       purposes.

1196 _____. The golden stairs. New York: Doubleday,
       1968.
              Journey of an English woman of 35 and three
       children in her charge during the exodus from
       Burma in 1942.

1197 _____. The rope bridge. New York: Doubleday,
       1964.
              Social and emotional pressures upon a lovely
       English girl living in Bhutan hills with her huntress
       mother, and her love for an Indian whose parents
       have other plans for him.

1198 Lewis, Alun. In the green tree. London: Allen and
       Unwin, 1948.
              Contains six short stories.

1199 Lewis, Reba. The Brahmin and the belle. Berlin:
       Seven Seas, 1969.

1200 Lidchi, Maggi. Earthman. London: Gollancz, 1967.

1201   A European's experience with Vedanta, Indian
         mysticism, and an Indian girl. (U. S. title: Man of
         earth.)

1202 Lillie, Arthur. An Indian wizard. London: Simpkin,
         1887.
         A lieutenant's life during the Mutiny.

1203 _____. The workshop of religions. London: Swan
         Sonnenschein, 1906.
         A long narrative with evangelical digressions of
         the first Christian age.

1204 Littlejohn, Neil. The mountain laughed. London:
         Chapman and Hall, 1928.
         Domestic difficulties of a British couple.

1205 Lloyd, Eyre. Lieutenant Beatrice Raymond, V. C.:
         a frontier novel. London: Andrew Melrose, 1920.
         A girl masquerades as a soldier of the Indo-
         Afghan frontier, and distinguishes herself.

1206 Locke, Dorothy Mary. Roses and peacocks: an Indian
         episode. London: Grayson, 1932.
         Incoherent story about an unpleasant English
         couple's domestic difficulties. Miss Locke probably
         wrote other novels using India as locale.

1207 Locke, Gladys Edson. The golden lotus. London:
         Page, 1927.
         Unscrupulous English knight steals a diamond,
         abducts a Rajput princess and dies in prison.

1208 Longley, Pearl Dorr. The rebirth of Venkata Reddi:
         a story. Philadelphia: Judson Press, 1939.
         Gradual emancipation from tradition and super-
         stition of a sudra family that converts to Christianity.

1209 Lovatt, William F. The curse of Kama. London:
         Houghton Publishing Company, 1932.
         Theft of a priceless ruby from an idol, and the
         effort of a fanatical Hindu seeking to restore it.

1210 Lowe, Thomas Alfred. Wine, women and soldiers.
         London: Methuen, 1932.
         Army life in India.

      Luck, Mary Churchill. See M. Hamilton.

1211 Lynn, Escott. <u>A hero of the Mutiny.</u> London: Chambers, 1913.

1212 Lyon, Christopher C. <u>Mr. Penriddick's progress.</u> Rochford, Essex: C. W. Daniel, 1956.
Religious experiences with many mystical movements including Indian Yoga.

1213 _____. <u>Wazir.</u> Rochford, Essex: C. W. Daniel, 1958.
Wazir is a Kashmiri mystic.

1214 MacCarthy, Justin Huntly. <u>A London legend.</u> 3 vols. London: Chatto and Windus, 1895.
Attempted murder of the son of an English victor by the son of a sepoy.

1215 Macculloch, William. <u>Bengali household tales.</u> London: Hodder and Stoughton, 1912.

1216 McDearmid, Andrew. <u>The man-eater of Rupaidha and other stories.</u> Bombay: Jaico, 1970.
Stories on big game hunting in India.

1217 Macdonald, James Middleton. <u>The baba log: a tale of child life in India.</u> London: D. Nutt, 1896.
European children's experiences and fancies in India. For young adults.

1218 McDonell, Gordon. <u>The clock tower.</u> Boston: Little Brown, 1951.
Tribal life in lower Himalayans, and clumsy efforts of a civil servant to build a clock tower.

1219 Macfarlane, Iris. <u>Tales and legends from India.</u> London: Chatto and Windus, 1965.

1220 Macfarlane, J. <u>Hartley House, Calcutta: a novel of the days of Warren Hastings.</u> Calcutta: No publisher given, 1908.

1221 Machray, Robert. <u>Sentenced to death: a story of two men and a maid.</u> London: Chatto and Windus, 1910.
English hero grapples with sedition and saves India; falls in love, and makes hairbreadth escape from vengeful Indians. The author probably wrote other mysteries with Indian settings.

1222 McInnes, Graham. <u>Sushila.</u> New York: Putnam's, 1957.
Daughter of a Hindu father and an American mother combines the best of two cultures; successful as an artist she avoids emotional contacts with men.

1223 Mackenzie, Compton. <u>Ben Nevis goes east.</u> London: Chatto and Windus, 1954.
Mystery set in an Indian princely state. There may be other mysteries with Indian settings by this author.

1224 Mackenzie, Helen (Mrs. Colin). <u>Life in the mission, the camp, and the zenana, or six years in India.</u> 3 vols. London: R. Bentley, 1853.
Nothing is left unseen between Bombay and Calcutta. Lamentable account of military society.

1225 Maclean, James N. M. <u>The ranee: a legend of the Indian mutiny.</u> London: Gustavus, Cohen and Co., 1887.
Many parallels with the Rani of Jhansi.

1226 Maclehose, Jesie Hagart. <u>Master key.</u> London: Blackie, 1958.
Conversion to Christianity. For young adults.

1227 Macmillan, Michael. <u>In wild Maratha battle: a tale of the days of Shivaji.</u> London: Blackie, 1905.

1228 _____. <u>Tales of Indian chivalry.</u> London: Blackie, 1901.

Also see, A. F. P. Harcourt.

1229 MacMunn, George Fletcher. <u>Azizu, the dancing girl, and other Indian stories.</u> London: Sampson Low, 1934.

1230 _____. <u>Black velvet, a drama of India and the bomb cult.</u> London: Sampson Low, 1934.
An English policeman, with an Indian mistress, tracks down seditionists. Glimpses of Simla life.

1231 _____. <u>A freelance in Kashmir: a tale of the great anarchy.</u> New York: Dutton, 1914.
English conquest of Kashmir in the 19th century.

1232   . The Ghilzai's wife and other stories of east
     and west. London: Sampson Low, 1936.

1233   . The king's pawns: being empire stories of
     the world war. London: Sheldon Press, 1930.

1234 McMurry, George H. Call to Murralla. New York:
     Harper, 1960.
          Story of a devout missionary family in India.

1235 Macnamara, Rachel S. Torn veils: an Anglo-Indian
     story. London: Hurst and Blackett, 1926.
          A scandal monger investigates the past of British
     officials and their families in India. Macnamara
     may have done other stories with Indian settings.

1236 Maddock, Eleanor. The snake in the sleeve. London:
     Hutchinson, 1927.
          An English girl born in India and educated in the
     United States meets an Indian prince, a graduate
     student at Harvard, and thoroughly westernised. He
     reverts back to wicked Indian way of life after
     marrying her and returning to his home.

1237 Madgulkar, Vyankatesh Digamber. The village had no
     walls. Trans. by Ram Deshmukh from Marathi
     novel Bangarwadi. Bombay: Asia, 1967.
          School teacher in a Maharashtrian village.

1238 Madhaviah, A. Clarida: a historical novel. Madras:
     Authors Press, 1915.
          Clarinda, widow of a Maratha brahmin, becomes
     the concubine of a British officer; after his death
     embraces Christianity and builds the first Christian
     church at Palamcottah.

1239   . Kaushika's short stories on marriage re-
     form and allied topics. Madras: Authors Press,
     1924.

1240   . Lieut. Panju: a modern Indian. Madras:
     Authors Press, 1924.
          A young Indian army officer overcomes racial
     handicaps and distinguishes himself.

1241   . Muthumeenakshi: the autobiography of a
     brahmin girl. Madras: Authors Press, 1915.

Sensitive life story of a brahmin girl who suffers
the cruelty of the step mother, the tyranny of the
mother-in-law, and misfortunes as a wretched widow.

1242 _____. Nanda, the pariah who overcame caste.
Madras: Indian Publishing House, 1923.
Excellent social document, poorly written.

1243 _____. Thillai Govindan: a posthumous autobiography. London: Fisher Unwin, 1916.
Habits, ideas and sorrows of a brahmin from
birth to death, who obtained university education,
served as government official, and finally found
peace in traditional Hinduism. Valuable for its
vignettes of South Indian village life.

1244 Mainwaring, M. The suttee or the Hindu converts.
3 vols. London: Newman, 1830.
Hindu family with many virtues and superstitions
converts to Christianity and combines western
humanism with Indian family virtues.

1245 Malet, H. P. Lost links in the Indian mutiny. London: Newby, 1867.
Scattered incidents of the Mutiny and Afghan wars.

1246 Malgonkar, Manohar. A bend in the Ganges. London:
Hamish Hamilton, 1964.
Quit India movement, partition, communal hatred.

1247 _____. Combat of shadows. London: Hamish
Hamilton, 1962.
Outrageously melodramatic and facile; tea gardens,
northwest Assam, 1938-40.

1248 _____. Distant drum. Bombay: Asia, 1961.
Indian army life.

1249 _____. The princes. London: Hamish Hamilton,
1963.
A princely ruler, ruffian of vintage, outwits the
nationalists with the aid of the British. But the
heir turns out to be unprincely. Anti-Congress in
tone; written from the inside about Indian princely
tradition.

1250 _____. Spy in Amber. Delhi: Hind Pocket Books,
n. d.

Secret service story dealing with Sino-Indian intrigues in a Tibetan monastery.

1251 Malhotra, Madan Lal. Quirks of fate. New Delhi:
Sunanda, 1970.
Fourteen stories.

Malik, Marcus Abraham. See Hazari.

1252 Mallick, Roop Lal. Even clouds feel thirsty. Calcutta: Lok Kalo Forum, n. d.

1253 Malya, K. G. The goddess of wealth. Chikodi:
Jeevan Jyoti, 1966.

1254 Manara, Balraj. The altar and other stories. Delhi:
Writers Forum, 1968.

1255 Manchester, William Raymond. Shadow of the monsoon. London: Cassell, 1956.
Himalayan valley where the power of the sadhu
remains unchecked by the Congress regime, and
where the Englishman still commands respect. Excellent description of a leopard hunt.

1256 Mandy, Colin R. Death of Ptolemy and other stories.
Bombay: Thacker, n. d.

1257 _____. Fleas and nightingale: stories. Bombay:
Thacker, 1945.

1258 _____. Guest of the baron. Bombay: Thacker,
n. d.

1259 _____. More laughter in court. Bombay: Thacker,
n. d.

1260 _____. Sunny hours. Bombay: Thacker, n. d.

1261 Manjappa, Kadidal. Martyr of Panjaravalli. Bang-
lore: Prakash and Mohan, 1966.

1262 Mann, Thomas. The transposed heads. London:
Secker and Warburg, 1941.
The most interesting novel on Hindu philosophy.
A woman loves the mind of one person, the body of
the other. She finds the heads of the two severed

from their trunks, and transposes these heads.
Does indentity go by the head or the trunk, or the
mind? A gem.

Mann, Violet Vivian. See Alex Stuart.

1263 Mannin, Ethel Edity. At sundown the tiger. London:
Jarrolds, 1951.
A hunter must give up hunting to marry a girl
who hates hunting. East triumphs over west. Miss
Mannin may have other novels on India.

1264 Mansford, C. J. Shafts from an eastern quiver.
London: Newmes, 1894.

1265 Mardaan, Ataullah. Devadasi. Paris: Olympia Press,
1957.
Pornography.

1266 _____ . Kama-houri. Paris: Olympia Press, 1956.
Likewise.

1267 Markandaya, Kamala. The coffer dams. New York:
John Day, 1969.
At a South Indian dam construction, Europeans
supervise the project, and Indians do the work; during the monsoon an Indian engineer saves the project
and winds up with the Englishman's wife.

1268 _____ . A handful of rice. New York: John Day,
1966.
Indian poverty.

1269 _____ . Nectar in a sieve. London: Putnam's,
1954.
Peasant life in South India.

1270 _____ . Possession. New York: John Day, 1963.
A rich English woman and a penniless Indian boy
meet, collide and learn from each other; a swami
plays a crucial role as the embodiment of Indian
spirituality.

1271 _____ . A silence of desire. New York: John Day,
1960.
A serene marriage suddenly beset by storms due
to the wife's interest in a swami.

1272 _____ . Some inner fury. London: Putnam's, 1955.
      The love of an Indian girl and an English boy
      comes to end in 1942.

1273 Marris, A. J. Through eastern windows: life stories
      of an Indian city. London: No publisher given,
      1919.
      In spite of strong missionary bias and propa-
      ganda, contains serious insights into Indian life style.

1274 Marryat, Augusta. Lost in the jungle: a story of the
      Indian mutiny. London: Griffith and Farrar, 1877.

1275 Marryat, Florence. Gup: sketches of Anglo-Indian
      life. London: No publisher given, 1868.

1276 _____ . Veronique, a romance. 3 vols. London:
      Guilford, 1869.
      Set in 'Ooty' and Madras it is critical both of
      India and the British men and women who serve it.

1277 Marsh, Richard. The mahatma's pupil. London:
      Henry and Co., 1893.
      Esoteric; inability of the occidentals to learn the
      mysteries of the orient. Marsh may have written
      other items on India.

1278 Marshall, Edison. Bengal tiger. New York: Double-
      day, 1952.
      First rate romance and adventure set at the time
      of the Mutiny.

1279 _____ . Darzee: a girl of India. New York:
      Kinsey, 1937.
      American engineer and a Bengali girl plunge into
      a maze of mystery and adventures.

1280 _____ . Gypsy sixpence. London: Frederick
      Muller, 1950.
      Based on Richard Burton's travels in Sind and
      the Frontier provinces; love, kidnapping, and
      mystery.

1281 _____ . The heart of little Shikara and other stories.
      London: Hodder and Stoughton, 1924.
      The title story is about an Indian boy who saves
      the life of an English hunter.

1282 _____. The jewel of Mahabar. London: Hodder
      and Stoughton, 1938.
         Jewel is lost; jewel is rediscovered.

1283 _____. Love stories of India. New York: Farrar
      Straus, 1950.

1284 Marshall, Ian. The vengeance of Kali. London:
      Nelson, 1930.
         Mystery.

1285 Marston, Louise. The call of the king. Madras:
      Christian Literature Society, 1915.

1286 Martin, David. The stones of Bombay. London:
      Wingate, 1950.
         Indian mysticism, Bombay police, a Swami and
      politics.

1287 Mascarenhas, Lambert. Sorrowing lies my land.
      Bombay: No publisher given, 1955.
         Life in Goa under the Portuguese.

1288 Mason, A. E. W. The broken road. London: Smith,
      Elder, 1907.
         Disastrous results, politically and socially, of
      sending an Indian prince to be educated in England
      to become hybrid Englishman; set in the 'Frontier'.

1289 _____. The drum. London: Hodder and Stough-
      ton, 1937.
         An original and excellent yarn of the northwest
      frontier.

1290 Mason, Francis Van Wyck. Himalayan assignment.
      Garden City: Doubleday, 1952.
         Ordinary mystery.

1291 Mason, Philip. Call the next witness. London: Cape,
      1945.
         Tortuous unreliability of Indian evidence and the
      dubious methods of Indian police in solving a murder
      mystery.

1292 _____. The island of Chamba. London: Cape,
      1950.
         Princely state, forced to introduce quick reforms,
      has a disaster.

1293 _____. The wild sweet witch. London: Cape, 1947.
    Steady deterioration of relations, over a period
of three generations, between an Indian family and
a succession of British civil servants, in Himalayan
foothills.

1294 Mason, Richard. The fever tree. London: Collins,
    1962.
    An inexperienced Indian girl falls in love with an
American, accomplice to murder; and his escape to
the Himalayas.

1295 _____. Wind cannot read. London: Hodder and
    Stoughton, 1946.
    A Japanese girl and a British intelligence officer
stationed in India fall in love during the war.

1296 Masters, John. Bhowani Junction. New York: Viking,
    1954.
    A modern Anglo-Indian girl is confused by her
racial status on the eve of India's independence.

1297 _____. Coromandel. New York: Viking, 1955.
    An Englishman goes to India in the seventeenth
century in search of adventure and fortune.

1298 _____. The deceivers. New York: Viking, 1952.
    India in 1825; British rule of law versus Indian
paternal despotism.

1299 _____. Far, far the mountain peak. New York:
    Viking, 1957.
    The hero is the grandson of General Savage of
Nightrunners of Bengal. The story of five men and
women who follow their destinies as they had out-
lined in one week at Cambridge. Period of 1902-22.

1300 _____. The lotus and the wind. New York:
    Viking, 1953.
    Sequel to Nightrunners of Bengal. Son of General
Savage continues the tradition of British officer in
India and follows in the footsteps of the father he
hates. Romance subordinated to adventure.

1301 _____. Nightrunners of Bengal. New York: Viking,
    1951.
    The Indian Mutiny; rise of General Savage.

1302 _____. To the coral strand. New York: Harper, 1963.
British general, nostalgic for imperial India, resigns his position with a British firm rather than lose it under new management, in 1947.

1303 _____. The venus of Konpara. New York: Harper, 1960.
Excavation of a dam in a Rajput princely state turns up a mysterious fragment of an ancient statue; the effect of this discovery on the prince, his mistress, and a handful of British residents in 1890.

1304 Mathai, K. E. (pseud. of Parappurath). Blood stained footprints: an army novel. tr. by N. Kunju. New Delhi: Army Educational Stores, 1970. Indian soldiers during World War II.

1305 Mather, Berkely (pseud. of John Evan Weston Davies). The gold of Malabar. London: Collins, 1967.

1306 _____. The pass beyond Kashmir. London: Collins, 1960.
Undercover spy story set in Kashmir where agents are looking for oil and an ex-army officer.

1307 _____. The road and the star. London: Collins, 1965.
Marathas versus Mughuls in 17th-century India.

Matheson, Sylvia Anne. See Max Mundy.

1308 Mathew, T. Hills and plains. 2 vols. London: Smith, Elder, 1861.

1309 Maugham, William Somerset. The razor's edge. London: Heinemann, 1944.
A young American flyer finds peace on visit to India.

1310 Mayo, Katherine. Maggot to man. London: ca. 1930.

1311 _____. Slave of the gods. London: Cape, 1929.
Twelve stories; lurid and ghastly, especially in regard to the treatment of women in India.

1312 Mazumdar, Sachindra. Creatures of destiny: short stories. Bombay: Jaico, 1956.

1313 Meacham, Ellis K. The East Indiaman. Boston:
      Little, Brown, 1969.
      A rousing historical sea novel about the Bombay
      buccaneers of 1800.

1314 _____. On the company's service. New York:
      Little, Brown, 1971.
      Further adventures of an officer in the naval
      service of the East India Company during the Na-
      poleonic Wars.

1315 Meer Ummun. Tale of the four durwesh. Translated
      from Urdu by Lewis Ferdinand Smith. Bombay:
      Portuguese Press, 1841.

1316 Meerza, Wasif Ali. A mind's reproduction. Calcutta:
      Newman, 1934.

1317 Mehta, D. R. Mystery of the monocle. Bombay: the
      author, 1935.

1318 Mehta, Perin C. Short stories. Bombay: Asian
      Printers, n. d.
      Presistence of Sitas and Savitris in modern India.

1319 Mehta, Rama. Life of Keshava: a family story from
      India. New York: McGraw Hill, 1969.

1320 _____. Ramu. New York: McGraw Hill, 1964.
      Both these titles are for young adults.

1321 Mehta, Rustam. How he got over: a story of English
      life. Bombay: The Author, 1918.

1322 Mehta, Ved. The delinquent chacha. New York:
      Harper, 1967.
      An Indian tries to become pucca sahib in England,
      is hauled into the court by his creditor, and saves
      himself through an anglicised Indian humor.

1323 Melwani, Murli Das. Stories of a salesman. Calcutta:
      Writers Workshop, 1967.

1324 Menen, (Salvator) Aubrey. The prevalence of witches.
      London: Chatto and Windus, 1947.
      Satire on modern civilization. In a remote part
      of India where civilization has hardly penetrated, a

man is accused of murder under British law but according to his own law he did not commit any crime.

1325 _____. The Ramayana. London: Chatto and Windus, 1954.
A marvellous satire on the Ramayana which offended the orthodox Hindu.

1326 _____. Shelah. New York: Random House, 1963.
World events considered from a state of nirvana; satire on Buddhism.

1327 Menon, Marath A. The sale of an island. London: Dobson, 1968.

1328 _____. The wound of spring. London: Dobson, 1966.
A Kerala Nayar marries a Harijan girl.

1329 Merriman, H. Seton (pseud. of Hugh S. Scott). Flotsam: the study of a life. London: Longmans, 1896.
Siege of Delhi during the Mutiny.

1330 Methley, Alice A. Baby sahib. London: Wells Gardner, 1928.
An English lad and his Indian servant companion. For children.

1331 Methley, Violet Mary. Three for luck: an Indian school story for girls. London: Pilgrim Press, 1927.

1332 Miles, Favell Mary. The red flame. London: Hutchinson, 1921.
An alluring redhead's marriage in India, and her distasteful episodes with her uncle.

1333 Miles, Pat. They came to a mountain. London: Chapman and Hall, 1951.
A young English writer is stranded in Kashmir and falls in love with an Indian girl who has developed social conscience. Authentic Indian background.

1334 Millington, Powell. In cantonments. Allahabad: Pioneer Press, 1897.

1335 Miln, Louise Jordan. The green goddess. New York:
     Stokes, 1922.

1336 Milton, C. R. The eyes of understanding. London:
     Andrew Melrose, 1919.
        Teacher in South India. Poor.

1337 _____. An Indian summer. London: Andrew Mel-
     rose, 1927.
        An English youth goes to South India to become a
     policeman; a vampire tries to lead him to destruc-
     tion, but he is saved by the right girl.

1338 _____. The sunset gun. London: Andrew Melrose,
     1920.
        Love story; South India.

1339 _____. Tiernay Blake's wife. London: Andrew
     Melrose, 1929.
        Mixed marriage; Eurasian girl seeks love.

1340 Minney, Rubeigh James. Across India by air. Alla-
     habad: Wheeler, 1921.

1341 _____. Clive. London: Jarrolds, 1931.
        Fictionalized biography.

1342 _____. Distant drums. London: Chapman Hall,
     1935.
        An Englishman's commercial life spent in Cal-
     cutta; Indian philosophy of negation versus Western
     philanthropy.

1343 _____. Excursions in ink. Allahabad: Wheeler,
     1921.

1344 _____. Governor General. London: Chapman
     Hall, 1935.
        Warren Hastings.

1345 _____. Governor's lady. London: Jarrolds, 1951.
        Hastings's romance with Marian on board ship to
     India.

1346 _____. Maki. London: John Lane, 1922.
        A young Indian girl raised in the zennana marries
     a prince, is considered insane, runs away, and

finds her beauty a curse. Excellent descriptions of
child marriage customs and the purdah.

1347 _____. Midst Himalayan mists. Calcutta: Butterworth, 1920.
Good geographic descriptions.

1348 _____. Night life of Calcutta. Butterworth, 1920.
Excellent knowledge of Calcutta bazaars.

1349 _____. The road to Delhi. London: John Lane,
1923.
An Indian village boy makes good and enters
political life. Powerful story.

1350 _____. Shiva: or the future of India. London:
Kegan Paul, 1929.
Indian preoccupations with sex.

1351 Mistry, Homi D. Rebels of destiny. Bombay: Hind
Kitabs, 1959.
Fifteen famous trials in dialogue form.

1352 Mitchell, Edmund. Towards the eternal snows. London: Hutchinson, 1896.
Eurasian life and love; fortunes and misfortunes
of Calcutta commercial houses.

1353 Mitchison, Naomi. Judy and Lakshmi. London:
Collins, 1959.
Two girls, one Indian, the other English, in
Madras. For school children.

1354 Mitford, Bertram. The heath hover mystery. London: Ward, Lock, 1911.
Good detective work. Mitford may have set some
of his other mysteries in India.

1355 _____. The sirdar's oath. London: G. Bell, 1904.
Northwest frontier.

1356 Mitra, Jatindra Nath. Towards the dawn. Lucknow:
Anglo-Oriental Press, 1922.

1357 Mitra, Narendra Nath. Mahanagar. Translated by
S. K. Chatterjee and M. F. Franda. Bombay:
Jaico, 1968.

Refugees from East Pakistan in Calcutta.

1358 Mitra, Piari Chand. The spoilt child: a tale of
      Hindu domestic life. Translated from the Bengali
      Alalar gharer dulal by G. D. Oswell. Calcutta:
      Thacker, 1893.
        Picaresque novel of two brothers, one good, the
      other spoilt, from Bengali gentry.

1359 Mitra, Premendra. Kaleidoscope, a novel. Calcutta:
      Purvasa, 1945.
        Peasantry and middle classes of Bengal under
      British rule in the 1930's.

1360 Mitra, S. M. Hindupore: a peep behind the Indian
      unrest: an Anglo-Indian romance. London: Luzac,
      1909.
        Anti-Muslim; anti-nobility; an Irish lord marries
      a Rajput princess.

1361 Mitter, Hari. Progressive film stories for producing
      new films. New Delhi: Author, 1959.
        Nine stories; Marxist flavor.

1362 Mitton, Geraldine Edith, and James George Scott.
      Under an eastern sky. Allahabad: Wheeler, 1924.
        Stories set in South India.

1363 Mofussilite (pseud. of John Lang.) Two clever by
      half, or the Harroways. London: No publisher
      given, 1853.

1364 Molesworth, K. I. By favor of the gods and other
      stories. Allahabad: Pioneer Press, 1896.

1365 Money, E. The wife and the ward; or a life's error.
      London: Routledge, 1859. Later published as
      Woman's fortitude: a tale of Cawnpore.
        Unhappy marriage; bravery; Cawnpore massacre
      during the Mutiny.

1366 Monkland, Mrs. Life in India: or the English at
      Calcutta. 3 vols. London: Henry Colburn, 1828.

1367 Mookerjea, Tarachand. The scorpions, or eastern
      thoughts. Allahabad, No publisher given, 1868.

1368 Moorad Ali Beg. <u>Lalun, the beragun, or the battle of</u>
     <u>Panipat.</u> Bombay: No publisher given, 1884.
     Panipat, 1761.

1369 Moorat, Mary A. C. <u>Alfred and Eliza Stark: a ro-</u>
     <u>mance from life in India.</u> Edited by G. Sircar.
     Calcutta: No publisher given, 1925.

1370 Morand, Paul. <u>The living Buddha.</u> Translated by
     Eric Sutton. New York: Knopf, 1927.
        Buddha is imagined to be living in Paris and
     New York. His reactions to the West.

1371 _____. <u>Montoceil: rajah of greater India.</u> Trans-
     lated by Tony White. London: Chapman and Hall,
     1962.
        A very funny novel. Raja of Oudore, on a visit
     to Vichy, with a ciphered document, finds that his
     father was a Bonapartist and the object of desire of
     an Indian begum.

1372 Mordecai, Margaret. <u>Indian dream lands.</u> London:
     Putnam's, 1925.
        Gaiety of British life in India.

1373 Morehead, Alan McRae. <u>Rage of the vulture.</u> London:
     Hamish Hamilton, 1948.
        Chaos in a Himalayan resort as the British pre-
     pare to leave. A British officer suffering from
     war neuroses cures himself as he copes with the
     turmoil.

1374 Morgan, W. G. Curtis. <u>A frontier romance.</u> Lon-
     don: Nash and Grayson, 1926.
        A wealthy American girl vacationing in India
     wishes excitement, travels to forbidden Pathan
     territory, and is abducted by the Pathans.

1375 Morris, Ira Victor. <u>The Bombay meeting: a novel of</u>
     <u>modern India.</u> New York: Doubleday, 1955.
        An American writer meets a Hindu girl at an
     international writers' conference.

1376 Morrow, Honore Willsie. <u>Splendour of God.</u> London:
     Hodder and Stoughton, 1930.
        East India Company's opposition to the establish-
     ment of the Baptist mission in India.

1377 Mortimer, Chapman. <u>Father goose.</u> London: Rupert
       Hart Davis, 1951.
              Two separate tales: one about a sepoy who finds
       a charm that can make anyone fall in love with the
       wearer; the other a peculiar love story told by a
       fakir living at the bottom of a well. Both stories
       are linked.

1378 Mountain, Isabel. <u>Salaam.</u> London: Heath Cranton,
       1917.
              Discomfort and inconveniences to an English girl,
       and her loneliness in the mofussil; good sketches of
       Indian servants.

1379 _____. <u>Tigress.</u> London: Heath Cranton, 1920.
              English romance partly laid in India.

1380 Mudaliar, C. T. Parathasarthi. <u>Bhima, the giant</u>
       <u>killer.</u> Madras: Macmillan, 1926.
              For children.

1381 Muddock, Joyce Emerson. <u>The great white hand: or</u>
       <u>the tiger of Cawnpore.</u> London: Hutchinson, 1896.
              Mutiny; Cawnpore.

1382 _____. <u>The star of fortune.</u> 2 vols. London:
       Chapman and Hall, 1894.
              Mutiny; Meerutt.

1383 Mukerji, Damodar. <u>Golden lotus or sonar kamal.</u>
       Translated from Bengali by R. P. De. Calcutta:
       Author, 1917.
              Thrilling romance! (Translator.)

1384 _____. <u>Ma-o-meye: or the mother and daughter.</u>
       Calcutta: Bose, 1906.

1385 Mukerji, Dhan Gopal. <u>Caste and outcaste.</u> London:
       Dent, 1923.
              Convincing picture.

1386 _____. <u>The chief of the herd.</u> London: Dent, 1929.

1387 _____. <u>Gay neck: the story of a pigeon.</u> London:
       Dent, 1928.

1388 _____. <u>Ghond: the hunter.</u> London: Dent, 1929.

1389 _____. Hari: the jungle lad. New York: Dutton,
        1924.

1390 _____. Jungle beasts and men. New York: Dent,
        1923.

1391 _____. Kari: the elephant. London: Dent, 1922.

1392 _____. My brother's face. London: Butterworth,
        1925.

1393 _____. Rama, the hero of India. London: Dent,
        1931.

1394 _____. Secret listeners of the east. London:
        Dutton, 1926.
        Mystery surrounding the death of a Boy Scout
        leader, resolved by an Indian doctor.

1395 Mukherjee, Anil Kumar. My mother. Ranchi: No
        publisher given, 1959.
        Bengali peasants vs. British administrators dur-
        ing World War II.

    Mukherji, Balachand. See Benophul.

1396 Mukherji, Prabhat Kumar. Stories of Bengalee life.
        Translated by M. S. Knight and the author. Calcutta:
        Indian Press, 1912.
        Love for life in spite of trials and sorrows.

1397 Mukherji, Santosh Kumar. Indian ghost stories.
        Allahabad: Wheeler, n. d.

1398 _____. The mysterious traders. Calcutta: Wheeler,
        n. d.

1399 Mukhopadhyaya, Tapati. Murder needs a staircase and
        six faces of Eve. Bombay: Jaico, 1963.

    Mull, Sanjhi. See Sanjhi Mull.

1400 Mullens, Mrs. and others. Prasanna and Kamini.
        London: Religious Tract Society, 1885.

1401 Mundy, Max (pseud. of Sylvia Anne Matheson). Death
        is a tiger. London: John Long, 1960.

1402 Mundy, Talbot. <u>Black light.</u> London: Hutchinson,
       1930.
       Young Englishman and his selfish mother go to
       India to find the daughter of an old school friend.

1403 _____. <u>Caves of terror.</u> London: Hutchinson,
       1932.
       King of the Khyber rifles continued. Captain
       King resigns from the army and joins an American
       concern.

1405 _____. <u>C. I. D.</u> London: Hutchinson, 1932.
       Indian political intrigue undone by the C. I. D.
       under 'Chullender' Ghose.

1406 _____. <u>Cock o' the north.</u> Indianapolis: Bobbs
       Merrill, 1929.
       A Scotsman, on the Indian frontier, is drawn
       into the powers of the ex-ranee of Jullunder, an
       amazingly beautiful English girl.

1407 _____. <u>Diamonds see in the dark.</u> London: Hutch-
       inson, 1936.
       Glamour of Indian princely life; mystery and in-
       trigue involving a white woman and an Indian man.

1408 _____. <u>East and west.</u> New York: Appleton Cen-
       tury, 1937.
       Unscrupulous Indian prince; a secret British
       officer; and a lovely American girl.

1409 _____. <u>Full moon.</u> New York: Appleton Century,
       1935.
       Bizarre adventure.

1410 _____. <u>Gunga Sahib.</u> London: Hutchinson, 1933.
       'Chullender' Ghose, Gunga Sahib and an Indian
       elephant overthrow the maharaja of an Indian state.

1411 _____. <u>Suns of the gods.</u> London & Indianapolis:
       Bobbs Merrill, 1921.
       Indian princess, partly Russian, makes political
       errors, but succeeds later.

1412 _____. <u>Gup Bahadur.</u> London: Hutchinson, 1929.
       Northwest India.

1413 _____. Hira Singh's tale. London: Cassell, 1918.
An Indian army officer at Flanders and then at
the Khyber.

1414 _____. The hundred days. London: Hutchinson,
1930.
Wild adventure across the Indian frontier; the
exploits of Pathan trans-border ruffian.

1415 _____. Jimgrim and Allah's place. London:
Hutchinson, 1933.
Thriller; Egypt and India.

1416 _____. Jungle jest. London: Hutchinson, 1931.
An English forester and the Moplah rebellion.

1417 _____. King of the Khyber rifles. London:
Constable, 1917.
Captain King must head off the mood of jihad
among the Afghan tribes where German agents are
active.

1418 _____. The nine unknown. London: Hutchinson,
1924.
Adventures of Father Cyprian with the thugs of
Delhi; excellent light on Indian magic and cunning;
and the Bengali babu.

1419 _____. OM, the secret of the Abhor valley. Indianapolis: Bobbs Merrill, 1924.
A secret service agent, posing as a brahmin,
goes to find his sister and brother-in-law who dis-
appeared in the north twenty years ago.

1420 _____. Red flame of Erinpura. London: Hutchinson, 1934.
'Chullender' Ghose again.

1421 _____. Rung ho. London: Cassell, 1914.
An untried English officer comes to India where
his father had met a hero's death, on the eve of
the Mutiny.

1422 _____. There was a door. London: Hutchinson,
1935.
A British general disappears in the Himalayas.

1423 _____. Told in the east. Indianapolis: Bobbs
        Merrill, 1920.
        Three stories set in Rajasthan.

1424 _____. The winds of the world. London: Cassell,
        1916.
        Detective story, World War I.

1425 Mungaji, V. The brilliant Simantak. Bombay: No
        publisher given, 1889.
        The diamond koh-i-noor.

1426 Munshi, Kanaiyalal Maneklal. Bhagwan Parushuram.
        Translated from Gujarati. Bombay: Bharatiya
        Vidya Bhavan, 1965.

1427 _____. Krishnavatara. 4 vols. Translated from
        Gujarati. Bombay: Bharatiya Vidya Bhavan, 1962-
        67.
        Life and legends of Sri Krishna.

1428 _____. Prithvi Vallabh. Translated from Gujarati
        by H. M. Patel. Bombay: Bharatiya Vidya Bhavan,
        1966.

1429 _____. Tapasvini or the lure of power. Trans-
        lated from Gujarati by H. M. Patel. Bombay:
        Bharatiya Vidya Bhavan, 1964.
        Probably the best novel that has yet appeared on
        the Gandhian age, 1919-37; coming of the provincial
        autonomy and different trends in Indian nationalism.

1430 Munshi, Motilal M. Beauty and joy. Surat: Gujarati
        Printing Press, 1914.
        Friendship between a Hindu, a Muslim and a
        Eurasian; many quotations from other writings and
        songs.

1431 Murphy, Charles Cecil Rowe. Stories and Adventures:
        being a miscellany of . . . . fiction, travel and
        adventure. Calcutta: Thacker Spink, 1909.

1432 Murray, William Hutchinson. Five frontiers. London:
        Dent, 1959. (Same as Appointment in Tibet.)
        Tibet, Nepal and the Himalayan foothills; Russo-
        Indian rivalry and the secret service in action.

1433 Murrell, Shirley.   Children under arms.   London:
       Hodder, 1958.
              British force at Cabul, 1841.

1434 Musbah Haidar.   Dawn beyond the tamarisks.   London:
       Hutchinson, 1953.
              First Sikh War, 1840.   A British officer's
       daughter is captured and imprisoned in a nautch
       establishment.   Battle of Ferozshah.   Excellent
       knowledge of Panjab history.

1435 Myers, Leopold Hamilton.   The near and the far.
       London: Cape, 1929.
              An extraordinary novel of the time of Akbar.

1436 _____.   The pool of Vishnu.   London: Cape, 1940.
              Mughal politics; spirituality versus secular
       power; community of persons versus a society of
       classes.

1437 _____.   Prince Jali.   London: Cape, 1931.
              Muslim princely life and politics; continues The
       near and the far.

1438 _____.   The root and the flower.   New York:
       Harcourt, 1935.
              Dilemma of Raja Amar Singh, a Rajput.   Should
       he support Prince Daniyal or Prince Selim?   Third
       in the trilogy dealing with Mughal politics in the
       days of Akbar.

1439 Nagarajan, K.   Athawar house.   Madras: Higgin-
       bothams, 1937.
              Enduring picture of Maratha family living in
       South India.

1440 _____.   Chronicles of Kedaram.   Bombay: Asia,
       1961.
              Life in a southern coastal town after World War
       I.

1441 _____.   Cold rice.   Madras: Shakti Karayalam,
       1945.
              12 stories; Coromandel coast; between two world
       wars.

1442 Nahal, C. L. The weird dance. New Delhi: Arya
      Book Depot, 1965.
      Stories mostly dealing with the partition of Pan-
      jab, but without rancor; inter-communal love rela-
      tionships.

1443 Naipaul, V. S. The mimic men. New York: Mac-
      millan, 1967.
      Partially deals with India.

1444 Namonarayana, (pseud.) Premanand and Pushpavati,
      or the purdah princess and her poet lover. Madras:
      Kanara Press, 1927.
      Rajput love story; really bad.

1445 Nanda, Gulshan. Air hostess. Translated by L. Hayat
      Bouman. New Delhi: Paradise Publications, 1968.

1446 _____. Frozen lips. Translated by Devendra
      Pratap Lahoti. Bombay: Pearl Publications, 1967.

1447 _____. Neel Kamal. Translated by P. P. Ma-
      heshwary. New Delhi: Paradise Publications, 1968.

1448 Napier, Elers. The linesman, or service in the
      guards and in the line during England's long peace
      and little wars. 3 vols. London: George Hyde,
      1856.

1449 Napier, Rosamund Lawrence. Conversation in heaven.
      London: Hodder and Stoughton, 1936.
      Warm love story set in a "criminal tribe"
      settlement.

1450 _____. Release. London: Methuen, 1921.
      Irish girl married to a civil servant twenty years
      her senior.

1451 Narain, Bishan. Devki's problem. Lahore: No pub-
      lisher given, n. d.

1452 Narasimha Sastri, Isukapalli Lakshmi. A pleasant
      surprise and other stories. Translated from Telugu
      by A. Muralidhar. Hyderabad: No publisher given,
      1961.

1453 Narayan, R. K. An astrologer's day and other stories.
      London: Eyre and Spottiswoode, 1947.

1454 _____ . The bachelor of arts. London: Nelson, 1937.
   College education informally continued.

1455 _____ . Cyclone and other stories. Madras: Rockhouse, 1944.

1456 _____ . The dark room. London: Macmillan, 1938.
   A domestic tragi-comedy, involving a couple and the other woman; the aggrieved wife retires to the "dark" room.

1457 _____ . Dodu and other stories. Mysore: Indian Thought Publications, 1943.

1458 _____ . The English teacher. London: Eyre and Spottiswoode, 1945.
   Domestic life as son, husband and father of an English language teacher.

1459 _____ . The financial expert. London: Methuen, 1952.
   A pathetic and absurd figure whose canniness amounts to stupidity.

1460 _____ . Gods, demons and other great tales from Indian myth and legend. New York: King, 1964.

1461 _____ . Grateful to life and death. Same as The English teacher.

1462 _____ . The guide. New York: Viking, 1958.
   A prisoner, recently released, takes shelter in a deserted temple and inadvertently becomes a holy man.

1463 _____ . Horse and two goats. New York: Viking, 1970.

1464 _____ . Lawley Road. Mysore: Indian Thought Publications, 1956.

1465 _____ . Malgudi days, short stories. Mysore: Indian Thought Publications, 1943.

1466 _____ . The man-eater of Malgudi. New York: Viking, 1961.
   A taxidermist intrudes in the quiet life of Malgudi.

1467 _____. Mr. Sampath. London: Eyre and Spottis-
        woode, 1949.
              A newspaper printer goes bankrupt. An idealistic
        editor and an eccentric printer become involved
        with the production of a movie.

1468 _____. The printer of Malgudi. Same as Mr.
        Sampath.

1469 _____. Swami and friends. East Lansing: Michigan
        State, 1954.
              Childhood of the Bachelor of arts hero.

1470 _____. The vendor of sweets. New York: Viking,
        1967.
              Son of a candy maker goes to the United States,
        returns with an American girl, and wants to manu-
        facture a "story writing machine" to evade taxes.
        Life-weary Gandhian.

1471 _____. Waiting for the Mahatma. London: Methuen,
        1955.
              Response of Indian humanity to the challenge of
        Gandhian revolution.

1472 Natesa Sastri, S. M. Tales of Tennaliram. Madras:
        Natesan, 1902.
              Witticisms of Tennali, the court jester.

     Natesan, T. L. See Shankar Ram.

1473 Nathaniel, Arthur. Virgin bouquet. Trivandurum:
        The Author, 1969.

1474 Natwar Singh, K. (editor). Tales from modern India.
        New York: Macmillan, 1966.
              Anthology of stories; seven from regional lang-
        uages.

1475 Nayak, K. S. Campus on fire. Bombay: New Great
        Printery, 196-.
              Student teacher relationships at a university.

1476 Neale, J. M. The bride of Ramcuttah. Oxford:
        Parker, n. d.
              16th-century historical novel for children; Neale
        may have written other children's stories with Indian
        setting.

1477 Newcomen, G. B. Blue moons. London: Selwyn
     and Blount, 1925.
        An Indian potentate takes an English girl, sus-
     pected of having oriental blood, to India, and makes
     her part of his harem.

1478 Newell, Robert (pseud. of O. C. Kerr) Ilderin the
     Afghan. (cited by Dixson.)

1479 Newnham-Davis, N. Three men and a god and other
     stories. London: Downey, 1896.

1480 Nikambe, Shevantibai. Ratanbai: a sketch of a Bom-
     bay high caste Hindu young wife. London: Marshall
     Brothers, 1895.
        Maratha Brahmin domestic life.

1481 Nirody, B. S. Nandini. Delhi: Publications Division,
     1967.

1482 Nisbet, Hume. The queen's desire. London: F. V.
     White, 1893.
        Critical of British role in the Mutiny; Meerutt,
     Delhi, Cawnpore, Lucknow, and Tantia are all
     there.

1483 Nityanandan, P. M. The long, long days. Bombay:
     Asia, 1960.
        Novel of college life; good satirical sketches.

1484 Noon, Firoz Khan. Scented dust. Lahore: Gulab
     Singh, 1942.
        A novel that seeks to portray the diversity and
     totality of Indian life; and fails.

1485 _____. Wisdom from fools: tales. Lahore:
     Gulab Singh, 1940.

Norway, Nevil Shute. See Nevil Shute.

1486 O'Beirne, Ivan. The colonel's crime: a story of to-
     day; and Jim's wife. Allahabad: Wheeler, 1889.

1486a _____. Major Craik's craze. Allahabad: Wheeler, 1892.

1487 O'Hind, Jan. Curse of the arhat. New Delhi: Delhi
     Press, 1961.

1488 _____ . Legacy: a historical novel. New Delhi:
        Delhi Book Co., 1962.

1489 _____ . Mughal night. New Delhi: Delhi Press,
        1965.
            Jehangir's era.

1490 Oles, B. and Darshan Singh. Burglars of hearts.
        Bombay: Jaico, 1969.

1491 Oliphant, Phillip Lawrence. Her serene highness.
        London: Methuen, 1912.
            Complete orientalization of an Englishman and
        his final return to "civilization".

1492 _____ . The little red fish. London: Arnold, 1903.
            An English officer with the help of "good" In-
        dians cleans up the administration of a princely
        state.

1493 _____ . Maya: tale of east and west. London:
        Constable, 1908.
            Daughter of an English soldier grows up in an
        Indian palace after the Mutiny, and serves in a
        temple to Vishnu.

1494 Ollivant, Alfred. Old forever: an epic beyond the
        Indus. London: Allen and Unwin, 1923.
            Clash between white and brown, east and west,
        on the Afghan frontier.

1495 Oman, J. Campbell. Where three creeds meet.
        London: Grant Richards, 1898.
            Muslim village life; kidnapping of a Hindu woman
        and Christian social reform.

1496 Ottley, Thomas Henry. Rustum Khan or fourteen
        nights' entertainment at Shah Bhag, or royal
        gardens at Ahemadabad. London: No publisher
        given, 1831.

1497 Owenson, Sydney. English homes in India. London:
        No publisher given, 1821.
            British military and civilian officials in India.

1498 _____ . Luxima: the prophetess, a tale of India.
        London: No publisher given, 1859. (Same as The

missionary in India tales.   3 vols.)
    Life and labors of a missionary family; love of
a Hindu girl for a missionary; and the conflict between Hindu and Christian sects.

1499 Padmanabha Iyer, P.   Indian tales.   Srirangam: Vani
     Vilas Press, 1924.

1500 Paintal, Veena.   Link in the broken chain.   New Delhi:
     Army Educational Services, 1967.

1501 _____ .   Roshni: portrait of love.   Dehradun:
     E. B. D. Publishing, 1967.

1502 _____ .   Serenity in storm.   Bombay: Allied Pub-
     lishers, 1966.
         Indian girl's unhappy and strange marriage to a
     police official; and her love for two army officers.

1503 Pal, Radha Ballav.   A glimpse of zennana life in
     Bengal.   Calcutta: S. C. Auddy, 1904.
         Reliable; good information on the use of Bhagvats
     in India's social and religious life.

1504 Panchapakesa Ayyar, Aiylam Subrahmanya.   Baladitya:
     a historical romance of ancient India.   Bombay:
     Taraporevala, 1930.

1505 _____ .   Chankya and Chandragupta: a historical
     novel.   Madras: Ramaswamy Sastrulu, 1951.

1506 _____ .   Famous tales of Ind.   Madras: Rama-
     swamy Sastrulu, 1954.

1507 _____ .   The finger of destiny and other stories.
     Mylapore: Alliance Co. , 1946.

1508 _____ .   Gripping tales of Ind.   Tenali: Orient
     Publishing, 1948.

1509 _____ .   Indian after dinner stories.   2 vols. Bom-
     bay: Taraporevala, 1926.

1510 _____ .   Jolly old tales of Ind.   Vellore: K. V.
     Press, 1945.

1511 _____. Kovalan and Kannaki: story of the famous
Tamil epic. Madras: Alliance, 1940.
Silappadikaram retold.

1512 _____. The legions thunder past. Same as Three
men of destiny.

1513 _____. Life is one long sacrifice. Madras:
Alliance, 1947.
Student life.

1514 _____. Manimekalai. Madras: Alliance, 1947.
A dancing girl resists attempts of a Cholan
prince and becomes a Buddhist nun.

1515 _____. Musician shut the gate: stories. Madras:
Alliance, n. d.

1516 _____. Poor man's son and other stories. Madras:
Ramaswamy Sastrulu, 1963.

1517 _____. The royal jester or Tenali Rama: tales.
Vellore: K. V. Press, 1943.

1518 _____. Sense in sex and other stories of Indian
woman. Bombay: Taraporevala, 1927.

1519 _____. Tales of Ind. Mylapore: Alliance, 1944.

1520 _____. Three men of destiny. Madras: C. C.
Naidu, 1939.
Full length portraits of Alexander, Chandragupta
and Chanakya.

1521 Panchkouree Khan. Revelations of an orderly. Benares:
Lazarus, 1866.

1522 Panjabi, Khooshie L. Nevertheless I love her still.
Bombay: Punkul, 1944.

1523 _____. Will you marry me, please? Bombay:
Punkul, 1944.

Parappurath. See K. E. Mathai.

1524 Patel, Baburao. The rosary and the lamp. Bombay:
Girnar, 1966.
Ten stories of Krishna devotees.

1525 Patel, Dossabhoy. Carl Cornwall, a point four
        American in Malwa, India. Karachi: Pakistan,
        1962.

        Patton, James B. See Edmund White.

1526 Paul, Dhirendra Nath. The mysteries of Calcutta.
        Edited by M. Sen. 3 vols. Calcutta: Datta, Bose,
        1925.
            Pampered aristocracy and their fleshpots.

1527 _____. The mysteries of the Mogul court. Cal-
        cutta: Datta, Bose, 1920.
            Jahangir and the sinister influence of Nur Jahan.

1528 _____. Mysteries of the Mogul durbar: a historical
        romance. Calcutta: Datta, Bose, 1921.
            Shah Jahan and his daughters Jahanara and
        Roshanara.

1529 Payne, Pierre Stephen Robert. Blood royal. New
        York: Prentice Hall, 1952.
            Tavernier at the court of Shah Jehan: struggle
        for royal power.

1530 _____. The emperor. Same as Blood royal.

1531 _____. The lord comes: a novel on the life of the
        Buddha. London: Heinemann, 1948.

1532 _____. Maharajah. New York: World, 1951.
            A terrorist comes to a Himalayan state to kill
        the ruler and to paralyse the state.

1533 _____. Young emperor. New York: Macmillan,
        1950.
            Shah Jahan.

1534 Pearce, Charles, E. The bungalow under the lake.
        London: Stanley Paul, 1910.
            The Mutiny.

1535 _____. Love besieged: a romance of the residency
        in Lucknow. London: Stanley Paul, 1909.

1536 _____. Red revenge: a romance of Cawnpore.
        London: Stanley Paul, 1911.

1537 _____. A star of the east. London: Stanley Paul,
      1912.
          A dancing girl in a palace is recognized to be a
      lost English girl; climax is the Mutiny at Delhi.

1538 Peard, Frances M. The flying months. London:
      Smith Elder, 1909.
          Secret of a young man's parentage. Peard may
      have written other novels with Indian setting.

1539 Peethambar, C. The forgotten serenade and other
      stories. Bellary: No publisher given, 1970.

1540 Pegg, Eleanor. The brand of Kali. London: Sheldon
      Press, 1929.
          Romance and adventure set in Nilgiri Hills;
      blood curdling at times.

1541 _____. Red pepper or the zennana mystery.
      London: Sheldon Press, 1929.
          Mystery; South India.

1542 _____. Star maiden: a tale of South India.
      London: Sheldon Press, 1926.
          Missionary story of a half-Muslim, half-English
      girl.

1543 Pemberton, Max Joseph. Hindoo Khan. London:
      Mills and Boon, 1922.
          Afghan border; romance and adventure.

1544 Pennell, Alice M. The begum's son. London: John
      Murray, 1928.
          A virtuous Muslim prince, his equally virtuous
      wife; and an impossibly wicked aunt in a palace in-
      trigue.

1545 _____. Children of the border. London: John
      Murray, 1926.
          Noble savages of the Afghan border mountains.

1546 _____. Doorways of the east. London: John
      Murray, 1931.
          A young Hindu is modernized; and a young Indian
      girl joins the revolutionary movement.

1547 Penny, Fanny Emily Farr. Caste and Creed. 2 vols.

London: White, 1890.
Eurasian life; good rendering of Vishnu worship.

1548 _____. Chowra's revenge. London: Hutchinson,
1937.
Continues The familiar stranger.
Tragedy in which Indian superstition and magic
play role.

1549 _____. Dark corners. London: Chatto and
Windus, 1908.

1550 _____. Desire and delight. London: Chatto and
Windus, 1919.
Life of a nurse in Bangalore.

1551 _____. Diamonds. London: Hodder and Stoughton,
1920.
Elihu Yale; early years of the East India Company.

1552 _____. Dilys. London: Chatto and Windus, 1903.
Indian gypsies.

1553 _____. The elusive bachelor. London: Hutchinson, 1935.
A Madras romance.

1554 _____. The familiar stranger. London: Hutchinson, 1936.
Twin daughters of a rich British merchant are
orphaned, come in the custody of a Hindu woman,
and one is found missing. The other goes to England and has two unfortunate love affairs.

1555 _____. A forest officer. London: Methuen, 1900.
A forester in the Madras presidency.

1556 _____. Get on the wooing. London: Hodder and
Stoughton, 1931.
Axed navy officer goes to a tea plantation in
India, and finds himself too poor to marry the girl
he loves. Wicked Hindu is also there.

1557 _____. The inevitable law. London: Chatto and
Windus, 1907.
Tragedy of a cultured Indian married to an un-

cultured girl; Indian nationalism in which Congress
is "a mere bladder inflated by cheap gas. "

1558 _____. Jackals and others. London: Mills and
Boon, 1939.
Nine stories from South India.

1559 _____. Living dangerously. London: Hodder and
Stoughton, 1925.
Death of an Englishman; native superstitious at-
mosphere.

1560 _____. Love by an Indian river. London: Chatto
and Windus, 1916.
English officer in love with an American girl
while a tree in which the spirit of the River God
lives is being cut to make way for a bridge.

1561 _____. Love in a palace. London: Chatto and
Windus, 1915.
Englishman teaches an Indian the meaning of love.

1562 _____. Love in the hills. London: Chatto and
Windus, 1913.
Nilgiris, that is.

1563 _____. A love tangle. London: Chatto and Windus, 1917.
East versus west in ethics, and in marriage.

1564 _____. Magic in the air. London: Hodder and
Stoughton, 1933.
An Indian jungle seer changes human beings into
animals.

1565 _____. The Malabar magician. London: Chatto
and Windus, 1912.
Adventures and misadventures of an Indian hypnotist.

1566 _____. Missing. London: Chatto and Windus, 1917.
A Rajput raja is missing.

1567 _____. A mixed marriage. London: Methuen,
1903.
The unhappiness of an educated Indian who cannot accept an Indian wife, and whose English love
is not accepted by society.

1568 _____. The old dagoba. London: Hodder and Stoughton, 1934.
   A girl and her two suitors; she chooses wrongly but amends before it is too late. Largely Ceylon.

1569 _____. On the Coromandel coast. London: Smith Elder, 1908.

1570 _____. One of the best. London: Hodder and Stoughton, 1923.
   An English judge who had passed sentence on a high born Indian for murder is himself murdered.

1571 _____. The outcaste. London: Chatto and Windus, 1912.
   An Indian convert to Christianity and the social miseries to which he is subjected; repugnance towards the theory of transmigration and rebirth.

1572 _____. Patrick. London: Hodder and Stoughton, 1934.
   Taming of elephant; school and church life; romance.

1573 _____. Pulling the strings. London: Hodder and Stoughton, 1927.
   Crime and detection; police officer and a mysterious stranger who tries to cure him of his shyness.

1574 _____. A question of colour. London: Hodder and Stoughton, 1926.
   Inter-racial love affair.

1575 _____. A question of love. London: Hodder and Stoughton, 1928.
   An English girl becomes governess in a Hindu zennana of Coimbatore. Good descriptions of the zennana.

1576 _____. The rajah. London: Chatto and Windus, 1911.
   An English educated Rajah and the vexing problem of love in India.

1577 _____. The rajah's daughter. London: Hodder and Stoughton, 1921.

Educated Indian girl, married to a coarse zamindar, elopes with a rajah.

1578 _____. The romance of a nautch girl. London:
Swan Sonnenschein, 1898.
Fine picture of intertwined Indian and English
lives.

1579 _____. Sacrifice. London: Chatto and Windus,
1910.
Contains a thorough and sympathetic account of
the beliefs of the Khonds.

1580 _____. The sanyasi. London: Chatto and Windus,
1904.
Life of British officials in India and the mysterious identity of an ascetic.

1581 _____. A spell of the devil. London: Hutchinson,
1935.
An Englishman living in hemp country becomes
addicted to hashish.

1582 _____. The swami's curse. London: Hodder and
Stoughton, 1922.
High caste Hindu converts to Christianity; con-
tains detailed information on Hindu customs.

1583 _____. The tea planter. London: Chatto and
Windus, 1906.
Indian magician at work.

1584 _____. Treasure, love and snakes. London: Mills
and Boon, 1938.
Nine stories; South India.

1585 _____. The two brides. London: Hodder and
Stoughton, 1929.
Indian girl after "acculturation" in England be-
comes a model wife to a Western educated Hindu.

1586 _____. The unlucky mark. London: Chatto and
Windus, 1909.
A race horse, shady transactions, and a wealthy
contractor's son, educated in England, out for mis-
chief.

1587 _____ . The wishing stone. London: Hodder and
Stoughton, 1930.
A Eurasian beauty wants to marry an Englishman.

1588 Pereira, Arthur. Spicy Stories. Allahabad: St. Paul,
1959.

1589 Pereira, Michael. Stranger in the land. London:
G. Bles, 1967.

1590 Perrin, Alice. The Anglo-Indians. London: Methuen,
1912.
The author who lived in India for many years
generally writes about "Anglo-Indian" and Eurasian
life, and the tragedy of Anglo-Indians in the moffusil.
This is one of her best.

1591 _____ . The charm. London: Methuen, 1910.
An Englishman marries a Eurasian widow.

1592 _____ . East of Suez. London: Treherene, 1901.
Powerful and pathetic tale of Anglo-Indian life.

1593 _____ . A free solitude. London: Chatto and
Windus, 1907.
An Englishman inherits property at the foot of
the Himalayas; also Eurasian life.

1594 _____ . Government House. London: Cassell, 1925.
Governor falls in love with his children's
governess.

1595 _____ . The happy hunting ground. London: Methuen,
1914.
English girls go to India to find husbands.

1596 _____ . Idolatry. London: Chatto and Windus, 1909.
Two types of missionaries in India. Step-
daughter of one of them, reared in England, penniless, goes to India to win a suitor. The second
missionary exhibits selflessness.

1597 _____ . Into temptation. 2 vols. London: F. V.
White, 1894.

1598 _____ . The mound. London: Methuen, 1922.
The influence of the Buddha on an Englishman who
has supposedly discovered the master's burial place.

1599 _____. Other sheep. London: Benn, 1932.
      The heroine marries the wrong man and is es-
tablished in a missionary settlement.

1600 _____. Red records: tales. London: Chatto and
Windus, 1906.
      Of the 17 stories the only two that are not
tragedy are tart; occult influences, superstitions.

1601 _____. Rough passages. London: Cassel, 1926.
      Stories; from the Mutiny to reincarnation.

1602 _____. Separation. London: Cassell, 1917.
      Clara detests India.

1603 _____. The spell of the jungle. London: Treherene, 1902.
      Tiger shooting; love making.

1604 _____. A star of India. London: Cassell, 1919.
      Young girl married to an old colonel tragically
falls in love with a young officer.

1605 _____. The stronger claim. London: Eveleigh
Nash, 1903.
      Englishman with a trace of Hindu in his blood
goes inadvertently to serve a town where he had
been born; and comes under the influence of superstitions of his mother's ancestral gods.

1606 _____. Tales that are told. London: Skeffington,
1917.
      Stories; the one on "old Ayah" is a gem.

1607 _____. The vow of silence. London: Cassell,
1920.
      Artless tale of love, fidelity and murder.

1608 _____. The waters of destruction. London: Chatto
and Windus, 1905.
      Romance.

1609 _____. The women in the bazaar. London:
Cassell, 1914.
      Stereotyped dull jealous husband, frivolous wife,
and a glamorous young man. No one can guess the
ending.

1610 Perry, George B. Uncle Peter's trust. New York:
      Harper, 1912.
      Mutiny.

1611 Peters, Ellis. Mourning raga. New York: William
      Morrow, 1970.
      Suspense; chaperone of the teen-age daughter of
      a movie star is taken to her father in New Delhi;
      but the father is gone, and the girl vanishes too.

1612 Peterson, Margaret. Just because. London: Andrew
      Melrose, 1915.
      English parson's daughter marries the familiar
      subaltern. Miss Peterson may have written other
      romances with Indian setting.

1613 Phadke, N. S. Leaves in the August wind: a novel
      with the Indian upheaval of August 1942 for its
      background. Bombay: Hind Kitabs, 1947.
      First published in Marathi in 1943, it was pro-
      scribed in 1944. A married woman does not love
      her husband or his ideology, but another man with
      a different ideology. Hindu Mahasabha versus
      Congress.

1614 _____. Where Angels sell eggs and other stories.
      Bombay: Hind Kitabs, 1957.

1615 _____. Whirlwind. Translated from Marathi.
      Bombay: Jaico, 1956.
      Quit India movement.

1616 Phillimore, E. E. A million for soul. London: John
      Lang, 1915.
      The first chapter contains strange Latin and even
      stranger Irish. Girl goes to India, gets married,
      and takes to drink.

1617 _____. Two women and a maharaja. London:
      John Lang, 1907.

1618 Phipps, C. M. Katherine. Douglas Archdale: A tale
      of Lucknow. London: Literary Society, 1885.

1619 Pilcher, T. D. East is east: stories of Indian life.
      London, John Lane, 1922.
      Three stories; unfavorable view of Indians.

1620 Pilkington, Mary. The Asiatic princess. 2 vols.
      London: No publisher given, 1800.
          Vol. II, Chap. 3 on Calcutta and Indian abomi-
      nations.

1621 Piper, Anne. The hot years. London: Heinemann,
      1955.
          Delhi, Rangoon, and English girls; very proper.
      Good insights into British war time racial mentality.

      Piper, David. See Peter Towry.

1622 Planter's Mate, pseud. A new clearing: a medley of
      prose and verse. Madras: Vest & Co., 1884.
          Planters and plantations, of course.

1623 Pollard, Eliza Fanny. The silver hand: a story of
      India in the eighteenth century. London: Blackie,
      1908.
          English, French, Hyder Ali, Scindia and Maratha
      political rivalries simplified.

1624 _____. The white dove of Amritzir. London: No
      publisher given, 1896.
          Good descriptions of Amritsar and Sikh life.
      English girl in India on the marriage path.

1625 Ponder, Stephen Einar Gilbert. A daughter of Atropos.
      London: Stanley Paul, 1945.
          Frontier romance.

1626 _____. Daughter of destiny. London: Stanley
      Paul, 1955.
          Set during the reign of Akbar; the love of a Mus-
      lim prince for a Rajput princess.

1627 _____. Frontier tapestry. London: Stanley Paul,
      1943.
          Frontier romance: superb picture of a Pathan
      prostitute and her lovers.

1628 _____. A mughul miniature. London: Stanley
      Paul, 1948.
          Romance around the life of Emperor Akbar.

1629 _____. A rose of Hindustan. London: Stanley
      Paul, 1946.
          Romance, again during Akbar's reign.

1630 _____. Valleys of the ungodly. London: Stanley
       Paul, 1947.
       Panjab and the Sikhs.

1631 _____. Waters of chastisement. London: Stanley
       Paul, 1947.
       Murder in princely India.

1632 Pon-Ratnam, Schwartz. Spotten green: Indian ghost
       stories. London: Stockwell, 1935.

1633 Pook, Peter. Pook sahib: a light satire on all things
       eastern including the English who go there. London:
       Hale, 1965.

1634 Potter, Margaret Horton. The flame gathers. Lon-
       . don: Macmillan, 1904.
       Romance of India; thirteenth century.

1635 Prabha, pseud. Purdah woman abode. Bombay:
       Popular, 1962.

1636 Prem Chand (pseud. of Dhanpat Rai Srivastava). The
       chess players and other stories. Translated by
       Gurdial Mallik. Delhi: Hind Pocket Books, 1967.

1637 _____. The gift of a cow. Translation of Godaan
       by Gordon C. Roadarmel. Bloomington: Indiana
       University Press, 1968. Another translation is by
       Jaya Ratan Lal and P. Lal. Bombay: Jaico, 1957.
       Most realistic interpretation of Indian village so-
       ciety; hungry and semistarved people, yet hopeful
       and optimistic. Set in Uttar Pradesh.

1638 _____. A handful of wheat. Translated from Urdu.
       New Delhi: Peoples Publishing House, 1955.

1639 _____. The secret of culture and other stories.
       Translated from Hindi by Madan Gupta. Bombay:
       Jaico, 1960.

1640 _____. Short stories of Prem Chand. Translated
       from Hindi by Gurdial Mallik. Bombay: Nalanda
       Publications, 1946.

1641 _____. The world of Prem Chand. Selected stories
       translated by David Rubin. Bloomington: Indiana Uni-
       versity Press, 1969.

1642 Prichard, Iltudus Thomas. Chronicles of Budgepore;
      or sketches of life in upper India. 2 vols. London:
      no publisher given, 1870.
         A truly remarkable work of the pre-Kipling
      period; life of the red tape and the bureaucratic
      white wash; dedicated to the theory that Indians are
      clever to make a fool of their white masters.

1643 _____ . How to manage it. 3 vols. London: No
      publisher given, 1864.
         White civil servant and his friendship with a
      nawab, who is forced to join the Mutiny. Excellent
      descriptions of Calcutta life. Convincing romance.

1644 [Prinsep, Augustus] The baboo and other tales de-
      scriptive of society in India. 2 vols. London:
      Smith Elder, 1834.
         Sahibs, 'nabobs', their servants, babus, and
      women of the zennana, in Calcutta.

1645 _____ . Eva and Forester: a tale of India. 2 vols.
      London: Smith Elder, 1840.
         Excellent on the babus.

1646 Prior, Lilian Faith Loveday. The horse of the sun.
      London: John Murray, 1945.
         Dynastic intrigues in Rajput states at the turn of
      the century.

1647 Pritam, Amrita. Doctor Dev. Translated by Krishan
      Gujral. Delhi: Hind Pocket Books, 1968.

1648 _____ . The skeleton and other writings. Trans-
      lated by Khushwant Singh. Bombay: Jaico, 1964.
         Four short stories plus the novelette Pinjar.

1649 _____ . Two faces of Eve. Translated by P.
      Machwe and G. S. P. Suri. Delhi: Hind Pocket
      Books, n. d.
         Two novels translated from Panjabi deal with
      communal and inter-racial love.

1650 Prokosch, Frederick. The Asiatics. London: Chatto
      and Windus, 1935.
         An American on the move in Asia, receptive to
      any experience whether physical or emotional, find-
      ing in Asia the final tragic end, and the endless
      desire for the beautiful.

1651 _____. The dark dancer. New York: Farrar,
     Strauss, 1964.
     Set in the time of Emperor Shah Jahan.

1652 Pryde, Anthony and Rose Kirkpatrick Weekes. The
     purple pearl. London: Allen and Unwin, 1923.
     Mystery about purple pearls handed to English
     lords by lovelorn Indian begums.

1653 Punt, Ram Krishna. The boy of Bengal. London:
     No publisher given, 1866.

1654 Puri, Meenakshi. Pay on the first. Delhi: Sidd-
     hartha, 1968.

1655 Purwar, G. In the P(ublic) W(orks) D(epartment).
     Bombay: No publisher given, 1888.

1656 Pymm, L. Calcutta by night. Simla: No publisher
     given, no date.

1657 Quin, Michael Joseph. Nourmahal, an Oriental ro-
     mance. 3 vols. London: Henry Colburn, 1838.
     Jahangir and Nur Mahal in Kashmir.

1658 Rae, Mrs. Milne. A bottle in the smoke: a tale of
     Anglo-India. London: Hodder and Stoughton, 1912,
     Eurasian hero is contrasted with a pukka sahib
     who is unscrupulous; later it is detected that the
     Eurasian is pure white, but the sahib is not.

1659 Raeside, Ian (translator). The rough and the smooth.
     Bombay: Asia, 1966.

1660 Rafter, Michael. The rifleman: or the adventures of
     Percy Blake. London: No publisher given, 1858.

1661 _____. Savindroog or the queen of the jungle.
     3 vols. London: No publisher given, 1848.
     Hindu-Muslim prejudices and the chivalry of the
     Bhils.

1662 Raina, Vimala. Ambapali. New York: Asia, 1962.
     A court dancer, daughter of sin and pleasure,
     becomes the first woman to join the Buddhist sangha.

1663 _____. Indian love legends. Bombay: Popular,
        1967.

1664 Raines, G. P. Terrible times: a tale of the Mutiny.
        London: Routledge, 1899.
        Meerutt in the 1850's.

1665 Raj, Hilda. The house of Ramiah. Lucknow: Luck-
        now Publishing House, 1967.
        Four generations of a South Indian Christian
        family at Tirunelveli.

1666 Raja Rao. The cat and the Shakespeare. New York:
        Macmillan, 1965.
        Soul must rely on God as the kitten relies on its
        mother; clerk seeks simple life in a South Indian
        town during World War II.

1667 _____. The cow of the barricades and other stories.
        Bombay: Oxford University Press, 1947.

1668 _____. Kanthapura. London: Allen and Unwin,
        1938.
        Gandhian movement reaches a South Indian village.
        Magnificient.

1669 _____. Serpent and the rope. New York:
        Pantheon, 1963.
        Perhaps the greatest novel of Hindu India. A
        Brahmin marries a French girl but is not at home
        with her or in Europe. Rich in Vedanta philosophy.

1670 Rajagopalachari, Chakravarti. The fatal cart and
        other stories. New Delhi: Hindustan Times, 1946.
        16 stories, translated from Tamil. South India.

1671 _____. Stories for the innocent. Bombay: Bhartiya
        Vidya Bhavan, 1963.

1672 Rajah, H. D. Is it a crime? Bombay: Young Lib-
        erator Office, 1933.
        Prison life.

1673 _____. Sparks from our life. Madras: National
        Literature Publishing Co., 1934.
        Stories; Indian social reform.

1674 Rajam Aiyar, B. R.   True greatness or Vasudeva
      Sastri. Madras: Thompson, 1905.
          Religious life in Tamilnad in the late nineteenth
      century.

1675 Rajamani, Lalita. Sweet seventeen. Bombay: Jaico,
      1957.

1676 Rajan, Balchandra. The dark dancer. New York:
      Simon and Schuster, 1958.
          Anglicised Indian discovers his identity through
      private and public upheavels in 1947.

1677 _____. Too long in the west. London: Heine-
      mann, 1961.
          Splendidly comic story of a lively daughter of a
      university professor who after her American educa-
      tion returns to a tiny, remote village to acquire a
      bridegroom in the traditional way.

1678 Rajgopal, K. The faded flower. Madras: Rajagopa-
      lachari, 1924.
          Short story set in Tamil Nadu.

1679 Rajput, (pseud.) The advancing year. London: Hurst
      and Blackett, 1941.

1680 _____. Indian river. London: Hurst and Blackett,
      1939.

1681 _____. Khyber calling. London: Hurst and
      Blackett, 1938.
          Narrative of service in the Frontier province.

1682 Rakesh, Mohan. Lingering Shadows. tr. by Jai
      Ratan. Delhi: Hind Pocket Books, 1970.

1683 Ralli, Sidney. The Etna messages and other stories.
      Bombay: Hind Kitabs, 1945.

1684 Ram, Shanker (pseud. of T. L. Natesan). The
      children of Kaveri. Madras: Purnah, 1926.
          Subtle influence of the river on the life of people
      living on the banks of Kaveri.

1685 _____. Creatures all. 2 vols. Madras: Purnah,
      1933.
          Short stories; South Indian life.

1686 _____. The love of dust. Madras: Purnah, 1938.

1687 Ram Kumar. Stories. tr. from Hindi by Jai Ratan.
Calcutta: Writers Workshop, 1970.

1688 Ram Narain. The tigress of the harem. New York:
Macaulay, 1930.
Sensational goings on in a princely state.

1689 Rama Rao, Santha. Remember the house. New York:
Harper, 1956.
Uprooted, pseudo-sophisticated, westernized set
in Bombay versus serene tradition-based life in
Malabar.

1690 Rama Sharma, M. V. The stream. Masulipatam:
Triveni, 1956.
Man between two women and unable to achieve
satisfactory relationship with either.

1691 Ramabai, C. T. Victory of faith and other stories.
Ramnagar: Gopalkrishna Rao, 1935.

1692 Ramabhadran, N. Kettle drums. Mangalore: Basel
Mission Press, 1933.
Nineteen stories of considerable ethnographical
interest.

1693 Ramachandra Rao, D. S. Lakshmi's triumph: a
message from the stars. Madras: Natesan, 1936.
Harijan temple entry.

1694 Ramachandra Rao, P. The son-in-law abroad and
other Indian folk tales. Madras: Natesan, 1904.

1695 Ramakrishna, Pillai T. The dive for death. London:
George Allen, 1911.
Set in the 1600's; South Indian religious life.

1696 _____. Padmini: an Indian romance. London:
Swan Sonneschein, 1903.
A love story of the 16th century following the fall
of the Vijavanagar empire and the establishment of
the British at Madras.

1697 Ramamurthy, V. Fragrant Valley. Kurukshetra:
Hippie Books, 1969.

1698 Raman, Mariada. <u>Tales of Marianda Raman.</u> Translated by P. Ramachandra Rao. Madras: No
publisher given, 1902.

1699 Ramani, Hashoo Kewal. <u>Sindhi short stories.</u> Delhi:
Hashmat, 1964.
Twenty-one nostalgic memories of Sindh and its
Sufism.

1700 Ramappa, K. <u>The whirlwind.</u> Bangalore: The Author,
1966.

1701 Ramarau, Rama V. M. <u>Irascible, iridescent, iridium.</u>
Calcutta: Alpha Beta, 1963.

1702 _____. <u>The sands serenade the snows.</u> Calcutta:
Alpha Beta, 1964.
A daring novel of experimentation with a life of
pleasure and enjoyment.

1703 Ramnani, T. <u>Magnificient moghuls.</u> Bombay: Jaico,
1969.

1704 Ramzan, Muhammad. <u>The rajah.</u> No publisher given,
1929.

1705 Rana, J. <u>Alien there is none.</u> London: Hodder and
Stoughton, 1959.
English girl's difficulties in adjusting to India
following her marriage to an Indian.

1706 Randall, Margaret. <u>Getting rid of blue plastic.</u> Calcutta: Dialogue, 1969.

1707 Rankin, Louise. <u>Daughter of the mountains.</u> London:
Bodley Head, 1962.
A Tibetan girl journeys from Lhasa to Calcutta
to find her stolen dog. Young adults.

1708 Ransom, Josephine. <u>Indian tales of love and beauty.</u>
Adyar: Theosophical, 1921.
Women's life in ancient Indian legends.

1709 Rao, A. V. <u>The man in the red and other stories.</u>
Bombay: International Book House, 1942.

1710 Rao, K. R. <u>None shall live.</u> Rajkot: Kitabghar, 1945.
Tragic romance.

1711 _____. On the sands of Juhu. Rajkot: Kitabghar, 1945.

Rao, Raja. See Raja Rao.

Rao, S. V. Shiva. See Gulvadi.

1712 Rawley, Ratan Chand. Mr. John Bull speaks out. Bombay: Thacker, 1943.
    Indian politics; Europeans, princes, socialists of the 1930's are all there.

1713 Ray, Bani. Srilata and Sampa. Calcutta: Mitra and Ghosh, 1953.

1714 Ray, Lila (translator). Broken bread: short stories of modern Bengal. Calcutta: M. C. Sarkar, 1957.

1715 Redwood, Ethel Boverton. Wanderings and wooings east of Suez. London: John Long, 1913.
    More of a travelogue; good scenes of Benares, Bombay, Agra, Darjeeling and Simla.

1716 Rege, Purushottama Shivarama. Saviritri and Avalokita. Tr. from Marathi by Kumud Mehta. Bombay: Thacker, 1969.
    Two novelettes.

1717 Reid, C. Lestock. Masque of Mutiny. London: Temple, 1947.
    Mutiny, 1857.

1718 Reid, Mayne. The cliff climbers. London: C. H. Clarke, 1864.
    For the young.

Ressich, John Sellar Matheson and Eric Debonzie. See Gregory Baxter.

1719 Reuben, Bunny. Monkeys on the hill of God. Bombay: Pearl, 1969.

1720 Reyna, Ruth. Sukra: the story of truth. New Delhi: Sagar, 1969.
    Doctrines of Advaita Vedanta.

1721 Reynolds, G. W. M. Pope Joan or Female Pontiff.

2 vols. Ahmedabad: Sakalchand Amralal, 1917.

1722 Rhodes, Kathlyn. <u>Golden journey.</u> London: Hutchinson, 1926.
Beautiful Eurasian girl shows degrading influence of her mixed parentage!

1723 Rideout, Henry Milner. <u>Dulcarnon.</u> London: Hurst and Blackett, 1925.

1724 _____. <u>Man eater.</u> London: Hurst and Blackett, 1927.
A police officer on the northwest frontier, sympathetic to the tribesmen.

1725 _____. <u>No man's money: the story of Tin Couri Dass.</u> London: Jarrolds, 1919.
Mystery and adventure involving the lost heir of an Indian princedom.

1726 Rivers, R. N. <u>The call of the jungle.</u> London: Simpkin, Marshall, 1926.
A clinging divorced wife and an unscrupulous partner force the hero to abandon his plantation on the Brahmaputra; he retires to the hills, marries into the tribe, and discovers the joys of jungle life.

1727 Roberts, Emma. <u>Jerringham, or the inconstant man.</u> Calcutta: No publisher given, 1836.

1728 _____. <u>Scenes and characteristics of Hindostan with sketches of Anglo-Indian society.</u> 3 vols. London: No publisher given, 1835.

1729 Robinson, Philip Stewart. <u>Chasing a fortune.</u> London: No publisher given, 1884.

1730 _____. <u>In my Indian garden.</u> London: No publisher given, 1878.
Quite accurate picture of a bungalow household.

1731 _____. <u>The Indian garden series: tales and sketches.</u> 3 vols. London: Sampson and Low, 1884-86.

1732 _____. <u>Tigers at large.</u> London: No publisher given, 1884.

1733 _____. Under the punkah. London: No publisher
     given, 1881.

1734 _____. The valley of the teetotom trees. London:
     No publisher given, 1886.

1735 Robinson, Philip Stewart, E. Kay Robinson and H.
     Perry Robinson. Tales by three brothers. London:
     Ibister and Co., 1902.

1736 Robinson, R. E. The golden company: stories of the
     Buddha, etc. London: Humphrey Milford, 1926.

1737 Rooke, Daphne. Beti. Boston: Houghton Mifflin, 1959.
     Kidnapping, smuggling and banditry; told by a
     twelve-year-old girl.

1738 Roped In (pseud.) Reflections. Calcutta: Lal Chand,
     1921.
     On English life.

1739 Rose, Isabel Brown. Diana's Indian diary. New York:
     Richard Smith, 1930.
     Romance of a widow who goes to India; mission-
     ary settlement, leper colony, and a girls' school.

1740 Rothfeld, Otto. Indian dust. Oxford: Alden, 1909.
     Rajput life.

1741 _____. Life and its puppets: being stories from
     India and the west. Oxford: Alden, 1911.

1742 Rousselet, L. The serpent charmer. New York:
     Scribner, 1880.
     For children.

1743 Rouviere, Henrietta Mosse. Arrivals from India.
     4 vols. London: A. K. Newman, 1812.

1744 Row, C. S. The confessions of a bogus patriot.
     Madras: Gandhi House, 1923.

1745 _____. How I became a maharaja. Madras: No
     publisher given, no date.

1746 _____. Mysteries of the court of a maharaja.
     Madras: No publisher given, no date.

1747 Rowney, Horatio Bickerstaff. The young zemindar.
      London: Remington, 1883.
      Excellent sketches of 19th-century Permanent
      Settlement society.

1748 Roy, Dilip Kumar. Miracles still do happen. Bom-
      bay: Jaico, 1962.

1749 _____. The upward spiral. Bombay: Jaico, 1949.
      Philosophical discourse involving Bengalis from
      a resident of the Aurobindo Ashram.

1750 Roy, John (pseud. of Henry Mortimer Durand). Helen
      Trevenyan, or ruling race. 3 vols. London:
      Macmillan, 1892.
      Excellent descriptions of Simla life; war in
      Afghanistan; and of Delhi in 1877.

1751 Roy, Motilal. My life's partner. Translated from
      Bengali by D. S. Mahalanobis. Calcutta: Prabatak,
      1945.
      The story of a middle class joint family of Cal-
      cutta. Husband eventually joins Aurobindo; wife is
      a martyr.

1752 Rubin, David George. Cassio and the life divine.
      New York: Farrar, Straus, 1965.
      Adventures of an unconventional and foot-loose
      American with mystics, the New Left and the New
      Right.

1753 _____. Enough of this lovemaking. New York:
      Simon and Schuster, 1969.
      Two novellas; the title story is about a jet set
      waiting the guru's arrival; the other--"Love in the
      melon season"--deals with lodgers in a boarding
      house in Delhi playing musical chairs in games of
      love.

1754 _____. The greater darkness. New York: Farrar,
      Straus, 1963.
      An American sociologist on fellowship to India,
      and a westernised family.

1755 Runbeck, Margaret Lee. The year of love. London:
      Peter Davies, 1956.
      Fine portrait of a woman's life in a Central
      Indian village.

1756 Rushton, C. Dark amid the blaze. London: Herbert
     Jenkins, 1950.
          Agent 64 wages a battle in and around Delhi to
     save the state of Bhotiar from anarchy and tyranny.
     Crime and spy story. Rushton may have written
     other yarns on India.

1757 Sadoc, Lemuel. Zarina. London: Stockwell, n. d.
     Inter-racial love story.

1758 Sahgal, Nayantara. Storm in Chandigrah. New York:
     Norton, 1969.
          Partition of Panjab; conflict between a man of
     conscience and a man of action.

1759 _____. This time of morning. New York: Norton,
     1965.
          Government servants pursuing their private ends
     at comfortable social gatherings of Delhi.

1760 _____. A time to be happy. New York: Knopf,
     1958.
          Picture of urban life in Uttar Pradesh and Cal-
     cutta as led by upper class westernized Indians be-
     fore and after Independence.

1761 St. Clair, William (pseud. of William Ford). Baja
     the freebooter: vivid pictures of life in Hindostan.
     London: Hamilton Adams, 1886.

1762 _____. Bendish. London: Swan Sonneschein, 1905.

1763 _____. Prince Baber and his wives: and, the
     slave girl Narcissus and the nawab of Lalput. Lon-
     don: Swan Sonneschein, 1901.
          Like the preceding two, for young adults.

1764 St. Maur, Bratton. The moral element and other
     stories. Lahore: Civil and Military Gazette Press,
     1901.
          Five stories of British life on the Frontier.

1765 Saldanha, Sirley. My baby. Madras: Visual Graphics,
     1967.

1766 Sancho Panza, (pseud.) Wife or maid? a jubilee ro-

mance. Peshawar Commercial Press, 1897.
Fleshpots.

1767 Sanderson, E. M. Love in a mist. Calcutta: No
publisher given, 1924.
Tales for children.

1768 _____. Souls and stones. London: Hugh Rees,
1911.
Stones and statues have souls; an Indian god reveals a long lost will.

1769 Sanjhi Mull. The interesting story of Prince Poorun.
Delhi: No publisher given, 1886.

1770 Sankar Ram. The ways of man. Madras: Gauthama,
1966.

1771 Sarabhai, Mrinalini. This alone is true. London:
Meridian Books, 1952.
An upper class Indian girl flouts convention and
becomes a temple dancer.

1772 Sarasvati, Pandita. Ramabai: the high-caste Hindu
woman. London: Bell, 1890.

1773 Sastri, Hara Prasad. The triumph of Valmiki. Translated from the original Bengali by R. R. Sen. Chittagong: Sonaton Press, 1909.
Establishment of universal brotherhood based on
ethics rather than on intellect or physical force.

1774 Sathianandhan, Kamala. Detective Janaki. Bombay:
Thacker, 1944.
South Indian girl solves mysteries.

1775 Sathianandhan, Krupbai. Kamala: a story of Indian
life. Madras: Srinivasa Varadachari, 1894.
Unfortunate girl's marriage, Nasik district.

1776 Sathianandhan, Samuel and Krupbai. Stories of Indian
Christian life. Madras: Srinivasa Varadachari,
1898.

1777 Savi, Ethel Winifred. The acid test. London: Hurst
and Blackett, 1926.
Husband sails for India leaving his newlywed be-

hind and falls into the clutches of a vamp.

1778 _____. At close quarters. London: Hurst and
Blackett, 1933.
British India where communities are mixed but
nationalities are incapable of fusion. Story of a
white girl disowned by her father, but befriended
by his mistress.

1779 _____. Baba and the black sheep. London: Hurst
and Blackett, 1914.
An ex-convict loves Miss Baba, step-daughter of
his wife. Black sheep is her mother.

1780 _____. Back o' beyond. London: Hurst and
Blackett, 1929.

1781 _____. Banked fires. London: Putnam's, 1919.
British India. The unawakened child wife who
innocently misjudges; and a man once betrayed by a
woman who loses all faith in women.

1782 _____. Beloved autocrat. London: Hurst and
Blackett, 1938.
Romance.

1783 _____. Birds of passage. London: Hurst and
Blackett, 1939.

1784 _____. A blind alley. London: Digby Long, 1911.
An English wife separated from her husband at
church door, after flirtations and indiscretions
comes out incognito to India, woos and wins her
love, but is disappointed by her fate on the eve of
the honeymoon.

1785 _____. Blunder. London: Hurst and Blackett, 1932.
A young girl bred in ignorance of her parentage
is adopted to be an instrument of revenge.

1786 _____. By torchlight. London: Hurst and Blackett, 1931.
Eurasian girl and her un-English ways.

1787 _____. Daggers drawn. London: Hurst and
Blackett, 1929.
A girl's true love is her eccentric employer.

1788 _____. A daughter-in-law. London: Hurst and
Blackett, 1913.
White wife of an Indian is subjected to humiliation
by both Indian and European communities.

1789 _____. The devil drives. London: Putnam's, 1921.
Mystery; Bengal.

1790 _____. The devil's carpet: an Anglo-Indian romance. London: Hurst and Blackett, 1954.
Young English schoolmaster, influenced by happy
memories of his childhood in India, goes to India to
work in a princely state where he encounters rural
prejudices against modernization. Bengal.

1791 _____. Devil's playground. London: Hurst and
Blackett, 1941.
War time; takes to India after vicissitudes at
sea, and introduces an Indian noble and an English
planter whose destinies are interwined.

1792 _____. Dog in the manger. London: Hurst and
Blackett, 1928.
Anglo-Indian romance.

1793 _____. The door between. London: Hurst and
Blackett, 1930.
The English companion of a Muslim's wife be-
comes the object of his objectionable attention.

1794 _____. The fatalist. London: Hurst and Blackett,
1929.
Pathan chief beyond the Khyber; and a young
English girl who finally becomes acceptable to the
local society.

1795 _____. Fate's captive. Same as Blunder.

1796 _____. A fool's game. London: Hurst and Blackett, 1929.
An unhappy couple carry on with other men and
women.   True love is found between cousins.

1797 _____. A forlorn hope. London: Hurst and
Blackett, 1928.
An unsophisticated saintly girl wearing the halo
of renunciation becomes a nuisance to everyone.

1798   . The fragrance lingers. London: Hurst
        and Blackett, 1947.
        Romance in eastern Bengal.

1799   . Glamorous East. London: Hurst and
        Blackett, 1936.
        An Englishman marries a girl from motives of
        revenge and becomes the principal sufferer. Ex-
        cellent information on rural India.

1800   . God forsaken. London: Hurst and Blackett,
        1930.
        Northwest Bengal; love story.

1801   . The great gamble. London: Hurst and
        Blackett, 1928.
        A dark episode of his past mars the peace of an
        English adviser to an Indian nawab.

1802   . Hidden flames. London: G. Howard Watts,
        1933.

1803   . House party. London: Hurst and Blackett,
        1952.
        Indian waif living in England with a retired
        British civil servant is called to India. Excellent
        descriptions of Muslim household.

1804   . The human heart. London: Hurst and
        Blackett, 1948.
        Assam and Panjab on the eve of Partition.

1805   . Ill-gotten gains. London: Hurst and
        Blackett, 1938.
        Wealthy financier leaves his property to his
        daughter but the will is lost and her stepmother
        claims the property. But the girl finds happiness
        in India.

1806   . In desperation. London: Hurst and
        Blackett, 1931.
        Love in the mofussil.

1807   . Insolence of youth. London: Hutchinson,
        1935.
        A girl brought up indulgently in India is trans-
        ferred, by death and adversity, to the care of Eng-
        lish relatives and then her troubles begin.

1808 _____. Labelled dangerous. London: Hurst and
        Blackett, 1950.
        An English lawyer and his wife become entangled
        in the affairs of an emancipated Muslim widow,
        after Partition.

1809 _____. Lords of creation. London: Hurst and
        Blackett, 1945.
        Hindu rural village in Bengal during the nation-
        alist drive.

1810 _____. Mistress of herself. London: Hurst and
        Blackett, 1918.
        Two sisters love a blind war hero in India.

1811 _____. Mixed cargo: stories of Indian and English
        romance, adventure, and majesty. London: Wright
        and Brown, 1932.

1812 _____. Mock majest. London: Putnam's, 1923.
        A white girl's color prejudice destroys her love
        affair with the cultured son of a nawab.

1813 _____. Money and power. London: Hurst and
        Blackett, 1940.
        Remote Bengal.   Young man forced to enter
        family business marries secretly in England, and
        finds his wife ill treated by ambitious relatives in
        India.

1814 _____. Neither fish nor flesh. London: Hurst and
        Blackett, 1924.
        A white man's attempt to win his childhood
        Eurasian girl.

1815 _____. On the knees of the gods. London: Hutch-
        inson, 1932.
        A Hindu and a Muslim in love with Jenny, whose
        birth is shrouded in secrecy.

1816 _____. On trust. London: Hurst and Blackett,
        1928.
        Several love triangles involving two English girls
        in India.

1817 _____. Passionate problem. London: Hurst and
        Blackett, 1934.

Muslim heiress, left to the guardianship of her
English stepfather, becomes westernised and refuses
marriage to an Indian.

1818 _____. Price of loyalty. London: Hurst and
Blackett, 1953.
Set in the Panjab Hills after Partition. An
Englishman offers to hide the treasure of a wealthy
Muslim in flight to Pakistan. One Indian girl helps,
the other nearly destroys him.

1819 _____. A prince of lovers. London: Hurst and
Blackett, 1925.
A handsome Englishman seduces married and un-
married women in India.

1820 _____. Prisoners of necessity. London: Hurst
and Blackett, 1933.
Plantation life makes prisoners of necessity.

1821 _____. The reproof of chance. London: Digby
Long, 1910.
Calcutta and mofussil life.

1822 _____. The riddle of the hill. London: Hurst and
Blackett, 1936.
Muslim owner of a hill associated with Kali
seeks to put it to secular use; Hindu, Muslim and
European tensions.

1823 _____. Rulers of men. London: Putnam's, 1922.
Romance of a wealthy English zamindar; and a
picture of Indian unrest.

1824 _____. Sackcloth and ashes. London: Hurst and
Blackett, 1925.
An ex-airman, disfigured by war, perpetuates a
fraud on an English girl, and later marries her.

1825 _____. Satan finds. London: Hurst and Blackett,
1926.
A young grass widow picks up an official on fur-
lough, but he marries an old fashioned girl and returns to India, where the grass widow follows him.

1826 _____. The saving of a scandal. London: Hurst
and Blackett, 1929.

1827 _____. Sinners all. London: Hurst and Blackett, 1915.
The sinner loves most the girl he has wronged most.

1828 _____. The soothsayer. London: Hurst and Blackett, 1937.
Girl in a missionary settlement in rural Bengal falls in love with an autocratic English landowner and becomes his victim.

1829 _____. The splendid outcaste. New York: Curtiss, 1929.

1830 _____. The tree of knowledge. London: Hurst and Blackett, 1929.
A vamp tries to break up a rocky marriage.

1831 _____. The troublemaker. London: Hutchinson, 1953.
Brother and sister are left to take care of their adopted sister. Some parts set in India; mostly England.

1832 _____. The tyranny of freedom. London: Hurst and Blackett, 1935.
Englishman runs away to India to escape his stepmother's cruelty; returns to England to claim patrimony.

1833 _____. The unattainable. London: Hurst and Blackett, 1948.
True love wins back erring husband.

1834 _____. Unvarnished truth. London: Hurst and Blackett, 1951.
Engaging love story set in rural Bengal.

1835 _____. Vagrant love. London: Hurst and Blackett, 1927.
A girl makes unsuitable engagement on boat to India but soon becomes aware of a better possibility. Vivid descriptions of Calcutta and rural Bengal.

1836 _____. When the blood burns. London: Putnam's, 1920.
Boss takes his secretary to India, bored with her

he sends her back to England, and becomes lonely
and miserable.

1837 _____. White lies. London: Hurst and Blackett,
        1927.
        Amours of a girl visiting her uncle in India.

1838 Sawhney, Satya Pal. Hate not the sinner. New Delhi:
        Aspi, 1968, c1959.

1839 _____. Tryst with destiny. New Delhi: Aspi,
        1968, c1959.

1840 Sawyer, George Henry Vaughan. Sport of gods.
        London: Mills and Boon, 1910.
        Remarkable portrait of an Indian soldier and
        Waziri politics; and the loyalty of Sikh troops to
        their commander.

1841 Scharlieb, Mary Ann Dacomb. Yet a more excellent
        way. London: W. Gardner, 1929.
        An Englishman renounces comfort to join the
        Benedictine Order at Benares; discovers that
        Christianity is the true climax of Hinduism. Ex-
        cellent descriptions of Hindu family life and religion.

1842 Schorn, J. Arnold. Tales of the East and narratives
        of the Indian Mutiny. Allahabad: Pioneer Press,
        1893.

1843 Schultzky, O. The soul of India. Berlin: Susserott,
        1910.
        Overly sentimental description of Indian spirit-
        uality.

1844 Scinthya (pseud. of S. Thanumalayaperumal) The ear
        rings.   Trivandrum; St. Joseph's Press, 1952.

1845 Scott, Aimee. A prince in chains. London: Hutch-
        inson, 1928.
        Princely state; romance and intrigue.

Scott, Mrs. C., See M. J. Coloquhoun.

1846 [Scott, Helenus] Adventures of a rupee, wherein are
        interspersed various anecdotes Asiatic and European.
        London: Murray, 1782.

Hyder Ali; East India Company.   Useless.

Scott, Hugh. <u>See</u> H. Seton Merriman.

1847 Scott, Jack Denton.   <u>Elephant grass.</u>   New York:
Harcourt, Brace, 1969.
Clash of principles and emotions on an Indian
big game hunt.

1848 Scott, Paul.   <u>The alien sky.</u>   London: Eyre and
Spottiswoode, 1953.
Some Britishers feel they cannot leave India in
1947 because it has been their home, yet they cannot stay behind to bear Indians in positions superior
to theirs.   A superb novel.

1849   _____.   <u>The birds of paradise.</u>   London: Eyre and
Spottiswoode, 1962.
Mother India gives Oedipus complex to English-
men in India in 1947.

1850   _____.   <u>The day of scorpion.</u>   London: Heinemann,
1968.
Continues <u>The jewel in the crown.</u>

1851   _____.   <u>The jewel in the crown.</u>   London: Heine-
mann, 1966.
Decline of British in India; love affair between an
Indian bred in England, and an English girl who was
raped by a gang of Indians.   1942 and the fear of
Japanese invasion.

1852   _____.   <u>Johnnie Sahib.</u>   London: Eyre and Spottiswoode, 1952.
A British officer on the India-Burma front feels
that the welfare of his sepoys is more important
than victory over Japan.

1853   _____.   <u>The mark of the warrior.</u>   New York:
Morrow, 1958.
Aftermath of the conflict in Burma.

1854   _____.   <u>Six days in Marapore.</u>   Garden City:
Doubleday, 1953.
An American tries to solve the mystery of his
brother's rejection of a married woman who had
loved him desperately.

1855 Scott, Walter. Guy Mannering, or the astrologer.
      3 vols. Edinburgh: Ballantyne, 1815.
           Tragi-comical portrayal of a dying ancient house;
      Mannering's misfortunes occur in India.

1856 _____. St. Ronan's well. 3 vols. Edinburgh:
      Constable, 1824.
           As above; but much less concerned with India.

1857 _____. The surgeon's daughter. Edinburgh: Cadell,
      1827.
           A cheap historical melodrama. A Scottish sur-
      geon's daughter is taken to India by her lover to be
      given to Tipoo Sultan, but is finally rescued. Much
      information about the recruitment of English factors.

      Scott, Winifred Mary. See Pamela Wynne.

1858 Seamark, (pseud. of Austin J. Small). The silent six.
      London: Hodder and Stoughton, 1926.
           Thriller; a Hindu herbalist concocts a deadly
      poison.

1859 Seligman, Hilda. When peacocks called. London: John
      Lane, 1940.
           The rise of the Maurya empire and its climax
      under Asoka superbly rendered.

1860 Seljouk, Mahdi Ali. Corpses. London: Duckworth,
      1966.
           Stories of twelve men and women whose corpses
      the author has confronted from Hyderabad to East
      Pakistan. Very able sketches.

1861 Sell, Frank Reginald. Bhim Singh: a romance of
      Mughal times. London: Macmillan, 1926.
           Accurate knowledge of Mewar and Udaipur in the
      time of Aurangzib.

1862 Sellon, Edward Herbert. Breakspear: a legend of the
      Mahratta war. London: Whittaker, 1848.
           Jaswant Rao Holkar, the Peshwa, and the East
      India Company are the background for this romance.

1863 Sen, Dinesh Chandra. Sati: a mythological story.
      Translated from Bengali. Calcutta: Atul Chandra
      Chakravarti, 1912.

Story of Sati given in marriage to Siva, who unable to choose between her duty to her father and to
her husband, immolates herself.

1864 Sen, Ela. Darkening days, being a narrative of famine
stricken Bengal. Calcutta: S. Gupta, 1944.
Seven stories; Bengal, 1943.

1865 Sen, Makham Lal. A romance of the Moghul harem.
Calcutta: Dutt, Bose, 1933.
Anarkali and Salim (son of Emperor Akbar).

1866 Senapati, Fakir Mohan. Six acres and a half. Translated from Oriya by B. M. Senapati and A. M.
Senapati. Delhi: Publications Division, 1967.

1867 Sengupta, Naresh Chandra. The idiot's wife. Madras:
Natesan, 1935.

1868 Sengupta, Padmini. Red hibiscus. Bombay: Asia,
1962.
One of the better ones on Bengal on the eve of
Partition, 1947.

Serner, Gunnar. See Frank Heller.

1869 Seshadri, Pundi. Bilhanna: An Indian romance.
Madras: Srinivasa Varadachari, 1914.

1870 Sett, Adi K. Chameleons. Bombay: B. G. Gandbhir,
1928.
Several stories set on the Jhelum, Kashmir.

1871 Shah, A. A. Tiger of the frontier. London: Sampson, Low, 1939.
Shair Khan of the Khyber Pass.

Shahani, Ranjee. See Hassan Ali.

1872 Shamsuddin. The loves of Begum Sumroo and other
true romances. Delhi: Hind Pocket Books, 1967.

1873 Shannon, Alastair. The black scorpion. London: G.
Bles, 1926.
Terrorist conspiracy for the extermination of all
whites.

1874 Sharar, Dwan. The gong of shiva. London: Harrap, 1935.
   Sensitive portrait of middle class Hindu life.

1875 Sharma, M. P. Awakening: a selection of short stories. Allahabad: The Author, 1932.

1876 Sharma, Sant Ram. Withering moss: short stories. Solan: Kauser Book Depot, 1964.

1877 Sharp, Henry. The assassins. London: Faber and Gwyer, 1927.

1878 _____. The dancing god. London: Faber and Gwyer, 1928.
   A Hindu villain forges cheques in the name of an English officer.

1879 _____. Goodbye India. London: Oxford University Press, 1946.
   Stories.

   Also see Oliver Ainsworth.

1880 Sharpe, Elizabeth. Indian tales. London: Luzac, 1939.

1881 Shearwood, George Frederick Ferrier. Five Indian tales. London: S. C. M., 1925.
   Clever psychological studies.

1882 Sheean, James Vincent. Rage of the soul. London: Cassell, 1953.
   An American adrift in Indian mysticism.

1883 Sheepshanks, Beatrice. Robinetta. London: Selwyn and Blount, 1924.
   Romance, fine description of Srinagar, Kashmir.

1884 _____. The sword and the spirit. London: Ernest Benn, 1928.
   The tragedy of Anderi; nationalist struggle.

1885 Sheorey, Anant Gopal. The volcano. Translated from Hindi by the author. New York: Pageant Press, 1965.

1886 Sheppard, J. Smiles: a military miscellany. Karachi: Daily Gazette Press, 1924.

1887 Sherer, John Walter. A princess of Islam.   London:
      Swan Sonneschein, 1897.
        Excellent study of Indian women and their self
      sacrifice.   Muslim girl is given in marriage by her
      brother to an Englishman.

1888 Sherman, D. R. Old mali and the boy.   London:
      Gollancz, 1964.
        A beautiful tale of a young white boy's relation-
      ship with his mother's gardener.

1889 Sherring, Herbert.   Gopi. London: Methuen, 1911.
        A dozen first hand short stories.

1890 _____. Light and shade: tales and verse.   Cal-
      cutta: Thacker, 1884.

1891 Sherwood, Mrs. Little Henry and his bearer. London:
      No publisher given, 1836.
        Devotion of a thug to a white boy.

      Sherwood, Mary Martha. See Mary Martha Butt.

1892 Shinde, B. G.   Modern Marathi short stories.   Bom-
      bay: Saroj, n. d.
        Shinde, Phadke and others translated.

1893 Shipp, John.   The Khaunie Kineh wallah: or eastern
      story teller: a collection of Indian tales.   London:
      Longmans, 1832.

1894 Shome, J. and A. Shome. translators. Towards the
      dawn. Bombay: Bharatiya Vidya Bhavan, 1967.
        Sixteen Bengali short stories of the post-Tagore
      period.

1895 Shore, Juliet. Doctor memsahib. London: Mills and
      Boon, 1958.
        An English woman surgeon in India faces a scan-
      dal about her past. Miss J. Shore may have set
      some other novels in India.

1896 Shrawan Kumar. Hindi short stories. Bombay: Jaico,
      1970.

1897 Shrinagesh, Shakuntala. The little black box. London:
      Secker and Warburg, 1955.

A woman about to die in a tuberculosis sana-
torium tells the story of her life.

1898 Shute, Nevil (pseud. of Nevil Shute Norway). The
chequer board. London: Heinemann, 1947.
India as the home of spiritualism from which
West must learn.

1899 Silver, Joseph. Blue gardens. London: Ernest Benn,
1950.
Indigo plantation in Independent India is the scene
of this thriller and satire.

1900 Simeons, Albert Theodore William. The mask of a
lion. London: Gollancz, 1952.
A moving story of a man stricken with leprosy
and his life in the leper colony.

1901 Sinderby, Donald. Dogsbody: the story of a romantic
subaltern. London: Herbert Jenkins, 1928.
Subaltern and the general's daughter.

1902 _____. The jewel of Malabar. London: John
Murray, 1927.
Moplah rebellion, 1921; tragic love between an
English general and an Indian girl.

1903 _____. Mother-in-law India. London: Marriott,
1930.
A British socialist government gives independence
to India; as British troops march out of Madras, the
kings of Hyderabad and Mysore march into Madras
and proclaim an independent kingdom in South India.

1904 _____. The protagonists. London: John Murray,
1928.
Adventure and romance in Malabar.

1905 Singh, Gurvir Inder. Not seriously--short stories.
New Delhi: Army Educational Stories, 1963.

1906 Singh, Huthi. Maura. London: Constable, 1951.
Locale: a Rajput state; the hero: a eunuch; the
time: twentieth century.

1907 Singh, Jogendra. Kamla. London: Selwyn and Blount,
1925.

A beautiful hill girl is abducted by a raja's
agents; as a devotee of the Ganges she preserves
her chastity and has a good influence on the raja.
Much unintelligible metaphysics.

1908 _____. Kamni. Lahore: No publisher given, 1932.
The daughter of a village barber goes with her
father to a city, and after many adventures comes
into contact with a missionary.

1909 _____. Nasrin: An Indian medley. London: James
Nisbet, 1911.
Hedonist life of Oudh nawabs and taluqdars; good
sketches of the zennana.

1910 _____. Nur Jahan: the romance of an Indian queen.
London: James Nisbet, 1909.
Ends with the marriage of Nur Jahan to Jehangir;
little historical imagination.

1911 Singh, Khushwant. A bride for the sahib and other
stories. Delhi: Hind Pocket Books, 1967.

1912 _____. I shall not hear the nightingale. London:
Calder, 1959.
Story of two Indian families, one Hindu and the
other Sikh, and the disruptive events that engulf
them. Sikh father is pro-British, the son is a
terrorist.

1913 _____. Mano Majra. New York: Grove, 1956.
A Punjabi village on the border of India and
Pakistan, caught in the summer of 1947 when
violence accompanied the movement of refugees.

1914 _____. The mark of Vishnu and other stories.
London: Saturn, 1950.

1915 _____. Train to Pakistan. Same as Mano Majra.

1916 _____. The voice of God and other stories. Bombay: Jaico, 1957.

1917 Singh, Khushwant and Jaya Thadani, editors. Land of
the five rivers. Bombay: Jaico, 1965.
Nineteen stories by different Panjabi writers.

1918 Singh, Malkiat. Love and faith. New Delhi: Chand,
      1966.

1919 Singh, Narendrapal. Light stands aside. Translated
      from Gurmukhi. New Delhi: Vidya Prakashan
      Bhawan, 1968.

1920 Singh, Rajkumari. A garland of stories. Ilfracombe:
      Arthur Stockwell, 1960.

1921 Sinha, Krishna Nandan. Wait without hope. Calcutta:
      Writers Workshop, 1967.
          Problem of romantic love in a society where
      marriages are arranged. An Indian teacher of
      Shakespeare loses his village sweetheart to another
      man.

1922 Sinha, Purnendu Narayan. The Chandi, or the great
      plan. Madras: Theosophical Publishing House, 1922.
          Stories from Chandi.

1923 Sinha, Satyanarayan. Adrift on the Ganga. Bombay:
      Bharatiya Vidya Bhavan, 1964.
          Autobiographical novel of social and political
      forces in India in the 1960's.

1924 Sircar, Noel. An Indian boyhood. London: Hollis and
      Carter, 1948.

1925 Sivasankara Pillai, Thakazhi. Chemeen. Translated
      by Narayana Menon. New York: Harper, 1962.
          Young people growing up in a Kerala fishing
      village; tragic novel of Hindu-Muslim romance.

1926 _____. The unchaste. Delhi: Hind Pocket Books,
      1970.
          Crime of passion set in the atmosphere of peasant
      dissatisfaction in South India.

1928 Skottowe, C. F. G. The haunted house of Chilka.
      London: Digby Long, 1892.

1929 Sladen, Douglas. Zalim Singh the great. London:
      Hurst and Blackett, 1915.
          A Rajput collaborates with the British before
      Waterloo.

1930 Sleath, Frederick. <u>Red vulture.</u> London: Hutchinson, 1923.
   Indian conspiracy to destroy British empire un-earthed by a burglar turned secret agent.

1931 Slimming, John O. <u>The pepper garden.</u> London: Heinemann, 1968.

   Small, Austin J. <u>See</u> Seamark.

1932 Smith, Archibald William. <u>Bandar log</u>. Boston: Little Brown, 1930.
   Englishman has second thoughts about his love when he discovers his girl friend to be Eurasian.

1933 _____. <u>A captain departed.</u> London: Peter Davies, 1934.
   A young Englishman goes to India with a regiment.

1934 _____. <u>The sword and the rose.</u> London: Peter Davies, 1938.
   Hertforshire regiment's heroes and the clashing fortunes of their wives and sweethearts.

1935 _____. <u>West is west.</u> Same as <u>Bandar log</u>.

1936 Smith, Elizabeth Bruce Elton. <u>The East Indian sketch-book.</u> 1st series, 2 vols. 2nd series, 2 vols. London: No publisher given, 1830-32.
   Social morality of whites in India.

1937 Smith, Emma. <u>The far cry.</u> New York: Random House, 1950.
   Fourteen-year-old English girl is sent to India; unusual documentary information about Calcutta and Himalayan tea gardens.

1938 Smith, Jr., John. <u>Sketches in Indian ink.</u> Calcutta: Englishman Office, 1880.
   Crownless martyrdom of Indians.

1939 Snilloc (<u>pseud.</u> of R. S. Harper Collins). <u>Ashes of roses and other stories.</u> Bombay: Thacker, n. d.

1940 _____. <u>Asir of Asirgarh.</u> Bombay: Thacker, 1943.
   Romance set in Mughal times.

1941 _____ . Badmashes. Bombay: Thacker, n. d.

1942 _____ . East African and Indian jungle thrillers.
Bombay: Thacker, 1943.

1943 _____ . The honest bunch and other stories. Bombay: Thacker, 1943.

1944 _____ . Minute tale. Bombay: C. Murphy, 1943.
Contains a collection of tales by the Indian way-
side.

1945 _____ . Ten minute tales. Bombay: Thacker, 1943.

1946 Somers, Mark. And it happened. London: Hutchinson,
1928.
Romance and adventure; Indian hypnotist versus
an English policeman.

1947 _____ . The bridge. London: First Novel Library,
1902.
Ordinary English romance.

1948 _____ . End of the road. London: Hutchinson, 1923.
Misadventure, peril, and ultimate victory both in
love and on the Afghan frontier.

1949 Sorabji, Cornelia. Between the twilight. London:
Harper, 1908.
Fourteen stories about women's life in India.

1950 _____ . Indian tales of the great ones among men,
women and bird people. London: Blackie, 1916.

1951 _____ . Love and life behind the purdah. London:
Freemantle, 1901.
Stories.

1952 _____ . The purdah nashin. London: Thacker, 1918.

1953 _____ . Sun babies: studies in the child life of
India. London: John Murray, 1904.

1954 Sousa, Innocent. Radha: a romance and other tales.
Bombay: Taraporevala, 1904.
Caste and dowry system fairly well depicted.

1955 _____. Uncle Roland or looking for a wife. Bombay: Taraporevala, 1906.

1956 Southgate, D. H. As a man's hand: an Indian saga, 1876-1936. London: Methuen, 1937.
Cruelly intimate story of Brahmin child marriage and family life.

1957 _____. Great things God has done: stories from modern India. London: Livingston Press, 1936.

1958 _____. Root in the rock. London: Methuen, 1938.
A novel of three generations in India; reveals much of the horror due to class customs, especially child marriage.

1959 Spencer, Francis Angus. The four horned altar. London: Heath Cranton, 1913.
A novel of Sivaji; love and war.

1960 Sridhar Rao, K. The twain shall meet. Bangalore: Power Press, 1949.

1961 Srinivasan, C. M. Ananda Maya: a didactic fiction on a realistic background. Madras: Aiyar, 1966.

Srivasta, Dhanpat Rai. See Prem Chand.

1962 Stables, William Gordon. On to the rescue: a tale of Indian Mutiny. London: J. F. Shaw, 1895.
For children.

1963 Stace, Henry. The adventures of Count O'Connor in the dominions of the great Mogul. London: Rivers, 1907.
Ironical narrative of the exploits of an Irish adventurer and impostor at the court of Aurangzib, ca. 1700.

1964 Stanger, Henrietta Sophia. Thorns and thistles. London: Stockwell, 1918.

1965 Stanton, Coralie (pseud. of Alice Cecil Seymour Hosken) and Heath Hosken. The white horsemen. London: J. Lang, 1934.
Expedition to rescue a white woman who rode alone into the Afghan tribal territory.

1966 Star-Najnin (pseud. of K. A. K. Vakil). Victims of
        fate and fashion. Bombay: No publisher given, 1913.
        Parsi life.

1967 Steel, Flora Annie. The adventures of Akbar. Lon-
        don: Heinemann, 1913.
        Emperor Akbar, Rajput princes and an Afghan
        noble. For young adults.

1968 _____. The builder. London: John Lane, 1928.
        Shah Jahan and the Taj Mahal.

1969 _____. The flatterer for gain. London: Daily
        Mail, 1904.
        A "middle-fail" babu who takes pride in his Eng-
        lish.

1970 _____. The flower of forgiveness. London: Mac-
        millan, 1894.
        Indian stories full of pathos.

1971 _____. From the five rivers. London: Heinemann,
        1893.
        Five somewhat cynical stories depicting ignorance,
        misery, and superstition in the Panjabi village.

1972 _____. The hosts of the lord. London: Heinemann,
        1900.
        Indian rebellion against the British; life in the
        Himalayas.

1973 _____. In the guardianship of God. London: Heine-
        mann, 1903.
        Seventeen stories of the Hindu character, full of
        pathos.

1974 _____. In the permanent way, and other stories.
        London: Heinemann, 1898.

1975 _____. Indian scene: collected short stories.
        London: Arnold, 1933.

1976 _____. King errant. London: Heinemann, 1912.
        Babar, based on his memoirs; his affection for
        his sister.

1977 _____. The law of the threshold. London: Heine-

mann, 1924.
Indian nationalism: Bolshevik and German agents.

1978 _____. The mercy of the lord. London: Heinemann, 1914.

1979 _____. Miss Stuart's legacy. London: Macmillan,
1893.

1980 _____. Mistress of men. London: Heinemann,
1918.
Nurjahan, from her childhood to empress.

1981 _____. On the face of the waters. London: Heinemann, 1896.
Perhaps the most significant novel on the Mutiny
written in the 19th century; historical portion dealing
with the siege of Delhi is punctiliously accurate.

1982 _____. The potter's thumb. 3 vols. London:
Heinemann, 1894.
Panjab canal colony. Indians to whom birth and
death alike are the pivot on which the wheel of life
rests. One of the best 'period' novels.

1983 _____. A prince of dreamers. London: Heinemann, 1908.
Emperor Akbar.

1984 _____. Salt duty. London: Heinemann, 1904.
Iman Khan, major domo to many pukka sahibs in
India.

1985 _____. A tale of Indian heroes. London: Heinemann, 1923.
· From the Indian epics.

1986 _____. Tales of the Panjab. London: Macmillan,
1894.

1987 _____. Tales of the tides and other stories. London: Heinemann, 1923.

1988 _____. Voices in the night. London: Heinemann,
1900.
Deals with social and political problems of the
day.

1989 Steel, Flora Annie and Richard C. Temple. Wide
     awake stories. Bombay: Education Society Press,
     1884.

     Steele, Francesca Maria. See Darley Dale.

1990 Sterndale, Robert Armitage. The Afghan knife. Lon-
     don: Sampson Low, 1879.
     Cawnpore massacre, 1857.

1991 _____. Seonee, or camp life on the Satpura range:
     a tale of Indian adventure. Calcutta: Thacker, 1887.

1992 Stevens, Nina. The perils of sympathy. London:
     Fisher Unwin, 1902.
     A new English recruit to the ICS goes to a Ben-
     gal delta station and meets a Eurasian girl.

1993 Stevenson, Burton Egbert. The house next door.
     London: Hutchinson, 1932.
     Detective mystery; Indian philosophy and religion
     in the suburbs of New York. Stevenson may have
     written other mysteries with some Indian setting.

1994 Steward, T. F. The mascarenhas: a legend of the
     Portuguese in India. London: Smith Elder, 1839.
     Set in Aurangzib's time; Mughals, Portuguese,
     Marathas and Rajputs are ably delineated.

1995 Stewart, Frances (pseud. of James Reginald Wilmot)
     Justice of Allah and other stories. Bombay: Thacker,
     1943.

1996 _____. Rain in the desert: stories. Bombay:
     Thacker, 1944.

1997 Stewart, Hugh. The web. London: Hurst and
     Blackett, 1929.

1998 Stokes, Denny C. Way of the panther: a romance of
     India. London: John Murray, 1926.
     Coffee plantation of Mysore: English hero fights
     encroachments of "civilization" on the jungle paradise.

1999 Stoll, Dennis Gray. Comedy in chains. London: Gol-
     lancz, 1944.
     Sympathetic to Indian nationalism; young Eurasian

doctor, a temple dancer, an eminent Congress politician are well described.

2000 _____. Doctor and the dragon. London: Gollancz,
1947.
White state of mind in India, 1939-40.

2001 _____. The dove found no rest. London: Gollancz,
1946.
A sympathetic portrait of appalling social conditions in India where the British force a poor village family to leave its beloved village to live in the city.

2002 _____. Feed him with apricocks. London: Muller,
1957.
Benares and Bombay: what contrast can be greater?

2003 _____. Memory is the scar. London: Gollancz,
1949.
Smuggling in Bengal; intelligent view of Bengali life style.

2004 Strang, Herbert (pseud.) The air patrol: a story of
the northwest frontier. London: Hodder and
Stoughton, 1913.
For young adults.

2005 _____. Barclay of the guides: a tale of the Indian
mutiny. London: Hodder and Stoughton, 1909.
For young adults, also.

2006 _____. In Clive's command. London: Blackie, 1906.
1754-57 for the young.

2007 _____. One of Clive's heroes. London: Hodder
and Stoughton, 1906.

2008 Strange, N. K. Mistress of ceremonies. London:
Stanley Paul, 1930.
Satire of old European travellers who over-rated India's wealth.

2009 Strange, Thomas Bland. Gunner Jingo's jubilee. London: Remington, 1893.
Mutiny.

2010 Stratford, Barbara Wingfield. Beryl in India. Liver-
      pool: Books, 1920.
          Memsahibs lacking in dignity and fidelity. Indian
      women and children are charming.

2011 Stuart, Alan. Unwilling agent. London: Ward Lock,
      1955.
          Thriller, Calcutta.

2012 Stuart, Alex (pseud. of Violet Vivian Mann). Daughters
      of the governor. London: Mills and Boon, 1958.
          Two sisters in love with a captain who is in a
      feud with a Rajput raja.

2013 _____. Star of Oudh. London: Mills and Boon,
      1960.
          An old officer's stubborn faith in the loyalty of
      his sepoys destroys the post and the regiment.
      Mutiny, 1857.

2014 Stuart, Mary. The pangs of youth. Bombay: Thacker,
      1943.
          Romance of an Englishman born in India.

2015 Subba Rao, R. Venkata. Kamala's letters to her hus-
      band. Madras: English Publishing House, 1902.
          Essentially a tract on social evils like child mar-
      riage and polygamy, ban on widow remarriage.

2016 Subrahmanya Aiyar, C. Indira Devi: a romance of
      modern political India. Madras: Ganesh, 1930.
          Anticipates "1951" when the viceroy will step down
      and hand over power to an Indian parliament.

2017 _____. Life's shadows. Bombay: Taraporevala,
      1938.
          Life of Tamilian Brahmins.

2018 Subramanian, Vadakaymadam Krishnier. Love twigs.
      Madras: Higginbothams, 1969.

2019 Sukhlata Rao. Behula: an Indian myth. Translated by
      Rabindranath Tagore. Calcutta: U. Ray, 19--.

2020 Sun, Alexander. If winter comes. New Delhi: Eurasia,
      1963.

2021 Sundaram Aiyar, T. M. The story of the raya and
      Appaji. Madras: Natesan, 1908.
          The Vijayangar emperor and his diwan; sixteen
      stories.

2022 Sundarraj. The return of the panther. Secunderabad:
      Good News Literature, 1958.

2023 Sunity Devi. The beautiful Mughal princesses. Cal-
      cutta: Thacker, 1918.
          Five princesses and their influences on Akbar,
      Jehangir and Shahjahan.

2024 _____. Bengal dacoits and tigers. Calcutta:
      Thacker, 1916.

2025 _____. The life of princess Yashodhara; wife and
      disciple of the Lord Buddah. London: E. Mathers,
      1929.

2026 Surya Rao, Damaraju. The two visions: a novel of
      hopes and aspirations. Calcutta: Alpha-Beta, 1962.
          Andhra village family moves to the city.

2027 Sutherland, Joan (pseud. of Joan Collis Kelly). Cava-
      naugh of Kultann. New York: Harper, 1911.
          Best known of her Frontier novels.

2028 _____. Desborough of the northwest frontier.
      London: Hodder and Stoughton, 1920.
          Dull novel of an irrigation engineer's experiences.

2029 _____. The edge of the empire. London: Mills
      and Boon, 1916.
          Romance against the background of Chitral up-
      rising, 1895.

2030 _____. Wynnegate Sahib. London: Hodder and
      Stoughton, 1918.
          Frontier uprisings, and cholera outbreaks.

2031 Sutherland, W. A. An innocent thief: a romance of
      the British post office of India. Allahabad: Pioneer,
      1902.
          Eccentricities and idiosyncrasies of Railway Mail
      Service workers.

2032 _____. A murder by parcel post.   Allahabad:
       Pioneer, n. d.

2033 _____. My husband's night dream.   Allahabad:
       Pioneer, n. d.

2034 _____. A sorter's revenge.   Allahabad: Pioneer,
       n. d.

2035 Svarna Kumari Devi (Mrs. J. Ghosal).   To whom? an
       Indian love story.   Calcutta: S. K. Lahiri, 1910.

       Svoronos - Gigantes, M. K. and G. See M. P. Dean.

2036 Swabey, Hilda M.   The chief commissioner.   London:
       Methuen, 1912.
       A civil servant so devoted to his work and soli-
       tude that he deserts his family; but his eldest
       daughter invades it.

2037 Swaminathan, K. editor.   Plough and the stars: stories
       from Tamilnad.   Bombay: Asia, 1963.

2038 Swynnerton, Charles.   The adventures of the Panjab
       hero Raja Rasalu and other folk tales of the Panjab.
       London: No publisher given, 1884.

2039 _____. Indian nights' entertainments; or folk tales
       from the Upper Indus.   London: Elliot Stock, 1892.

2040 _____. Romantic tales from the Panjab.   West-
       minster: Constable, 1903.

2041 Symington, John.   In a Bengal jungle; stories of life on
       the tea gardens of northern India.   Calcutta: Noah
       Carol, 1935.

2042 Tagore, Rabindranath.   Binodini.   Translated by
       Krishna Kriplani.   New Delhi: Sahitya Akademi,
       1959.
       Bengali family life at the turn of the century.

2043 _____. Boundless sky.   Calcutta: Modern Review
       Press, 1964.
       Translation of selected stories and other writings.

2044 _____. Broken ties and other stories. London:
        Macmillan, 1925.
        The title story which takes more than one half of
        the volume gives a clue to Tagore's own religious
        viewpoint.

2045 _____. Chaturanga. Translated from Bengali by
        Asok Mitra. New Delhi: Sahitya Akademi, 1963.
        Fate of a heroine which is successively controlled
        by four men.

2046 _____. The cheese doll. Translated from Bengali
        by Nilima Devi. Calcutta: Signet Press, 1945.

2047 _____. Eyesore. Calcutta: Modern Review Press,
        1914.

2048 _____. Farewell my friend. Translation of Shesher
        Kavita (The Last Poem). Bombay: Hind Kitabs,
        1946.
        An ultra-modern Oxford educated Bengali whose
        western education and experience cause unhappy love.

2049 _____. Four chapters. Translated by Surendranath
        Tagore. Calcutta: Visva Bharati, 1950.
        Story of two modernized Bengali lovers, set dur-
        ing early Indian nationalist struggle.

2050 _____. Glimpses of Bengali life. Translated by
        Rajani Ranjan Sen. Madras: G. A. Natesan, 1913.
        Short stories.

2051 _____. The golden boat. Translated by Bhabani
        Bhattacharya. London: Allen and Unwin, 1932.

2052 _____. Gora. Translated into English. London:
        Macmillan, 1924.
        Tagore's best novel deals with removing caste
        barriers, and anticipates Gandhi's non-cooperation
        movement.

2053 _____. The home and the world. Translated by
        Surendranath Tagore. London: Macmillan, 1919.
        Upheaval in a Bengali raja's family during the
        Swadeshi movement. Tagore expresses his views
        on the theory and method of Bengali revolutionaries.

2054 _____. Hungry stones and other stories. Translated by C. F. Andrews and others. London: Macmillan, 1916.

2055 _____. Lipika. Translated by Indu Dutt. Bombay:
Jaico, 1969.
Short stories.

2056 _____. Mashi and other stories. Translated into
English. London: Macmillan, 1918.

2057 _____. More stories from Tagore. 2 vols. Calcutta: Modern Review Press, 1951.
All but two stories in the first volume appeared
in Hungry Stones, Mashi, and Broken ties.

2058 _____. The parrot's training. Translated by the
Author. Calcutta: Thacker Spink, 1918.
Four allegorical stories.

2059 _____. The runaway and other stories. Translated by Somnath Maitra, C. F. Andrews, W. W.
Pearson and others. Calcutta: Visva Bharati, 1959.

2060 _____. Stories from Tagore. Calcutta: Macmillan,
1918.

2061 _____. Two sisters. Translated by Krishna Krip-
lani. Calcutta: Visva Bharati, 1945.
Two sisters of contrasting characters: "the
mother kind and the beloved kind." The former
triumphs; the latter loses her husband.

2062 _____. The wreck. London: Macmillan, 1921.
The heroine is a true Indian woman with traditional virtues; male characters for the most part are
westernized upper class Hindus.

2063 Tagore, Sourindro Mohun. Taravati. Translated from
Bengali. Calcutta: No publisher given, 1881.

2064 Tagore, Subho. Blue blood turned red. Calcutta:
Century Press, 1953.
Episodic story of the revolt of a young Bengali
artist against traditional way of life during World
War II.

2065 [Entry deleted.]

2066 Tandon, Pratap Narayan. Rita. Translated from Hindi
     by the author. Calcutta: Alpha Beta, 1965.

2067 Taylor, Lucy. Sahib and sepoy: or saving an empire.
     A tale of the Indian Mutiny. London: Shaw, 1897.

2068 Taylor, Philip Meadows. Confessions of a thug.
     3 vols. London: Richard Bentley, 1839.
     A near classical story and a graphic, human in-
     terest tale of the community of robbers and assas-
     sins.

2069 _____. The fatal amulet. Bombay: Industrial
     Press, 1872.
     A legend of Ellichpoor in the Deccan.

2070 _____. A noble queen, a romance of Indian history.
     3 vols. London: Kegan Paul, 1878.
     Court life and career of Chand Bibi, sixteenth-
     century queen of Bijapur, and the heroic resistance
     during the siege of Ahmadnagar.

2071 _____. Ralph Darnell. 3 vols. London: Kegan
     Paul, 1865.
     Black Hole tragedy of 1757, and Clive's victory
     at Plassey are the setting of this novel.

2072 _____. Seeta. 3 vols. London: Kegan Paul, 1872.
     An English official marries a Hindu widow on the
     eve of the Mutiny and her gallant efforts against the
     rebellious Indians.

2073 _____. Tara: A Mahratta tale. 3 vols. London:
     Kegan Paul, 1863.
     Abduction and later release of a widowed girl
     dedicated as devadasi. Excellent knowledge of both
     Hindu and Muslim domestic life and Mughal court of
     the seventeenth century.

2074 _____. Tippoo Sultan: a tale of the Mysore war.
     3 vols. London: Kegan Paul, 1840.
     A powerful story of the Mysore war of 1788-89
     affording a complete and historical picture of the
     times.

2075 Temple, James. Leopard of the hills. London: Bell,
      1953.
          Sensitive biography of a leopard in Himalayan
      hills.

2076 Tennyson, Hallam. The dark goddess. London: Valen-
      tin, 1957.
          A young English teacheress falls in love with India
      of 1945.

      Tessier, Ernest Maurice. See Maurice DeKobra.

2077 Thackeray, William Makepeace. The history of Pen-
      dennis, his fortunes and misfortunes, his friends,
      and his greatest enemy. London: Bradbury and
      Evals, 1849.
          A few Anglo-Indian sketches.

2078 _____. The Newcomes: memoirs of a most re-
      spected family, edited by Arthur Pendennis, Esq.
      2 vols. London: Bradbury and Evans, 1854-55.
          A few Anglo-Indian characters exuberantly drawn.

2079 _____. The tremendous adventures of Major Ga-
      hagan. London: New Monthly Magazine, 1838-39.
          A burlesque in which almost all characters are
      cruel, cowardly, or treacherous; grotesque descrip-
      tions of an English soldier of fortune.

2080 _____. Vanity fair; a novel without a hero. Lon-
      don: Bradbury and Evans, 1848.
          Good descriptions of voyage between England and
      India.

      Thanumalayaperumal, S. See Scinthya.

2081 Thapar, Romila. Indian tales. London: Bell, 1961.

2082 Thillai, Villalan. Gone with the wind. Chidambaram:
      Thambi, 1965.
          Novelette; previously serialized in Homeland.

2083 Thomas, Dudley Hardress. The touchstone of peril: a
      tale of the Indian mutiny. 2 vols. London: Fisher
      Unwin, 1886.
          Life of a plantation family in the Upper Provinces
      during the Mutiny.

2084 Thompson, Edward John. An end of the hours. London: Macmillan, 1938.
The death of spiritual India and its degeneration through western progress.

2085 _____. A farewell to India. London: Ernest Benn, 1931.
Sincere Englishman who loved India is discarded by Indian students without a word of gratitude during the nationalist struggle; excellent reflections on the Gandhian techniques, and convincing portraits of Indian nationalists.

2086 _____. An Indian day. New York: Knopf, 1927.
An English judge, a true lover of India, and his judgment in a case which sets the English community against him. Superb portrait of Indian country life.

2087 _____. Night falls on Siva's hill. London: Heinemann, 1929.
Poetic description of the Indian jungle; tragedy of an English officer who married an Indian and lives in Assam jungles.

2088 _____. Reconstruction of India. Same as A farewell to India.

2089 _____. So a poor ghost. London: Macmillan, 1930.
A liberal Englishman returns to India after the war, to the same community that he had served earlier for two decades, and finds the woman he loves married to a dull British resident in a princely state, with whom he cannot renew his friendship. Very sympathetic to India.

2090 _____. The youngest disciple. London: Faber, 1938.
The last twenty-five years of the Buddha's life, pictured through the eyes of a herdsman. Though with an unconvincing plot, the narrative of people and places is extremely well rendered.

2091 Thompson, N. F. Intrigues of a nabob. London: No publisher given, 1780.
Eccentricities and vulgarities of a "nabob."

2092 Thorburn, Septimus Smet. David Leslie: a story of

the Afghan frontier. 2 vols. London: Blackwood,
1879.
    Life in a border district; affair of an army
officer with a Pathan girl and his later marriage to
an insipid English girl; has excellent examples of
Pathan pidgin English.

2093 _____. His majesty's greatest subject. West-
minster: Constable, 1897.
    A successful military officer on his death-bed is
afraid to confess an indiscretion he committed
earlier. Excellent sketch of NWFP.

2094 _____. India's saint and the viceroy. London:
Blackwood, 1908.
    High politics in Simla; and the viceroy comes in
for satire; deals with Pathan affairs.

2095 _____. Sir John's conversion. London: Kegan
Paul, 1913.
    Political and family activities of "Sir John Na-
pier", an Indian civil servant.

2096 _____. Transgression. London: C. A. Pearson,
1899.
    A military officer is successful in the NWFP but
loses his lady love; excellent for administration in
the frontier province.

2097 Thorne, E. P. The black sadhu, story of India. London: Wright and Brown, 1935.
    Mystery set in a "frontier" princely state; poor
knowledge of Jainism.

2098 _____. Ganges mud. London: Wright and Brown,
1936.
    Rawalpindi, mystics, Ganges, Tibet and assorted
Indian rishis.

2099 _____. Sinister sanctuary. London: Wright and
Brown, 1929.
    Mysterious mystics, a Bengali babu, and northern
hills.

2100 _____. Yoga mist. London: Wright and Brown,
1937.
    Again Tibet and India.

2101 Thwaytes, Edmund Charles. The latent force. London: John Ouseley, 1910.
        Politics and pleasures in a "residency" town; good descriptions of nautch girls and their influence on Muslim nobility.

2102 Tiddeman, Lizzie Ellen. Sahib's birthday. London: Blackie, 1899.
        For children.

2103 Time, Mark. A derelict empire. Edinburgh: Blackwood, 1912.
        The British withdraw from India but an English officer gets control of sufficient force to establish his authority. A fantasy.

2104 Todd, William Hogarth. Ian and Joan. London: Heath Cranton, 1931.
        Twenty-three artless chapters about a husband and wife who spend some time in India.

2105 _____. The old bungalow. Oxford: Alden Press, 1933.
        Animal stories.

2106 Towers, Robert. The necklace of Kali. New York: Random House, 1961.
        Americans in Calcutta during the month preceding the withdrawal of British Raj; weak plot; Calcutta vividly portrayed.

2107 Townsend, Leo. The peacock trees. London: Cape, 1958.
        A Hindu doctor on his way to Benares to die in peace meets and saves an English woman, falls in love with her, makes a passionate pilgrimage through village India, and has a tragic end.

2108 Towry, Peter (pseud. of David Piper). Trial by battle. London: Hutchinson, 1959.
        Army life in East India and East Asia during World War II.

2109 Tracy, Louis. Heart's delight or the great Mogul. New York: Clode, 1905.
        Sir Thomas Roe and the court of Jehangir.

2110 _____. The red year. New York: Clode, 1908.
Nana Sahib and the Cawnpore massacre.

2111 _____. Sirdar's sabre. New York: Clode, 1920.
A series of ten loosely connected adventure
stories. Tracy may have written other novels on
India.

2112 Travers, John (pseud. of Eva Bell). In the long run.
London: Hodder and Stoughton, 1925.
The "socialist" wife of a Panjab governor gets
mixed up with nationalist and Akali politics.

2113 _____. In the world of bewilderment. London:
Duckworth, 1912.
An English official in India torn between the love
of two women; excellent individual characterization.

2114 _____. The Mortimers. London: Hodder and
Stoughton, 1922.

2115 _____. Sahib log. London: Duckworth, 1910.
Dedicated to the proposition that the luxurious
East is a fraud; that English women there are pur-
poseful.

2116 _____. Second nature. London: Duckworth, 1914.

2117 _____. A servant when he reigneth. London:
Hodder and Stoughton, 1921.
Panjab during World War I; race relations.

2118 Trease, Robert Geoffrey. The land of the Mogul: a
story of the East India Company's first venture in
India. Oxford; Blackwell, 1938.
William Hawkins and Jehangir; well done.

2119 Trevelyan, George Otto. The competitionwallah. Cambridge: No publisher given, 1864.
British civil servant in India during the mid-
nineteenth century. Extremely valuable.

2120 Trevor, Charles. Drums of Asia. London: Lovat
Dickson, 1934.

2121 Trikamdas, Purshottam. The living mask. Baroda:
Padmaja, 1947.

Psychological possibilities if two heads were
transposed.

2122 Tripathi, Govardhanram Madnavram. Saraswatichandra.
Tr. from the original Gujarati. Bombay: N. M.
Tripathi, 1948-1950.

2123 Tucker, Charlotte. Beyond the black water. London:
Nelson, 1890.

2124 _____. Edith and her ayah. Edinburgh: No publisher given, 1872.

2125 _____. Futteypoor: the city of victory. London:
No publisher given, 1859.

2126 _____. Little bullets from Batala. London: Gall
and Inglis, 1880.

2127 _____. Pomegranates from the Panjab. London:
No publisher given, 1878.

2128 _____. The two pilgrims to Kashi and other stories.
Madras: No publisher given, 1901.

2129 _____. War and peace: a tale of the retreat from
Cabul. London: No publisher given, 1862.

2130 _____. A wreath of Indian stories. London: No
publisher given, 1876.
Good to excellent stories for children and adults; Mrs.
Tucker was a missionary in India.

2131 Turkhud, Nalini. The jagirdar of Palna. Poona:
Israelite Press, 1936.
Rich family suddenly reduced due to gambling and
business speculation leaves two young children behind; the girl overcomes her circumstances but the
boy doesn't.

2132 Turner, George Frederic. A bolt from the east.
London: Methuen, 1917.
A gifted mystery novel portraying the spiritual
journey of a Mephistophelian Mirza.

2133 Turner, W. The death of a nazi. Bombay: Noble
Publishing, 1943.

Nazi intrigues on the Indo-Afghan border.

Tutiet, Mary Gleed. See Maxwell Gray.

2134 Ullman, James Ramsey. And not to yield. New York:
      Doubleday, 1970.
      Novel about a man who dreamed of climbing a
      great Himalayan mountain.

2135 Ullmann, Richard. Coppelia. London: Jarrolds, 1947.

2136 Umrao Bahadur. The curse of society. Delhi: Print-
      ing and Stationery Depot, 1933.
      The curse "is the ban on widow remarriage, "
      but the widow does remarry. A social novel.

2137 _____. Destiny. Delhi: Printing and Stationery
      Depot, n. d.
      Romantic events in the life of an upper class
      north Indian Muslim family.

2138 _____. Freaks of fate. Delhi: Indraprastha Vedic
      Library, 1929.
      Domestic and religious life of north Indian Hindu
      family.

2139 _____. Janaki. Delhi: Indraprastha Vedic Library,
      1931.
      Glorifies Hindu womanhood.

2140 _____. Love and its charms. Delhi: Indraprastha
      Vedic Library, 1924.
      Hindu domestic life.

2141 _____. The unveiled court; a story of a prince's
      court. London: Arthur Stockwell, 1932.
      Exposes defects in the regimes of Indian princes.

2142 Upward, Allen. Athelstane Ford. London: C. A.
      Pearson, 1899.
      Clive's expedition to Bengal after the Black Hole
      incident, written for young adults. The author may
      have written other young adult fiction on India.

2143 Vachell, Horace Annesley. The fourth dimension.
      London: John Murray, 1920.
           Mystery involving a young Anglo-Indian girl living
      in rural India. The author may have written other
      mysteries.

2144 Vaid, Krishna Baldev. Steps in darkness. New York:
      Orion, 1962.
           Northwest Indian village family uprooted during
      the famine of the 1930's; the story of a young boy's
      search for happiness in a family atmosphere of bick-
      ering, poverty and hate.

2145 Vaidya, Suresh. Kailas. London: Queensway Press,
      1937.
           A Brahmin receives the gift of a sacred bull each
      year whom he cannot sell; his pilgrimage to
      Badrinath; and his realisation that he belongs to
      society, not to a monastic retreat.

2146 Vakil, K. A. K. The star of Switzerland. Bombay:
      No publisher listed, 1922.
           A Parsi in Bombay and in Europe.

      Also see Star-Najnin.

2147 Vance, L. J. The bronze bell. London: Grant
      Richards, 1909.
           Mystery; a young American on a hunting expedi-
      tion is mistaken for an Indian raja, and thereby re-
      ceives a precious antique from an Indian babu.
      Good portraits of the Indian C. I. D. The author
      may have written other mysteries with Indian back-
      ground.

2148 Vansittart, Jane. The so beloved: the story of Henry
      Lawrence and Honoria. London: Hodder and
      Stoughton, 1967.
           Historical novel.

2149 Varma, Bhagvati Charan. Chitraleka. Translated
      from the original Hindi by B. Karki. Bombay: Jaico,
      1957.
           A distinguished Hindi novel poorly translated.

2150 Vasamoorti. Here and beyond. Translated by V.
      Satyanarayanmurti. Amalpuram: Telugu Veluger
      Prachuranalu, 1967.

2151   Vaswani, Bulchand Jhamatmal. Beast of the east and
       other stories of war time Burma, China, India and
       Ceylon. Karachi: The Author, 1945.

2152   _____. Yanks and yogis: sensational stories of
       eerie events and uncanny adventures into yogiland
       by GI's in India, Burma, and Ceylon. Karachi:
       Modern Book Depot, 1945.

       Vatsyana, Sachchidanand Hiranand. See Agyeya.

2153   Venkataramani, K. S. A day with sambhu. Mylapore:
       Svetaranya Ashrama, 1929.
             Moral tales.

2154   _____. Jatadharan and other stories. Madras:
       Svetaranya Ashrama, 1937.

2155   _____. Kandan, the patriot. Mylapore: Svetaranya
       Ashrama, 1934.
             Swarajist movement of the 1930's in South India;
       events culminate in a riot.

2156   _____. Murugan, the tiller. Mylapore: Svetaranya
       Ashrama, 1927.
             A striking novel of village life in South India; the
       main characters are a government servant, a city
       lawyer, and Murugan.

2157   _____. Paper boats: sketches on Indian life and
       customs. Adyar: Theosophical Publishing House, 1921.
             Ten sketches; one on the Indian beggar worth
       reading.

2158   Venkatesa Iyengar, Masti. Short stories. 4 vols.
       Bangalore: Bangalore Press, 1943.
             Each volume has eight stories dealing for most
       part with Kannada village life; considerable
       ethnography.

2159   _____. Subbana. Bangalore: B. B. D. Power
       Press, 1943.

2160   Venkatesaiya Naidu, M. The princess Kamala; or,
       the model wife. Madras: A. L. V. Press, 1904.
             Court romance set in ancient India stressing
       virtues of Indian women.

2161 Venugopal, T. <u>Parvati.</u> Bezwada: No publisher
      given, 1934.
          Story of post-puberty marriage; social evils are
      well depicted.

2162 _____. <u>The tales of Kerala.</u> Tripunittura:
      Lakshmi Stores, 1943.

2163 Vera (pseud.) <u>Lotus; or the lily maid of the east.</u>
      Allahabad: Pioneer Press, 1909.
          An apology for the Eurasian life style.

2164 Verghese, M. <u>Villain.</u> Tiruvalla: The Author, 1958.

2165 Verne, Jules. <u>Works of Jules Verne.</u> Edited by
      Charles F. Horne. New York: Parke & Co. , 1911.

2166 _____. In volumes XI and XII are: <u>The five hun-</u>
      <u>dred millions of the Begum; The demon of Cawn-</u>
      <u>pore; and The steamhouse, or a trip across northern</u>
      <u>India.</u>

2167 Vetch, G. A. <u>The gong: or reminiscences of India.</u>
      Edinburgh: No publisher given, 1852.
          Meaningless sketch of military life in India.

2168 Vian, Pat. <u>Broken arcs.</u> London: Hutchinson, 1931.
          Love story of a girl who considers English
      morality to be false, and who finds happiness in
      India.

2169 _____. <u>Instead of the bier.</u> London: Hutchinson,
      1934.
          English girl marries for status, and English man
      marries her for love. Set in the Tamil country it
      has a moving portrait of an Indian lawyer.

2170 _____. <u>Set desire.</u> London: Hutchinson, 1932.

      Vidyabinod. <u>See</u> Chakravarti, Kedarnath.

2171 Vidyasagar, Ishwar Chandra. <u>The exile of Sita.</u> Trans-
      lated from Bengali by H. Jane Harding. London:
      Henry J. Drane, 1904.
          From Ramayana.

2172 Vittal Rao, Ananda. <u>Glamour and other stories.</u>

Bangalore: Power Press, 1950.

2173 _____. The man in the red tie and other stories.
      Bombay: Hind Kitabs, 1942.
          The first title has ten stories; the second has
      fifteen stories; all deal with upper class town people.

2174 Viyogi, Hari. A handful of flour. Delhi: Harijan
      Sevak Sangh, 1958.
          Harijan life.

2175 Waddy, Percival Stacy. The great Moghul: stories of
      Akbar. London: Constable, 1913.

2176 Wadhwa, Besant Lall. Spring of the deserts. Bom-
      bay: The Author, 1935.
          Contains two short stories, "The wandering girl"
      and "Daughter of the moon. "

2177 Walker, David Harry. Harry Black. Boston: Houghton
      Mifflin, 1956.
          Sentimental novel about a tiger hunt, and the
      sorrow of the hunter who is in love with the wife of
      his best friend. Much local color.

2178 Wallis, Arthur F. Slipped moorings. London: E. J.
      Larby, 1910.
          A clever, newly educated Indian causes unrest by
      using English mischief makers.

Wallis, Henry. See Ashton Hillier.

Warburton, Stanley. See S. Woods Hill.

2179 Waring, P. Alston. Peacock country. New York:
      John Day, 1948.
          Twenty-one stories, mostly from Orissa, showing
      the unusual bond between animals and people, from
      the maharaja down to the farmer. A book of deli-
      cate beauty.

2180 Warren, John Russell. A bride for Bombay. London:
      Ward, Lock, 1931.
          On the evening of her arrival in a princely state,
      an English girl finds her fiance mysteriously stabbed,
      and the pretender to the throne asking her to marry
      him. An improbable mystery.

2181 Wasi, Muriel. <u>Too high for rivalry</u>. Bombay: Kutub Popular, 1967.

2182 Weiss, Renee K. <u>The bird from the sea</u>. New York: Thomas Crowell, 1970.
   Juvenile. Story of a gamekeeper's daughter in an Indian village.

2183 Welfle, Richard A. <u>The ruined temple</u>. Patna: The Author, 1944.

2184 Wentworth, Patricia. <u>The devil's wind.</u> London: Andrew Melrose, 1912.
   During the Sepoy Mutiny an English girl marries an Indian to save her life, and is despised for it. Mentions the Cawnpore massacre. It is probable that Miss Wentworth wrote other mysteries using India as the background.

2185 Wernher, Hilda. <u>The land and the well.</u> London: Harrap, 1946.
   A totally Indian novel set in Rajputana containing not a single European character; solidly enthno-graphical. It is the story of a sister-in-law's effort to woo a boy away from his wife.

2186 _____. <u>My Indian family.</u> New York: Doubleday, 1945.
   The narrator's daughter is married to an Indian, and the story deals with her marriage and her attempts to adjust to the Muslim way of life. Several interesting insights.

2187 _____. <u>My Indian son-in-law.</u> New York: Double-day, 1949.
   Continuation of <u>My Indian family</u>. In diary form this novel begins when the narrator's son-in-law returns from his second honeymoon. Story of a household where Western ideas are not always in harmony with Indian traditions.

2188 _____. <u>Story of Induraja.</u> New York: Doubleday, 1948.
   A young widowed princess who becomes an ardent and unconventional social reformer. Superficial.

2189 Westermayr, Arthur Joseph. <u>Power of innocence.</u>

New York: Fenno, 1909.

2190 _____. Rudra, a romance of ancient India.   New
      York: Dillingham, 1912.
          Excellent use of historical material; set in
      Hastinapura in the imperial age of Kanauj.

2191 _____. Udara, prince of Bidur; a romance of India.
      New York: Dillingham, 1913.
          A Hindu prince for the love of his Christian
      slave relinquishes the throne to his hated cousin but
      returns triumphantly and with popular support.

2192 Weston, Christine. Bhimsa: the dancing bear.   New
      York: Scribners, 1945.
          Wonderful children's story involving an Indian
      boy, his western friend, and his tame bear.

2193 _____. The hoopoe.   New York: Harper, 1970.
          Girl brought up in India marries an American
      and goes to live with Boston brahmins.

2194 _____. Indigo.   New York: Scribners, 1943.
          Friendship of four young persons of different na-
      tionalities and backgrounds, set in eastern India
      during the nationalist movement.

2195 _____. There and then.   New York: Scribners,
      1948.
          Fifteen short stories.

2196 _____. The world is a bridge.   New York:
      Scribners, 1950.
          India on the eve of British withdrawal, and in an
      atmosphere of hate, fear and violence sweeping the
      country in 1946.

2197 Westwood, Anne McDougal. Elfinstorm.   London:
      Hurst and Blackett, 1931.
          One hundred and fifty years of unbroken resi-
      dence, on the banks of the Ganges, has evil effects
      on pure European stock.

2198 _____. The flying firs.   London: Hurst and
      Blackett, 1930.
          An English baby girl found by a Eurasian railway
      guard amid the debris of a train wreck is adopted

(or stolen) by him.   The life of the Eurasian under-
world is vividly described.   Anti-Eurasian.

2199 _____. Quinlan. London: John Murray, 1933.
A Eurasian police officer in India poses as an
Englishman; murder mystery.

2200 _____. To what purpose? London: John Murray,
1936.
Again Eurasian life.

2201 Westwood, Anne McDougal and Jack Westwood. Ali
Baba and the lonely leopard. London: Blackie, 1951.
For children.

2202 Whish, Charles William. The man who died for India.
Bombay: Eagle Printing, 1907.
Silly anti-Indian diatribe.

2203 White, Charles. The Cashmere shawl. 3 vols. London: No publisher given, 1840.
Quasi-historical narrative of Indian chivalry in
the time of Maharaja Ranjeet Singh of Panjab.

2204 White, D. S. Recollections of an ex-detective of
Madras police force. Madras: C. Foster, 1876.

2205 White, Edmund (pseud. of James B. Patton). Bijli the
dancer. London: No publisher given, 1898.
Tragic and wonderful story of an Indian dancer
torn between her longings as a woman and her am-
bitions as an artist.

2206 _____. The heart of Hindustan. London: Methuen,
1910.
Portrayal of English administrative machinery,
Hindu-Rajput and Muslim life in Rohilkand. Very
good.

2207 _____. The path, an Indian romance. London:
Methuen, 1914.
A Rohila romance. A neo-Muslim returns after
many years in the west and starts a new this-worldly
religion.

2208 _____. The pilgrimage of Premnath. London:
Methuen, 1918.
A Hindu banker's search for salvation.

2209 White, J. Dillon. Brave Captain Kelso. London:
        Hutchinson, 1959.
            Kelso is commander of an East Indiaman fighting
        ship in action against Maratha pirate Angria in the
        eighteenth century.

2210 _____. Young Mr. Kelso. London: Hutchinson,
        1963.
            Story of a fourth-mate on an East Indiaman.

2211 White, Michael. Lachmi Bai, Rani of Jhansi. New
        York: J. F. Taylor, 1901.

2212 White, Robin. All in favor say no. New York:
        Farrar Strauss, 1964.
            Son of a San Francisco missionary goes to India
        for graduate study.

2213 _____. Elephant hill. New York: Harper, 1959.
            A middle-aged spinster goes to India to visit her
        missionary sister and to find love.

2214 _____. Foreign soil, tales of South India. New
        York: Atheneum, 1962.
            Fourteen stories with a touch of irony.

2215 _____. House of many rooms. New York: Harper,
        1958.
            Missionary family in south India is subjected to
        the equivocal moral climate of Hinduism.

2216 _____. Men and angels. New York: Harper, 1961.
            India born Englishman returns to India and falls
        in love with an Indian girl; excellent descriptions of
        Indian middle class life.

2217 Whitelaw, David. The girl from the east: a romance.
        London: Greening and Co., 1912.
            Mystery. The author may have written other
        crime and detective novels.

2218 Wilfred, Russel. Indian summer. Bombay: No pub-
        lisher given, 1953.

2219 Wilkins, W. J. The brahmin's plot or the story of
        two friends. London: Religious Tract Society, 1893.
            Travels from Calcutta to Delhi, and the "saving of
        a soul."

2220 Williamson, Geoffrey. Grand trunk knight. London:
       Hutchinson, 1933.
              Adventures of a Eurasian vagabond in India.

2221 _____. The lovable outlaw. London: Heinemann,
       1930.
              A six-foot-seven Eurasian joins the Indian
       criminal investigation department and is an instant
       success.

2222 Willmer, John Henry. The transit of souls, a tale of
       Lucknow. London: John Long, 1910.
              A novel of the occult based on transmigration
       and rebirth.

     Wilmont, James Reginald. See Frances Stewart.

2223 Wilmot, J. M. Zora, the invisible. Bombay: Ham-
       ilton, 1933.
              Mystery.

2224 Wilson, Alexander Douglas. The crimson dacoit.
       London: Herbert Jenkins, 1933.
              A mystery; worth reading.

2225 _____. The devil's cocktail. London: Longmans,
       1928.
              Secret service in action against the Bolsheviks
       in Lahore; people are divided into three categories;
       sahibs, snobs, and sinners.

2226 _____. The mystery of tunnel 51. London: Long-
       mans, 1928.
              A courier from Simla to Delhi is murdered on
       the mountain railroad and secret papers are stolen.
       Mr. Wilson probably wrote other mystery novels on
       India.

2227 Wilson, Christine. Mountain road. London: Hurst
       and Blackett, 1958.
              Set in Kashmir and Himalayan valleys, this is an
       ordinary story of adventure and love during World
       War II.

2228 Wilson, Dorothy Clarke. House of earth. Philadel-
       phia: Westminster Press, 1952.
              A village Brahmin finally accepts Christianity.

2229 Wilson, Margaret.   The daughters of India.   New
        York: Harper, 1928.
             Rare classic of missionary fiction; life in a mis-
        sion and a poor bustee; intimate understanding of
        Harijan women.

2230 _____.   Trousers of taffeta: a novel of the child
        mothers of India.   New York: Harper, 1929.
             An American missionary doctor tells of the hap-
        piness Indian Muslim women derive in the bearing
        of children which they consider the chief end of
        human existence.

2231 Wollaston, Nicholas.   Pharoah's chicken.   London:
        Hodder, 1969.
             Sardonic travelogue probing the chasm between
        India and the west.   A young English operative of
        Famine Fund of London goes to India to find out why
        the charity is not working.

2232 Wolpert, Stanley.   An error of judgment.   New York:
        Little Brown, 1969.
             General Dyer and the Jalianwallah Bagh massacre
        of April 1919.

2233 _____.   The expedition.   London: Cassell, 1967.
             Search for the abominable snowman; Nepal and
        India.

2234 _____.   Nine hours to Rama.   New York: Random
        House, 1962.
             Nine hours in the life of Godse immediately pre-
        ceding the firing of shots that killed Gandhi.   Super-
        cilious in parts.

2235 Wood, J. Claverdon (pseud. of Thomas Carter).   When
        Nicholson kept the border.   London: Boys Own
        Paper Press, 1922.
             Mutiny story for young adults.

     Woodruff, P.   See Philip Mason.

2236 Woolf, S. H.   Ordeal on the frontier.   London: Put-
        nam's, 1928.
             English girl falls in love with an Indian nobleman
        and also with an English captain.   Hill and frontier
        society frowns on her first love.

2237 Wren, Percival Christopher.   Beggar's horses.   London: John Murray, 1934.
   A secret service story that begins in India.

2238 _____.   Dark woman.   London: John Murray, 1943.
   Six British officers deserted by their sepoys
   seek advice from a yogi; in return for their promise
   to forego hunting the yogi grants them each one wish
   and tells them to beware of the dark woman.

2239 _____.   Dew and mildew: semi-detached stories
   from Karabad, India.   London: Longmans, 1912.
   In the lead story, an old fakir curses a Parsee
   who tore down a shrine to build a bungalow; for a
   number of generations the curse worked.

2240 _____.   Driftwood spars.   London: John Murray,
   1916.
   Duality of Eurasian character.   A half-Pathan,
   half-Scotsman murders an Englishman because of
   his Pathan character; and falls in love with an English girl but has a tragic outcome.

2241 _____.   Explosion.   London: John Murray, 1935.
   Historical: an explosion incident in Sind.

2242 _____.   Father Gregory of lures and failures: a
   tale of Hindostan.   London: Longmans, 1913.
   Humorous adventures of Father Gregory.

2243 _____.   The man of a ghost.   Same as The spur of
   pride.

2244 _____.   Odd, but even so: stories stranger than
   fiction.   London: John Murray, 1941.

2245 _____.   The snake and the sword.   London: Longmans, 1914.
   Eurasian boy degenerates in Indian environment
   because of the Indian fear of snakes.

2246 _____.   The spur of pride.   London: Houghton,
   1937.
   A disgraced English officer becomes a secret
   agent in the Indian intelligence service and acquires
   valuable information about the Indo-Afghan border
   situation.

2247 _____. To the hilt. New York: Houghton, 1937.
       Sequel to The spur of pride.

2248 _____. Worthwhile. London: John Murray, 1937.

2249 _____. The young stagers. London: Longmans,
       1917.
       Stories in continuation of Dew and mildew.

2250 Wylie, Elinor. Jennifer Lorn: a sedate extravaganza.
       New York: Doubleday, 1923.
       In this satirical novel several pages are given to
       a journey through northern India in the eighteenth
       century.

2251 Wylie, Ida Alexa Ross. The daughter of Brahma.
       London: Mills and Boon, 1912.
       Woman's way of looking at religion in India.

2252 _____. Hermit doctor of Gaya. New York: Put-
       nam, 1916.
       A retired Swedish dancer comes into the English
       colony at Gaya, and chooses unwisely between two
       men, half brothers, both of whom are in love with
       her.

2253 _____. Native born. Same as The rajah's people.

2254 _____. The rajah's people. London: Mills and
       Boon, 1910.
       English army colony at Meerut has tangled rela-
       tions with the local raja.

2255 _____. Temple of dawn. London: Mills and Boon,
       1915.
       Frivolity and adventure in English colony in the
       "Frontier" province.

2256 _____. Tristram Sahib. London: Mills and Boon,
       1915.
       Major Tristram's duty and sacrifice, romance
       and adventure in Bihar.

2257 Wylie, Max. Hindu heaven. London: Gollancz, 1933.
       Satire on the activities of American missionaries
       and the hypocrisy of their Indian converts; good
       portrait of a north Indian town and its missionary
       college.

2258 Wynne, May. The secret of the zennana. London:
Greening, 1913.

2259 Wynne, Pamela (pseud. of Winifred Mary Scott).
Ashes of desire. London: Macaulay, 1925.
A young English girl goes off to India disguised
as a boy.

2260 _____. East is always east. New York: Doubleday, 1930.
A fascinating widow with two beautiful twin
daughters sets out to India to join her brother, and
has thrilling experience.

2261 _____. Love's lotus flower. London: Collins, 1939.
A young girl runs away to India because her boy
friend in England is indifferent to her. Miss Wynne
has probably written other novels dealing with India.

2262 Xenox (pseud.) Echoes of the east. Allahabad: Pioneer Press, 1904.
Tales and sketches of Indian and Burmese life.

2263 Yadav Reddy, S. Storm over Hyderabad. Hyderabad:
No publisher given, 1964.
Political novel of contemporary India, college
students and their problems; interesting example of
Indian English.

2264 Yashpal. Short stories of Yashpal: author and patriot.
Tr. by Corinne Friend. Philadelphia: University of
Pennsylvania Press, 1969.

2265 Yates, Edward. Olives are scarce. London:
Heinemann, 1931.
A romantic novel dealing with two Englishmen.
Boy meets girl of high social position in Calcutta,
is separated and then united with her.

2266 Yeats, Sidney Kilner Levett. A galehad of the creeks
and other stories. London: Longmans, 1897.
The title story deals with the Burmese war of
1852.

2267 _____. The romance of guard Mulligan and other

stories.   Allahabad: Wheeler, 1893.
Light stories of India and Burma.

2268 Yeats-Brown,   Francis.   The lives of a Bengal lancer.
New York: Viking, 1930.

2269 York, Eden.   A prince of Kashmir.   London: Film
Story Publishing Company,   1923.
Founded on the powerful Stoll film version of
Indian love lyrics.

2270 Younghusband, Francis.   But in our lives; a romance
of the Indian frontier.   London: John Murray, 1926.
A philosophical romance by the hero of Chitral
written as a biography of Captain Lee and his devoted service at the northwest frontier.   Lacks
imagination.

2271 Zinkin, Taya.   The faithful parrot and other folk
stories.   London: Oxford University Press, 1968.

2272 _____ .   Rishi: the story of a childhood in India.
London: Methuen, 1960.
Both are stories for children.

TITLE INDEX

The abbey of bliss. (Chatterji, B.)
Abdication. (Chandler)
Abdul Aziz. (Goldinho)
Abdullah and his two strings. (Hukk)
Above what he could bear. (Cress)
The achievements of John Carruthers. (Cox)
The acid test. (Savi)
An acre of green grass (Bose, B.)
Across India by air. (Minney)
Across the black waters. (Anand, M. R.)
Adrift on the Ganga. (Sinha, S.)
The advanced guard. (Grier)
The advancing year. (Rajput)
The adventure of Mrs. Russell. (Bannerjea)
Adventurer in the Punjab. (Anon)
Adventures in India. (Kingston)
Adventures of a fair girl. (Gazdar)
Adventures of a rupee, wherein are interspersed various
    anecdotes Asiatic and European. (Scott, H.)
The adventures of Akbar. (Steel)
The adventures of an A. D. C. (Bradley)
The adventures of an Arcot rupee. (Kirby, C.)
The adventures of Count O'Conner in the dominions of the
    great Mogul. (Stace)
The adventures of Sherlock Holmes. (Doyle)
The adventures of the gooroo noodle. (Beschi)
The adventures of the Panjab hero Raja Rasalu and other
    folk tales of the Panjab. (Swynnerton)
The Afghan knife. (Sterndale)
The after cost. (Edge)
After my own fashion. (Elder)
After the knock. (Chitera)
Ahana. (Edge)
Aijah. (Cooper, P.)
Air hostess. (Nanda)
The air patrol: a story of the northwest. (Strang)
Ajanta. (Abbas)
Ajanta: a historical novel. (King, E. T.)
Alfred and Eliza Stark: a romance from life in India.
    (Moorat)

226

Ali Baba and the lonely leopard.   (Westwood)
The alien sky.   (Scott, P.)
Alien there is none.   (Rana)
All about H. Hatterr.   (Desani)
All in favor say no.   (White, R.)
All men are brothers.   (Anand, M. R.)
The altar and other stories.   (Manara)
Amba pali.   (Raina)
An American girl at the durbar.   (Bradley)
An American girl in India.   (Bradley)
Amitabha: a story of Buddhist theology.   (Carus)
Amrita.   (Jhabvala, R. P.)
Amy Vivian.   (Greenhow)
Ananda maya: a didactic fiction on a realistic background.
     (Srinivasan)
The anchorite and other stories.   (Kincaid, C. A.)
And gazelles leaping.   (Ghose, S. N.)
And it happened.   (Somers)
And not to yield.   (Ullman)
And other stories.   (Kipling)
Androcles, the tiger and other short stories.   (Gay)
Angel: a sketch in Indian ink.   (Croker)
Angel of gaiety.   (Hitrec)
Anglo-India.   (Holmes)
Anglo-Indian life in the sixties.   (Holmes)
The Anglo-Indians.   (Perrin)
Angry dust.   (Isvaran)
The angry goddess.   (Jai Ratan)
Anguish.   (Krishna Kutti)
Another sun, another home.   (Croft)
The anthology of Indian tales.   (Kincaid, C. A.)
Arrivals from India.   (Rouviere)
As a man's hand: an Indian saga, 1876-1936.   (Southgate)
As it happened.   (Hilliers)
As the clock struck twenty.   (Anon)
Ashes of desire.   (Wynne, P.)
Ashes of roses and other stories.   (Snilloc)
The Asiatic princess.   (Pilkington)
The Asiatics.   (Prokosch)
Asir of Asirgarh.   (Snilloc)
The assassins.   (Sharp)
An astrologer's day and other stories.   (Narayan)
At bay: a book for king and parliament.   (Ingrestone)
At close quarters.   (Savi)
At government house.   (Beamen)
At sundown the tiger.   (Mannin)
Athawar house.   (Nagarajan)

Athelstane Ford. (Upward)
Autobiography of a spinster. (Edwood)
Autobiography of an Indian army surgeon, or the leaves
        turned down from a journal. (Anon)
An avatar in Vishnu land. (Hill, S. W.)
Awakening: a selection of short stories. (Sharma, M. P.)
Awakening: a study in possibilities. (Diver)
Azizu, the dancing girl, and other Indian stories. (MacMunn)

Baba and the black sheep. (Savi)
The baba log: a tale of child life in India. (Macdonald)
Babes in the wood. (Croker)
The baboo and other tales descriptive of society in India.
        (Prinsep)
Baboo Hari Bungasho Jabberjee, B. A. (Anstey)
Baby sahib. (Methley, A. A.)
The bachelor of arts. (Narayan)
Back o'beyond. (Savi)
Back to the soil. (Karnath)
A backward place. (Jhabvala, R. P.)
Badmashes. (Snilloc)
The bag of diamonds. (Fenn, G. M.)
Bahadur Khan, warrior. (Afghan)
Bahadur means hero. (Klass)
Baja the freebooter: vivid pictures of life in Hindostan.
        (St. Clair)
Baladitya: a historical romance of ancient India. (Pan-
        chapakesa Ayyar)
Bandar log. (Smith, A. W.)
Banked fires. (Savi)
Banked fires and other stories. (Duggal)
Banker's wife. (Gore)
Bar sinister. (Hall, G. P.)
The barber's trade union and other stories. (Anand, M. R.)
Barclay of the guides: a tale of the Indian mutiny. (Strang)
A bayard from Bengal. (Anstey)
Beads of silence. (Bamburg)
Bears and the dacoits: a tale of the ghauts. (Henty)
Beast of the east and other stories of wartime Burma,
        China, India, and Ceylon. (Vaswani)
The beautiful Mughal princesses. (Sunity Devi)
Beauty and joy. (Munshi, M.)
The beauty; Bengali novel Rupavati. (Basu, M.)
Before the British raj: a story of military adventures in
        India. (Griffith)
Beggar's horses. (Wren)

The black Buddha.   (Chitty)
Black light.   (Mundy, T.)
Black narcissus.   (Godden, R.)
Black prince and other stories.   (Bowlong)
The black sadhu, story of India.   (Thorne)
The black scorpion.   (Shannon)
Black shadow.   (Fenn, G. M.)
The black sun and other stories.   (Abbas)
Black velvet, a drama of India and the bomb cult.   (Mac-
    Munn)
A blind alley.   (Savi)
Blood and stones.   (Abbas)
Blood royal.   (Payne)
Blood stained footprints; an army novel.   (Matai, K. E.)
Blue blood turned red.   (Tagore, S.)
The blue devils.   (Leslie)
Blue gardens.   (Silver)
Blue moons.   (Newcomen)
Bluestocking in India.   (Heston)
Bluff.   (Bowlong)
Blunder.   (Savi)
Boatman of the Padma.   (Bannerjee, M.)
A bolt from the east.   (Turner, G. F.)
The Bombay meeting: a novel of modern India.   (Morris)
Bombay murder.   (Chettur)
The bond of blood.   (Forrest)
Bond of blood.   (Ganguli, J. M.)
The border of blades.   (Foran)
The border line.   (Burn)
A bottle in the smoke: a tale of Anglo-India.   (Rae)
Bound in shallows.   (Hill, K.)
Boundless sky.   (Tagore, R.)
The bow of fate.   (Greenhow)
The boy of Bengal.   (Punt)
The brahmin and the belle.   (Lewis, R.)
The brahmin's plot or the story of two friends.   (Wilkins)
The brahmin's prophecy.   (Anon)
The brahmin's treasure.   (Bechhofer)
The brahmin's treasure or Colonel Thorndyke's secret.(Henty)
The brand of Kali.   (Pegg)
Brave Captain Kelso.   (White, J. D.)
Brave girl: true story of the Indian mutiny.   (Jackson)
Breakfast with Nikolides.   (Godden, R.)
Breakspear: a legend of the Mahratta war.   (Sellon)
Brenda's experiment.   (Greenhow)
A bride for Bombay.   (Warren)
A bride for the sahib and other stories.   (Singh, K.)

life in India.   (Anon)
The case of the laughing Jesuit.   (Burt)
The cashmere shawl.   (White, C.)
Cassio and life divine.   (Rubin)
Caste.   (Fraser, W. A.)
Caste and creed.   (Penny)
Caste and outcaste.   (Mukerji, D. G.)
The cat and the Shakespeare.   (Rao, R.)
Catch 'em alive.   (Burt)
Cats of Benares.   (Halls)
The cat's paw.   (Croker)
Cavanaugh of K.   (Sutherland, J.)
The cave of Hanuman.   (Hampden, H.)
Caves of terror.   (Mundy, T.)
Cecilia Kirkham's son.   (Combe)
Chameleons.   (Sett)
The chandi, or the great plan.   (Sinha, P. N.)
Chandra Shekhar.   (Chatterji, B. C.)
Chandrahasa: an ancient Indian monarch; a romance. (Anon)
Chandranath (Queen's gambit).   (Chatterji, Sarat Chandra)
Chand's little sisters.   (Batley)
The changeling.   (Ali, H.)
Chankya and Chandragupta: a historical novel.   (Panchapa-
    kesa Ayyar)
Character sketches.   (Anon)
The charm.   (Perrin)
Chasing a fortune.   (Robinson, P. S.)
Chaturanga.   (Tagore, R.)
The cheese doll.   (Tagore, R.)
Chemeen.   (Sivasankara Pillai)
The chequer board.   (Shute)
The chess players and other stories.   (Prem Chand)
Chi-chi.   (Hemingway)
The chief commissioner.   (Swabey)
The chief of the herd.   (Mukerji, D. G.)
Childhood in India, or English children in the East. (Anon)
Childish brides.   (Dean)
The children of Kaveri.   (Ram, S.)
Children of the border.   (Pennell)
Children under arms.   (Murrell)
Chindwin mission.   (Baillie)
Chingling.   (Deshpande)
Chinna etc.   (Hampden, H.)
Chitraheen.   (Chatterji, S. C.)
Chitraleka.   (Varma)
Chowra's revenge.   (Penny)
Chronicles of Budgepore: or sketches of life in upper India.
    (Prichard)

The crimson dacoit. (Wilson, A. D.)
Crooked corner. (Ferguson, M.)
Cruel interlude. (Anand, B. S.)
The crusaders of Tibet. (Bambi)
Cry the peacock. (Desai)
Curry and rice. (Atkinson, G. F.)
The curse of Kali. (Greening)
The curse of Kama. (Lovatt)
The curse of society. (Umrao Bahadur)
Curse of the arhat. (O'Hind)
Cyclone and other stories. (Narayan)

Daggers drawn. (Savi)
Damaris. (Harrison)
Damfool Sahib. (Irvine)
Dance of Shiva and other folk tales from India. (Ghosh, O.)
The dancing fakir and other stories. (Eyton)
The dancing god. (Sharp)
Dancing princess. (Bothwell)
Dangerous derelict. (Bayley)
Dark amid the blaze. (Rushton)
Dark corners. (Penny)
The dark dancer. (Prokosch)
The dark dancer. (Rajan)
Dark dealing. (Brown, A. C.)
The dark goddess. (Tennyson)
The dark room. (Narayan)
Dark woman. (Wren)
Darkening days, being a narrative of famine stricken Bengal.
     (Sen, E.)
Darzee: a girl of India. (Marshall, E.)
A daughter-in-law. (Savi)
A daughter of Atropos. (Ponder)
The daughter of Brahma. (Wylie, I. A. R.)
Daughter of destiny. (Ponder)
A daughter of India. (Huddleston)
Daughter of the Dahl. (Campions)
Daughter of the mountains. (Rankin)
The daughters of India. (Wilson, M.)
Daughters of the governor. (Stuart, A.)
A daughter's shadow. (Guru-kumara)
David Leslie: a story of the Afghan frontier. (Thorburn)
David's bond. (Batley)
Dawn beyond the tamarisks. (Musbah Haidar)
The day of scorpion. (Scott, P.)
The day the soldier died. (Gillespie, S.)

Diffidence. (Eyton)
The dilemma. (Chesney)
Dilys. (Penny)
The disinterested nabob. (Anon)
Dismiss. (Brown, C. H.)
The disputed V. C. (Gibbon)
Distant drum. (Malgonkar)
Distant drums. (Minney)
The dive for death. (Ramakrishna)
Divided heart. (Abbas)
Divinations of Kala Persad. (Hill, H.)
Doctor and the dragon. (Stoll)
Dr. Claudius. (Crawford)
Doctor Dev. (Pritam)
Dr. Hermoine. (Curwen)
Doctor memsahib. (Shore)
Doctor sahib. (Kerry)
Dodu and other stories. (Narayan)
Dog in the manger. (Savi)
Dogsbody: the story of a romantic subaltern. (Sinderby)
The doings of Berengaria. (Bradley)
The door between. (Savi)
Doorways of the east. (Pennell)
The double house. (Green)
Douglas Archdale: a tale of Lucknow. (Phipps)
The dove found no rest. (Stoll)
The dream prevails. (Diver)
The dreamer. (Krishan Chander)
Dreams and delights. (Beck)
Driftwood spars. (Wren)
The drought and other stories. (Chatterji, S. C.)
The drum. (Mason, A. E. W.)
Drums of Asia. (Trevor)
Dual lives. (Chillington)
Duet in Kerath. (Harvey, G. T. B.)
Duke of Albany's own highlanders. (Grant, J.)
The duke's own. (Groves)
Dulcarnon. (Rideout)
Dullal the forest guard. (Gouldsbury)
Durbar. (Kincaid, D. C. A.)
A durbar bride. (Cameron)
Durga-Das, the Rahtore. (Anonymous)
Durgesh Nandini, or the chieftain's daughter. (Chatterji,
    B. C.)
The dust of desire, or in the days of the Buddha. (Karney)
Dust upon wind. (Ferguson, M.)
Dwellers in the jungle. (Casserly)

Dynamite.   (Bayley)

The ear rings.   (Scinthya)
Earthman.   (Lidchi)
East African and Indian jungle thrillers.   (Snilloc)
East and west.   (Mundy, T.)
The East Indiaman.   (Meacham)
The East Indian sketch-book.   (Smith, E. B. E.)
East is always east.   (Wynne, P.)
East is east: stories of Indian life.   (Pilcher)
East of Suez.   (Perrin)
Eastern clay.   (Gracias)
Eastern legendary tales and Oriental romance.   (Daniell)
Echoes of the east.   (Xenos)
The edge of the empire.   (Sutherland, J.)
Edith and her ayah.   (Tucker)
Eight days.   (Forrest)
Ekada.   (Gopal)
The eldest sister and other stories.   (Chatterji, S. C.)
The elephant.   (Barrass)
The elephant god.   (Casserly)
Elephant grass.   (Denton)
Elephant hill.   (White, R.)
Elfinstorm.   (Westwood, A. M.)
Elsie Ellerton: a novelette of Anglo-Indian life.   (Edwood)
The elusive bachelor.   (Penny)
The emerald clue.   (Bothwell)
The emergency man.   (Candler)
The emperor.   (Payne)
The emperor's design.   (Greenhow)
The empire of the Nairs, or the rights of women: an
     utopian romance.   (Lawrence)
The emporium.   (Holmes)
End of a marriage.   (Hukk)
An end of the hours.   (Thompson, E. J.)
End of the road.   (Somers)
England hath need of thee.   (Grier)
An English girl in the east.   (Kirby, M.)
English homes in India.   (Owensen.)
The English in India.   (Hockley)
The English in India and other sketches.   (Anon)
The English teacher.   (Narayan)
The Englishwoman.   (Askew)
Enough of this lovemaking.   (Rubin)
Epoch's end.   (Banerjee, T.)
An error of judgment.   (Wolpert)

Esmond in India.   (Jhabvala, R. P.)
The eternal lotus.   (Banerjee, T.)
The Etna messages and other stories.   (Ralli)
The Eurasians.   (Bruce)
Eva and Forester: a tale of India.   (Prinsep)
Even clouds feel thirsty.   (Mallick)
Every inch a soldier.   (Coloquhoun)
Excursions in ink.   (Minney)
The exile of Sita.   (Vidyasagar)
Expectancy.   (Eyton)
Expedition.   (Wolpert)
Exploits of Asaf Khan.   (Afghan)
The exploits of Kesho Naik, dacoit.   (Cox)
Explosion.   (Wren)
The eyes of understanding.   (Milton)
Eyesore.   (Tagore, R.)

The faces of courage.   (Duncan, M.)
The faded flower.   (Rajgopal, K.)
Fairer than a fairy.   (Grant, G.)
The faithful parrot and other folk stories.   (Zinkin)
A fallen idol.   (Anstey)
The familiar stranger.   (Penny)
A family likeness; a sketch in the Himalayas.   (Croker)
Famous tales of Ind.   (Panchapakesa Ayyar)
Fancy tales.   (Isvaran)
Far away from home.   (Barret)
The far cry.   (Smith, E.)
Far, far the mountain peak.   (Masters)
Far to seek: a romance of England and India.   (Diver)
Farewell my friend.   (Tagore, R.)
A farewell to India.   (Thompson, E. J.)
The fatal amulet.   (Taylor)
The fatal cart and other stories.   (Rajagopalachari)
The fatal garland.   (Ghosal)
The fatalist.   (Savi)
Fate's captive.   (Savi)
Father goose.   (Mortimer)
Father Gregory or lures and failures: a tale of Hindostan.
     (Wren)
The fear of retribution.   (Bedi, K. S.)
Feed him with apricocks.   (Stoll)
Ferrol Bond.   (Easton)
The fever tree.   (Mason, R.)
A few Indian stories.   (James)
The fiddler and the elves, and other stories.   (Carnoy)

Fifty. (Bradley)
The final image. (Kincaid, D. C. A.)
The financial expert. (Narayan)
The finger of destiny and other stories. (Panchapakesa
    Ayyar)
The fire. (Chatterji, S. C.)
Fire on the snows of Himalayas. (Ganguli, J. M.)
The fire worshippers. (Bharucha)
Firebrand fakir: tales of adventure in India and Afghanistan.
    (Harding, R.)
Fires of passion. (Anderson, K.)
First love and last love: a tale of the Indian Mutiny.
    (Grant, J.)
The fisherman of Kerala. (Ganguli, J. M.)
Fitch and his fortunes: an Anglo-Indian novel. (Dick)
Five frontiers. (Murray)
Five Indian tales. (Shearwood)
Flame and the flower. (Krishna Chander)
The flame gathers. (Potter)
Flame of the forest. (Eustace)
The flame of the forest. (Ghose, S. N.)
Flashman: from the flashman papers. (Fraser, G. N.)
The flatterer for gain. (Steel)
Fleas and nightingale: stories. (Mandy)
A flight of falcons. (Eaubonne)
The flight of the arrow and other stories. (Anon)
Flight of the white crows. (Berry)
Floods along the Ganges. (Home)
Flotsam: the study of a life. (Merriman)
The flower of forgiveness. (Stool)
The flute of Asoka. (Forster)
The flying firs. (Westwood, A. M.)
The flying months. (Peard)
Folk tales from Rajasthan. (Birla)
Folk tales of Bengal. (Day)
Folk tales of Sind and Guzarat. (Kincaid, C. A.)
The folklore of Bombay. (Enthoven)
Fool's delight. (King, A. J.)
A fool's game. (Savi)
For infamous conduct. (Lambert)
For name and fame. (Henty)
For the old flag. (Fenn, C. R.)
Forasmuch. (King, P. J.)
Foreign soil, tales of South India. (White, R.)
The foreigner. (Bell)
The foreigner. (Joshi)
The forest goddess. (Basu. M.)

A forest officer. (Penny)
The forgotten land. (Hunt)
The forgotten serenade and other stories. (Peethamber)
A forlorn hope. (Savi)
The 49 days of death. (Ballinger)
Forty-three years: Jayant and Tara. (Barret)
A foster son, a tale of the Indian mutiny. (Langton)
Fountain of inspiration. (Chitrabhanu)
Four chapters. (Tagore, R.)
The four horned altar. (Spencer)
The fourth dimension. (Vachell)
Foxes have holes. (Eyre)
The fragrance lingers. (Savi)
Fragrant valley. (Ramamurthy)
Freaks of fate. (Umrao Bahadur)
A free lance in a far land. (Compton)
A free solitude. (Perrin)
A freelance in Kashmir: a tale of the great anarchy.
    (MacMunn)
From the five rivers. (Steel)
Frontier fires. (Bayley)
A frontier romance. (Morgan)
Frontier tapestry. (Ponder)
Frozen lake. (Gillespie, S.)
Frozen lips. (Nanda)
Full moon. (Mundy, T.)
The further adventures of Jungle John. (Budden)
A fury in white velvet. (Compton)
Futteypoor: the city of victory. (Tucker)

A galehad of the creeks and other stories. (Yeats)
Gamblers in happiness. (Endrikar)
Gana devata. (Banerjee, T.)
Ganges mud. (Thorne)
The garden creeper. (Chatterjee, Sita)
A garland of stories. (Singh, R.)
Gay neck: the story of a pigeon. (Mukerji, D. G.)
Gems from the mine. (Batley)
The general plan. (Candler)
The general's wife. (Hamilton, M.)
The genial anecdote. (Dutt, R. K.)
Geoffrey Castleton, passenger. (Blaker)
Get on the wooing. (Penny)
Get ready for battle. (Jhabvala, R. P.)
Getting rid of blue plastic. (Randall)
The ghilzai's wife and other stories of east and west. (MacMunn)

The good man's wife. (Baker, A. J.)
Gopi. (Sherring)
Gora. (Tagore, R.)
Government house. (Gillespie, S.)
Government house. (Perrin)
Governor general. (Minney)
Governor Hardy. (Blair)
Governor's lady. (Minney)
Govinda Samanta, or the history of a Bengal Raiyat. (Day)
The grand Panjandrum and other stories. (Barkataki)
The grand rebel: an impression of Sivaji, founder of the
      Maratha empire. (Kincaid, D. C. A.)
Grand trunk knight. (Williamson)
Grateful to life and death. (Narayan)
The great amulet. (Diver)
The great gamble. (Savi)
The great leviathan. (Barker)
The great Moghul: stories of Akbar. (Waddy)
The great proconsul: the memoirs of Mrs. Hester Ward,
      formerly in the family of Hon'ble Warren Hastings.
      (Grier)
Great things God has done: stories from modern India.
      (Southgate)
The great white hand: or the tiger of Cawnpore. (Muddock)
The greater darkness. (Rubin)
Green afternoon. (Ferguson, M.)
Green and gold: stories and poems from Bengal. (Kabir)
The green goddess. (Miln)
The grey squirrel: a story founded on Indian myth. (Batley)
Grim fairy tales and other facts and fancies. (Khosla,
      G. D.)
Gripping tales of Ind. (Panchapakesa Ayyar)
Guest of the baron. (Mandy)
The guide. (Narayan)
Gun-running in the gulf and other adventures. (Austin)
Gunga Sahib. (Mundy, T.)
Gunner Jingo's jubilee. (Strange, T. B.)
Guns of the gods. (Mundy, T.)
Gup Bahadur. (Mundy, T.)
Gup: sketches of Anglo-Indian life. (Marryat, F.)
Gurney married. (Hook)
Guy Mannering, or the astrologer. (Scott, W.)
Gypsy sixpence. (Marshall, E.)

The half-hearted. (Buchan, J.)
A handful of flour. (Viyogi)

Himalayan view.   (Gillespie, S.)
Hindi short stories. (Shrawan Kumar)
Hindoo holiday. (Ackerley)
Hindoo Khan. (Pemberton)
Hindu heaven. (Wylie, M.)
The Hindu wife, or the enchanted fruit.   (Devi)
Hindupore: a peep behind the Indian unrest: an Anglo-Indian
     romance. (Mitra, S. M.)
Hira Singh's tale. (Mundy, T.)
Hirimba's wedding. (Dass)
His honour and a lady. (Cotes, E.)
His majesty's greatest subject. (Thorburn)
His majesty's shirt sleeves. (Cailloux)
His only love. (Gour)
The history of George Desmond. (Butt, M. M.)
The history of Pendennis, his fortunes and misfortunes, his
     friends, and greatest enemy. (Thackeray)
The holders of the gate. (Fairley)
The home and the world. (Tagore, R.)
The honest bunch and other stories. (Snilloc)
Hoopoe. (Weston, C.)
The horoscope cannot lie and other stories. (Khosla)
Horse and two goats.   (Narayan)
Horse leeche's daughter. (Forster, D. K.)
The horse of the sun. (Prior)
The hosts of the lord. (Steel)
Hot water. (Bell)
The hot years. (Piper)
The house at Adampur. (Lall)
A house full of people. (Basu, R.)
The house next door. (Stevenson)
House of earth. (Wilson, D. C.)
The house of fulfillment. (Beck)
House of hatred. (Bayley)
House of many rooms. (White, R.)
The house of Ramiah. (Raj)
The house of sleep. (Burt)
House party. (Savi)
The householder. (Jhabvala, R. P.)
How can I bear suffering. (Christlieb)
How he got over. A story of English life. (Mehta, Rustum)
How I became a maharaja. (Row)
How to manage it. (Prichard)
How will it end. (Anon)
The human heart. (Savi)
The hundred days. (Mundy, T.)
Hungry hearts. (Home)

Hungry stones and other stories. (Tagore, R.)

I am a smuggler. (Evelyn)
I cannot die: a story of Bengal. (Krishan Chander)
I shall not hear the nightingale. (Singh, K.)
I take this woman. (Bedi)
Ian and John. (Todd)
Ida Craven. (Cadell, H. M.)
The idiot's wife. (Sengupta, N. C.)
Idolatry. (Perrin)
If I lived in India. (Christlieb)
If winter comes. (Sun)
Ilderin the Afghan. (Newell)
Ill gotten gains. (Savi)
The image and the search. (Baxter, W.)
Immersion. (Isvaran)
Immortal garland. (Ferguson, M.)
In a Bengal backwater. (Hamilton, J.)
In a Bengal jungle: stories of life on the tea gardens of
      northern India. (Symington)
In a dark bungalow: a collection of short tales. (Denning)
In a Simla season. (Irvine)
In black and white. (Kipling)
In cantonments. (Millington)
In Clive's command. (Strang)
In desperation. (Savi)
In extenuation of Sybella. (Beckett)
In furthest India: the narrative of Edward Carolyn of the
      Hon'ble East India Company's service. (Grier)
In my Indian garden. (Robinson, P. S.)
In old Madras. (Croker)
In tent and bungalow. (Cuthell)
In times of peril. (Henty)
In the Company's service. (Anon)
In the crimelight. (Aiyar)
In the days of the mutiny. (Henty)
In the green jungle. (Casserly)
In the green tree. (Lewis)
In the guardianship of God. (Steel)
In the heart of the storm. (Gray, M.)
In the kingdom of Kerry and other stories. (Croker)
In the long run. (Tavers)
In the permanent way and other stories. (Steel)
In the P(ublic) W(orks) D(epartment). (Purwar)
In the world of bewilderment. (Travers)
In transit. (Chitale)

In wild Maratha battle: a tale of the days of Shivaji.
    (Macmillan)
The incendiaries. (Drury)
Incidents of Indian life. (Browne)
Inconstant moon. (Ferguson, M.)
The Indian adventurer, or the true story of Mr. Vanneck.
    (Anon)
Indian after dinner stories. (Panchapakesa Ayyar)
Indian artifax. (Bayley)
An Indian boyhood. (Sircar)
An Indian day. (Thompson, E. J.)
Indian detective stories. (Banerjea)
Indian dream lands. (Mordecai)
Indian dust. (Rothfeld)
Indian file. (Foster)
The Indian garden series, tales and sketches. (Robinson,
    P. S.)
Indian ghost stories. (Mukherji, S. K.)
Indian Gup: untold stories of the Indian mutiny. (Baldwin,
    J. R.)
The Indian heroes. (Kincaid, C. A.)
The Indian heroine. (Anon)
Indian idylls. (Abbott, A.)
Indian idylls. (Cuthell)
Indian ink. (Beal)
Indian interlude. (Beercroft)
Indian life: a tale of the Carnatic. (Hartley)
Indian love legends. (Raina)
An Indian mystery. (Andrews)
Indian neighbors. (Christlieb)
Indian nights' entertainment; or folk tales from the upper
    Indus. (Swynnerton)
An Indian outcaste: the autobiography of an untouchable.
    (Hazari)
Indian police. (Fisher)
Indian river. (Rajput)
Indian scene: collected short stories. (Steel)
The Indian stories of F. W. Bain. (Bain)
An Indian summer. (Milton)
Indian summer. (Wilfred)
Indian tales. (Anderson, E. L.)
Indian tales. (Padmanabha)
Indian tales. (Sharpe)
Indian tales. (Thapar)
Indian tales, etc. (Banerjea)
Indian tales of love and beauty. (Ransom)
Indian tales of the great ones among men, women and bird

The jewel in the crown.   (Scott, P.)
The jewel of Malabar.   (Marshall, E.)
The jewel of Malabar.   (Sinderby)
Jimgrim and Allah's place.   (Mundy, T.)
John Carruthers: Indian policeman.   (Cox)
John Hobbs: a tale of British India.   (Drage)
John Sikander.   (Eyre)
Johnnie Sahib. (Scott, P.)
Jolly old tales of Ind.   (Panchapakesa Ayyar)
Jones of the 64th: a tale of the battles of Assaye.   (Brere-
     ton)
The journey homeward.   (Hanley, G.)
The judge.   (Banerjee, T.)
The judgment of the sword: the tale of the Kabul tragedy.
     (Diver)
Judy and Lakshmi.   (Mitchison)
Jungbir - secret agent.   (Dunbar)
Jungle beasts and men.   (Mukerji, D. G.)
The jungle book.   (Kipling)
Jungle born.   (Eyton)
The jungle girl.   (Casserly)
Jungle jest.   (Mundy, T.)
Jungle John.   (Budden)
Jungle tales.   (Croker)
Just because.   (Peterson)
Just flesh.   (Karaka)
Justice of Allah and other stories.   (Steward, F.)
The justice of the white sahibs.   (Fairley)
Justine Gay.   (Horsman)

Kailas.   (Vaidya)
Kaleidoscope, a novel.   (Mitra, P.)
Kali's jewels.   (Fairley)
Kalyani's husband.   (Krishnaswamy)
Kama-houri.   (Mardaan)
Kamala: a story of Indian life. (Sathianandhan, K.)
Kamala's letters to her husband.   (Subba Rao)
Kamalina.   (Gokhale)
The kamini bush: a story of Bengal.   (Batley)
Kamla.   (Singh, J.)
Kamni.   (Singh, J.)
Kandan, the patriot.   (Venkataramani)
Kanthapura.   (Rao, R.)
Kari: the elephant.   (Mukerjii, D. G.)
Karma: a story of early Buddhism.   (Carus)
Kashmir princess.   (Karnik)

Lalappa, an Indian story.   (Christlieb)
Lalun, the beragun, or the battle of Panipat.   (Moorad Ali
      Beg)
Lament on the death of a master of arts.   (Anand, M. R.)
Lamp in the desert.   (Dell)
The land and the well.   (Wernher)
The land of regrets.   (Currie)
Land of the five rivers.   (Singh, K.)
The land of the Mogul: a story of the East India Company's
      first venture in India.   (Trease)
The last long journey.   (Cleeve)
The last Mughal.   (Khosla)
The last of the peshwas: a tale of the third Maratha war.
      (Harcourt)
The last thug.   (DeWohl)
The latent force.   (Thwaytes)
Laughs at life.   (Bali)
The law of the threshold.   (Steel)
Lawley road.   (Narayan)
Leaf in the wind.   (Baker, A. J.)
Lean brown men.   (Burt)
Leaves in the August wind; a novel with the Indian upheaval
      of August 1942 for its background.   (Phadke)
Legacy: a historical novel.   (O'Hind)
The legions thunder past.   (Panchapakesa Ayyar)
Lengthening shadows.   (Handa)
Leonie of the jungle.   (Conquest)
Leopard of the hills.   (Temple)
The leopard's leap.   (Boxwallah)
The liberation.   (Chakravarti, K.)
The library of anecdotes.   (Dutt, H.)
Lieutenant Beatrice Raymond, V. C. : a frontier novel.
      (Lloyd)
Lieut. Panju: a modern Indian.   (Madhaviah)
Lieut. Suresh Biswas: his life and adventures.   (Datta, H.)
Life and its puppets: being stories from India and the
      west.   (Rothfeld)
Life goes on.   (Kapur, V.)
Life in an Indian outpost.   (Casserly)
Life in India: or the English at Calcutta.   (Monkland)
Life in the mission, the camp, and the zenana, or six
      years in India.   (Mackenzie, H.)
Life is one long sacrifice.   (Panchapakesa Ayyar)
The life of a Mogul princess.   (Butenschon)
Life of Keshav: a family story from India.   (Mehta, Rama)
Life of my heart.   (Crosse)
The life of princess Yashodhara: wife and disciple of the

Lotus, or the lily maid of the east.   (Vera)
Louisa.   (Hampden, H.)
The lovable outlaw.   (Williamson)
Love and faith.   (Singh, M.)
Love and its charms.   (Umrao Bahadur)
Love and life behind the purdah.   (Sorabji)
Love besieged: a romance of the residency in Lucknow.
        (Pearce)
Love by an Indian river.   (Penny)
Love for a doctor.   (Cole)
Love in a mist.   (Sanderson)
Love in a palace.   (Penny)
Love in the hills.   (Penny)
The love of dust.   (Ram, S.)
The love of Kusuma, an eastern love story.   (Bala Krishna)
Love stories of India.   (Marshall, E.)
A love tangle.   (Penny)
Love twigs.   (Subramanian)
The lovely and the damned.   (Collier)
The lovers of the market place.   (Dehan, R.)
Love's legend.   (Fielding)
Love's lotus flower.   (Wynne, P.)
The loves of Begum Sumroo and other true romances.
        (Shamsuddin)
The luck Udaipur: a romance of old Devon, Hindustan, and
        the fringe of the blue Pacific.   (Emery)
Luxima, the prophetess, a tale of India.   (Owensen)

Ma-o-meye: or the mother and daughter.   (Mukerji, D.)
The mad rani and other sketches of Indian life and thought.
        (Ashby)
Maggot to man.   (Mayo)
Magic in the air.   (Penny)
Magnificent Moghuls.   (Ramnani)
Mahanagar.   (Mitra, N.)
Maharajah,   (Banks)
Maharajah.   (Payne)
Mahatma.   (Hill, S. W.)
The mahatma's pupil.   (Marsh)
The maid and the idol: a tangled story of Poona.   (Fforde)
Major Craik's craze.   (O'Beirne)
Maki.   (Minney)
The Makra mystery.   (Campbell, H.)
The Malabar magician.   (Penny)
Malgudi days, short stories.   (Narayan)
Man and God.   (Bhondi)

Men and monsoon.   (Bothwell)
Men and rivers.   (Kabir)
Mera nam joker.   (Abbas)
The mercy of the lord.   (Steel)
Mess stories.   (Daly)
Midst Himalayan mists.   (Minney)
A million for a soul.   (Phillimore)
The mimic men.   (Naipaul)
Minari.   (Dalal)
A mind's reproduction.   (Meerza)
Minute tale.   (Snilloc)
Miracles still do happen.   (Roy, D.)
Mirror of dreams.   (Ganpat)
Missing.   (Penny)
The missing violin.   (Bothwell)
A mission for Betty Smith.   (Cooper, B.)
The missionary in Indian tales.   (Owensen)
Mr. and Mrs. John Brown at home.   (Brown, J.)
Mr. Ass comes to town.   (Krishan Chander)
Mr. Isaacs: a tale of modern India.   (Crawford)
Mr. Jervis: a romance of the Indian hills.   (Croker)
Mr. John Bull speaks out.   (Rawley)
Mr. Penriddick's progress.   (Lyon)
Mr. Ram.   (Eyton)
Mr. Sampath.   (Narayan)
Miss Stuart's legacy.   (Steel)
Mistress of ceremonies.   (Strange)
Mistress of herself.   (Savi)
Mistress of men.   (Steel)
Misunderstood and other sketches of Indian life.   (Banerjea)
Mixed cargo: stories of India and English romance, adven-
       ture, and mystery.   (Savi)
A mixed marriage.   (Penny)
Mock majesty.   (Savi)
Modern Marathi: short stories.   (Shinde)
The moles of death.   (Dellbridge)
Money and power.   (Savi)
Monkey god.   (Casserly)
Monkeys on the hill of God.   (Reuben)
Monsoon.   (David)
Monsoon.   (Jacob)
Monsoon.   (Johnston)
Monsoon bird.   (Knight, W. K.)
Monsoon murder.   (Cooper, B.)
Montoceil: rajah of greater India.   (Morand)
Mooltiki: stories and poems from India.   (Godden, R.)
The moon in Rahu.   (Baig)

My nine lives. (Abdullah)
My purdah lady. (Eustace)
My year in an Indian fort. (Guthrie)
The mysteries of Calcutta. (Paul)
Mysteries of the court of a maharaja. (Row)
The mysteries of the Mogul court. (Paul)
Mysteries of the Mogul durbar: a historical romance. (Paul)
The mysterious traders. (Mukherji, S. K.)
Mystery at the house-of-the-fish. (Bothwell)
Mystery of the monocle, a novel. (Mehta, D. R.)
The mystery of tunnel 51. (Wilson, A. D.)

The nabob at home. (Anon)
The nabob's jewel. (Alington)
The nabob's wife. (Anon)
Nadir shah, a romance. (Durand)
Nails and flesh. (Duggal)
Naked shingles. (Isvaran)
Nanda, the pariah who overcame caste. (Madhaviah)
Nandini. (Nirody)
Nasrin: an Indian medley. (Singh, J.)
Native born. (Wylie, I. A. R.)
The native wife; or Indian love and anarchism; a novel.
    (Bruce)
The nature of passion. (Jhabvala, R. P.)
The Naulakha. (Kipling)
The near and the far. (Myers)
The necklace of Kali. (Towers)
Nectar in a sieve. (Markandaya)
Neel Kamal. (Nanda)
The neighbour's wife and other stories. (Bond)
Neither fish nor flesh. (Savi)
Nellie's vows. (Chew)
The nest hunters or adventures in the Indian Archipelago.
    (Dalton)
Never let her go. (Crosby)
Nevertheless I love her still. (Panjabi)
A new book of tribal fiction. (Elwin)
A new clearing: a medley of prose and verse. (Planter's
    Mate)
The Newcomes: memoirs of a most respected family, edited
    by Arthur Pendennis, Esq. (Thackeray)
Night falls on Siva's hill. (Thompson, E. J.)
Night in Bombay. (Bromfield)
Night life of Calcutta. (Minney)
Nightrunners of Bengal. (Masters)

A nine day's wonder.   (Croker)
Nine hours to Rama.   (Wolpert)
Nine lives.   (Channing)
Nine-tiger man.   (Blanch)
The nine unknown.   (Mundy, T.)
1957.   (Blair)
The ninth vibration and other stories.   (Beck)
Nirgis: a tale of the Indian mutiny; and Bismillah; or happy
      days in Cashmere.   (Allard)
Nirvana: a story of Buddhist philosophy.   (Carus)
No actress: a stage door keeper's story.   (Besemeres)
No anklet bells for her.   (Isvaran)
No man's money: the story of Tin Courie Dass.   (Rideout)
A noble queen, a romance of Indian history.   (Taylor)
None shall live.   (Rao, K. R.)
North and south.   (Gaskell)
North from Bombay.   (Gillespie, S.)
Northwest frontier.   (Harman)
Northwest mail.   (Bayley)
Not all lies.   (Abbas)
Not at home.   (Cooper, B.)
Not seriously--short stories.   (Singh, G. I.)
Nourmahal, an oriental romance.   (Quin)
Now I can see: stories of Christians in South India. (Coch-
      ran)
Nur Jahan and Jahangir.   (Caunter)
Nur Jahan: the romance of an Indian queen.   (Singh, J.)

Oakfield.   (Arnold)
Obsession.   (Goddard)
Ocean of night.   (Ali, Ahmed)
Odd, but even so: stories stranger than fiction.   (Wren)
Odds & ends.   (Croker)
Of cabbages and kings.   (Kabir)
Of life and love; short stories.   (Broker)
Officer's children.   (Abbot, M.)
The old bungalow.   (Todd)
The old cantonment and other stories of India and elsewhere.
      (Croker)
The old dagoba.   (Penny)
Old Deccan days.   (Frere)
Old forever: an epic beyond the Indus.   (Ollivant)
Old mali and the boy.   (Sherman)
The old man and the cow.   (Anand, M. R.)
The old missionary.   (Hunter, W.)
An old score.   (Hilliers)

Old stories.   (Christlieb)
Old Tanjore.   (Gopalan)
Olives are scarce.   (Yates)
Olivia in England, the adventures of a Chota Mis Sahib.
      (Douglas)
Olivia in India, the adventures of a Chota Mis Sahib.
      (Douglas)
OM, the secret of the Abhor valley.   (Mundy, T.)
Omen for a princess.   (Bothwell)
On Kali's shoulder.   (Ayscough)
On the company's service.   (Meacham)
On the Coromandel coast.   (Penny)
On the face of the waters.   (Steel)
On the Irrawaddy: a story of the first Burmese war.
      (Henty)
On the knees of the gods.   (Harcourt)
On the knees of the gods.   (Savi)
On the march: a tale of the Deccan.   (Harvey, G.)
On the sands of Juhu.   (Rao, K. R.)
On to the rescue: a tale of Indian mutiny.   (Stables)
On trust.   (Savi)
The one-eyed knave.   (Ganpat)
One immortality.   (Fielding)
One of Clive's heroes.   (Strang)
One of the best.   (Penny)
One thousand nights on a bed of stones and other stories.
      (Abbas)
1001 Indian nights: the trials of Narayan Lal.   (Ghose,
      S. K.)
One virginity.   (Brown, C. H.)
Only an ensign.   (Grant, J.)
The openers of the gate; stories of the occult.   (Beck)
The optimist and other stories.   (Gulvadi)
Ordeal on the frontier.   (Woolf)
The orphan of Nepaul: a tale of Hindustan.   (Anon)
Other sheep.   (Perrin)
The otto of roses.   (Devasher)
Our picnic at Chordi.   (Anon)
Out of evil.   (Ganpat)
The outcaste.   (Penny)

Padmini: an Indian romance.   (Ramakrishna)
The pagoda tree.   (Croker)
The painted leopard.   (Greave)
Painted tigers.   (Isvaran)
Palace of intrigue.   (Craig)

Pink lotus: a comedy in Kashmir. (Crommelin)
Pioneer Jack and other stories. (Harding, R.)
Plain tales from the hills. (Kipling)
A pleasant surprise and other stories. (Narasimha)
Plough and the stars: stories from Tamilnad. (Swaminathan)
The point of the bayonet: a tale of the Maratha war. (Henty)
Poison and passion. (Home)
The poison mountain: a tale of the Indian secret service.
    (Harding, R.)
Poison of Kali. (Harding, R.)
The poison tree. (Chatterji, B. C.)
Poisoned arrow. (Dunbar)
The poisoned mountain. (Channing)
Pomegranates from the Panjab. (Tucker)
Pook Sahib: a light satire on all things eastern including the
    English who go there. (Pook)
Pool in the desert. (Cotes, S. J.)
The pool of Vishnu. (Myers)
Poor Elisabeth. (Hamilton, M.)
Poor man's son and other stories. (Panchapakesa Ayyar)
Pope Joan or female pontiff. (Reynolds)
Poppied sleep. (Fletcher)
Possession. (Markandaya)
Potpourri: a series of short tales. (Hanli)
Potter's clay. (Brown, C. H.)
The potter's thumb. (Steel)
Power of darkness and other stories. (Anand, M. R.)
Power of innocence. (Westermayr)
The power of the keys. (Grier)
Prasanna and Kamini. (Mullens)
Pratab Singh - the last of the Rajputs. (Dutt, R. C.)
Prem. (Gordon)
Premanand and Pushpavati, or the purdah princess and her
    poet lover. (Namonarayana)
Pretty Miss Neville. (Croker)
The prevalence of witches. (Menen)
The price of a wife. (Khosla)
The price of empire. (Hampden, E.)
Price of loyalty. (Savi)
The priceless jewels. (Batley)
Primers in India. (Coloquhoun)
The primeval and other stories. (Bannerjee, M.)
Prince Baber and his wives: and, the slave girl Narcissus
    and the nawab of Lalput. (St. Clair)
A prince in chains. (Scott, A.)
Prince Jali. (Myers)
The prince of Balkh: a tale of the wars of Aurangzeb. (Har-
    court)

Radha: a romance and other tales.   (Sousa)
Radharani.   (Chatterji, B. C.)
Rage of the soul.   (Sheean)
Rage of the vulture.   (Moorehead)
Rain in the desert: stories.   (Stewart, F.)
The rains came: a novel of modern India.   (Bromfield)
The rajah.   (Penny)
The rajah.   (Ramzan)
The rajah's casket.   (Christie)
The rajah's daughter.   (Penny)
The rajah's guests.   (Gillespie, S.)
The rajah's heir.   (Despard)
The rajah's people.   (Wylie, I. A. R.)
The rajah's second wife.   (Hill, H.)
Rajani.   (Chatterji, B. C.)
Rajmohan's wife.   (Chatterji, B. C.)
Rajni.   (Kapur, P.)
The rajpoot's rings.   (Knight, F. A.)
Rajput rani.   (Dastur)
Ralph Darnell.   (Taylor)
Rama, the hero of India.   (Mukerji, D. G.)
Ramabai: the high class Hindu woman.   (Sarasvati)
The Ramayana.   (Menen)
Ramji: a tragedy of the Indian famine.   (Anon)
Ramu.   (Mehta, Rama)
Randall Davenant: a tale of the Mahrattas.   (Bray)
Randolph Methyl: a story of the Anglo-Indian life.   (Ireland)
Random short stories.   (Ahmad)
The ranis: a tale of the Indian mutiny.   (Maclean)
The rani's dominion.   (Barker)
Rapture.   (Fakhruddin)
Ratanbai: a sketch of a Bombay high caste Hindu young wife.
       (Nikambe)
The razor's edge.   (Maugham)
The real India.   (Begbie)
Rebels of destiny.   (Mistry)
The rebirth of Venkata Reddi: a story.   (Longley)
Recollections of an ex-detective of Madras police force.
       (White, D. S.)
Reconstruction of India.   (Thompson, E. J.)
The recruit.   (Basu, B.)
The recruit.   (Kaikini)
The red flame.   (Miles, F. M.)
Red flame of Erinpura.   (Mundy, T.)
Red hibiscus.   (Sengupta, P.)
Red pepper or the zennana mystery.   (Pegg)
The red rajah.   (Kent)

Red records: tales. (Perrin)
Red revenge: a romance of Cawnpore. (Pearce)
Red sap. (Easton)
The red scarf. (Bothwell)
Red tea. (Daniel)
Red vulture. (Sleath)
The red year. (Tracy)
The redemption of the Brahmin. (Garbe)
Reflection on the golden bed and other stories. (Anand,
    M. R.)
Reflections. (Roped In)
Release. (Napier, R. L.)
Religion and folklore of Northern India. (Crooke)
Remember the house. (Rama Rao)
The reminiscences of a retired Hindu official. (Balakrishna
    Mudaliyar)
The reproof of chance. (Savi)
The republic of Pompapur. (Dikshit)
The residency; an Indian novel. (Bruce)
The resignation. (Jainendra Kumar)
The return of Sherlock Holmes. (Doyle)
The return of the panther. (Sundarraj)
Revelations of an orderly. (Panchkouree Kahn)
Rice and other stories. (Abbas)
Rickshawallah. (Isvaran)
The riddle of the dead. (Bamburg)
The riddle of the frontier. (Harding, R.)
The riddle of the hill. (Savi)
The riddle of the purple emperor. (Hanshew)
Ride, Zarina, ride. (Bothwell)
The rifleman: or the adventures of Percy Blake. (Rafter)
Ring of fate. (Bothwell)
Rishi: the story of a childhood in India. (Zinkin)
Rita. (Tandon, P. N.)
The river. (Godden, R.)
The road. (Anand, M. R.)
The road and the star. (Mather)
The road to Delhi. (Minney)
Road to roundabout. (Burt)
Roads to peace. (Ganpat)
Robinetta. (Sheepshanks)
A rolling stone. (Croker)
Romance in sacred lore: 22 stories translated from the Pali
    literature. (Bhagwat)
The romance of a nautch girl. (Penny)
The romance of a zenana. (Fernandez)
A romance of bureaucracy. (Anon)

The romance of guard Mulligan and other stories.   (Yeats)
A romance of Indian crime.   (Anon)
A romance of the Moghul harem.   (Sen, M. L.)
Romantic tales from the Panjab.   (Swynnerton)
Romany girl.   (Bothwell)
Romoni's daughters: a story of India.   (Batley)
The room on the roof.   (Bond)
The root and the flower.   (Myers)
Root in the rock.   (Southgate)
The rope bridge.   (Leslie)
The rosary and the lamp.   (Patel, B.)
Rose Clarendon: or the trials of true love. (Anon)
A rose of Hindustan.   (Ponder)
Roses and peacocks: an Indian episode.   (Locke, D. M.)
Roshanara of the seven cities.   (Foran)
Roshinara, a historical romance.   (Lahiri)
Roshni: a portrait of love.   (Paintal)
The rough and the smooth.   (Raeside)
Rough passages.   (Perrin)
Royal flash.   (Fraser, G. M.)
The royal jester of Tenali Rama: tales.   (Panchapakesa
    Ayyar)
A royal rascal: episodes in the career of Col. Sir Theo-
    philius St. Clair, K. C. B.   (Griffith)
The ruby of Rajasthan: an Indian tale.   (Forrest)
Rudra, a romance of ancient India.   (Westermayr)
The ruined temple.   (Welfe)
Rujeeb the juggler.   (Henty)
A ruler of India.   (Dickson and Pechell)
Rulers of men.   (Savi)
Ruler's morning and other stories.   (Hitrec)
Rumor's daughter.   (Hill, K.)
The runaway and other stories.   (Tagore, R.)
Rung ho.   (Mundy, T.)
Rural ghost.   (Chaudhuri, B. C.)
Rustam Khan or fourteen nights' entertainment at Shah Bhag
    or royal gardens at Ahemadabad.   (Ottley)

Sackcloth and ashes.   (Savi)
The sacred crocodile.   (Bradley)
The sacred falls.   (Channing)
Sacrifice.   (Penny)
Safe conduct.   (Bell)
The safety curtain and other stories.   (Dell)
The saffron veil.   (Bhattacharya, B.)
Sahib and sepoy; or saving an empire.   (Taylor, L.)

Sentenced to death: a story of two men and a maid.
      (Machray)
Seonee, or camp life on the Satpura range: a tale of Indian
      adventure.   (Sterndale)
Separation.   (Perrin)
Serenity in storm.   (Paintal)
Serpent and the rope.   (Raja Rao)
The serpent charmer.   (Rousselet)
A servant when he reigneth.   (Travers)
The servants of the Goddess.   (Campbell, H.)
Set desire.   (Vian)
Set in authority.   (Cotes, S. J.)
Seven faces of London.   (Krishan Chander)
The seven islands.   (Godden, J.)
Seven summers; the story of an Indian childhood.   (Anand,
      M. R.)
Seven times proven.   (Ganpat)
The seventh wave, and other stories.   (Bishop)
Shadow from Ladakh.   (Bhattacharya, B.)
The shadow of Abdul.   (Gordon)
Shadow of the monsoon.   (Manchester)
Shadow of the moon.   (Kaye, M. M.)
Shadows from the east.   (James)
Shadows in the sunshine.   (Bhattacharjee)
Shadows on the wall.   (Hutheesingh)
Shafts from an eastern quiver.   (Mansford)
Sharavan Kumar.   (Daryani)
Shasta of the wolves.   (Baker, O.)
She wore a star.   (Bonnell)
Shelah.   (Menen)
Ships of youth: a study of marriage in modern India.   (Diver)
Shiva: or the future of India.   (Minney)
Shorna's day.   (Batley)
The short march in Telangana.   (Larneuil)
Short stories.   (Alvares)
Short stories.   (Das, M.)
Short stories.   (Mehta, P.)
Short stories. (Venkatesa Iyengar)
Short stories of Prem Chand.   (Prem Chand)
Short stories: social and historical.   (Ghosal)
Shri Krishna of Dwaraka and other stories.   (Kincaid, C. A.)
Shut out the sun.   (Alroy)
The shuttles of the loom.   (Edge)
Siddhartha.   (Hesse)
Siege perilous and other stories.   (Diver)
The sign of four.   (Doyle)
The sign of the snake.   (Fforde)

Soldiers three. (Kipling)
Solitary witness. (Collier)
Some Indian stories. (Anon)
Some inner fury. (Markandaya)
Some like the hills. (Duncan, R. A.)
Son of Jesus, Sister Pauline at the cross road, the lean
      lamb and other stories. (Ganguli, J. M.)
Son of power. (Comfort and Dost)
Son of the moon. (Hitrec)
Song for Sunday and other stories. (Das, M.)
A song of Araby. (Guisborough)
The song of surrender: an Indian novel. (Bruce)
The song of the stars. (Holmes)
The son-in-law abroad and other stories. (Ramachandra
      Rao, P.)
Sons of tumult. (Dellbridge)
The soothsayer. (Savi)
Sorrowing lies my land. (Mascarenhas)
The sorrows of a subpostmaster: a story from life.
      (Chattopadhyaya, R. C.)
Sorry, no room. (Laxman)
A sorter's revenge. (Sutherland, W. A.)
The soul of India. (Schultzky)
The soul of the Orient. (Cavalier)
Souls and stones. (Sanderson)
The space, time, and I. (Jose)
Sparks from our life. (Rajah)
The speakers in silence. (Ganpat)
Special relationship. (Clark)
The spell of Aphrodite and other stories. (Chettur)
A spell of the devil. (Penny)
The spell of the jungle. (Perrin)
Spellbound: the story of Arthur Denniston Claire. (Kennedy,
      S. A.)
The sphinx has spoken. (Dekobra)
Spicy stories. (Pereira, A.)
Spiritual stories from India. (Chaman, Lal)
The splendid outcaste. (Savi)
The splendour of Asia. (Beck)
Splendour of god. (Morrow)
The spoilt child: a tale of Hindu domestic life. (Mitra,
      P. C.)
Sport of gods. (Sawyer)
Spotten green: Indian ghost stories. (Pon-Ratnam)
Spring of the deserts. (Wadhwa)
The spur of pride. (Wren)
Spy in Amber. (Malgonkar)

The story of the raya and Appaji. (Sundaram Aiyar)
Strange island. (Kaye, M.)
Strange men; strange places. (Bond)
Strange roads. (Diver)
The strange thirteen. (Gamon)
Stranger in the land. (Pereira)
Stray leaves from a military man's notebook. (Hartigan)
The stream. (Rama Sharma)
Stretton. (Kingsley)
The striking force. (Christie)
The stronger claim. (Perrin)
A stronger climate. (Jhabvala, R. P.)
A study in scarlet. (Doyle)
The subaltern, the policeman, and the little girl. (Fforde)
Subbana. (Venkatesa Iyengar)
Sublime though blind: a tale of Parsi life. (Banaji)
Sugar in spice. (Ferguson, M.)
Sugirtha. (Chinna Durai)
Sukra: the story of truth. (Reyna)
Sultan and Nihalde. (Birla)
Sun babies: studies in the child life of India. (Sorjabji)
Sun in the morning. (Cadell, E.)
Sunia and other stories. (Diver)
Sunlight on a broken column. (Hosain)
Sunny hours. (Mandy)
The sunset gun. (Milton)
The surgeon's daughter. (Scott, W.)
Susanna. (Brown, C. H.)
Sushila. (McInnes)
The suttee or the Hindu converts. (Mainwaring)
Swami and friends. (Narayan)
The swami's curse. (Penny)
Sweet seventeen. (Rajamani)
The sword and the rose. (Smith, A. W.)
The sword and the sickle. (Anand, M. R.)
The sword and the spirit. (Sheepshanks)
The sword of Azreal: a chronicle of the great mutiny.
    (Forrest)

Tale of a Soviet biologist. (Dhar)
A tale of Indian heroes. (Steel)
The tale of my exile. (Ghose, B. K.)
The tale of Nala. (Jarrett)
Tale of the four durwesh. (Meer Ummun)
Tales of the Panjab. (Steel)

Tender observation. (Christie)
Terrible times: a tale of the mutiny. (Raines)
Terry of Tangistan: a story of the N. W. frontier. (Christie)
Thakur Pertab Singh and other tales. (Crosthwaite)
That little owl: a tale of a lunatic, a loafer, and a lover.
      (Fforde)
Their heart's desire. (Grant, C.)
Their ways divide. (Kincaid, D. C. A.)
There and then. (Weston)
There lay the city. (Karaka)
There was a door. (Mundy, T.)
They came to a mountain. (Miles, P.)
They found God. An account of some little known holy lives.
      (Christlieb)
Thief of love. (Dimock)
Thieves in my house. (Vatuk)
Thillai Govindan: a posthumous autobiography. (Madhaviah)
Thirteen men. (Fraser, W. A.)
This alone is true. (Sarabhai)
This time of morning. (Sahgal)
Thorn harvest. (Ferguson, M.)
Thorns and thistles. (Stranger)
Thorns on a canvas and the captives. (Currimbhoy)
Those young married people. (Bell)
Three for luck: an Indian school story for girls. (Methley,
      V. M.)
Three men and a god and other stories. (Newham-Davis)
Three men of destiny. (Panchapakesa Ayyar)
The three R's. (Ganpat)
Three stories. (Kabir)
Three women had made him a saint and "I'm polluted" she
      told him. (Ganguli, J. M.)
Through eastern windows: life stories of an Indian city.
      (Marris)
Through sunlight and gloom. (Biswas, A. C.)
Through the furnace: a tale of the northwest frontier.
      (Hervey, H. J. A.)
Through the Sikh war: a tale of the conquest of the Panjab.
      (Henty)
Through three campaigns. (Henty)
Tiernay Blake's wife. (Milton)
Tiger girl. (Casserly)
Tiger in the north. (Harvester)
The tiger of Bargunga. (Emery)
The tiger of gold. (Jenkins)
The tiger of Mysore: a story of the war with Tippoo Sahib.
      (Henty)

Train to Pakistan.   (Singh, K.)
A traitor's wooing.   (Hill, H.)
Transgression.   (Thorburn)
The transit of souls, a tale of Lucknow.   (Willmer)
The transposed heads.   (Mann)
Trappings of gold.   (Basu, M.)
Treasures, love, and snakes.   (Penny)
The tree of knowledge.   (Savi)
The tremendous adventures of Major Gahagan.   (Thackeray)
Trial by battle.   (Towry)
Trials of glory.   (Biswas, A. C.)
A triangular view.   (Dilip)
Tribal folk-tales of Assam.   (Barkataki)
Tristam Sahib.   (Wylie, I. A. R.)
The triumph of Valmiki.   (Sastri)
A tropical romance.   (Barnby)
The trotter.   (Fforde)
Trouble on the frontier.   (Christie)
The troublemaker.   (Savi)
Trousers of taffeta: a novel of the child mothers of India.
    (Wilson, M.)
True greatness of Vasudeva Sastri.   (Rajam Aiyar)
The true history of Zoa.   (Anon)
A true reformer.   (Chesney)
The twain shall meet.   (Sridhar Rao)
Twilight in Delhi.   (Ali, Ahmed)
Twin giants.   (Forster, D. K.)
The two brides.   (Penny)
Two faces of Eve.   (Pritam, A.)
Two leaves and a bud.   (Anand, M. R.)
Two little wanderers.   (Hampden, H.)
Two measures of rice.   (Sivasankar Pillai)
Two mothers.   (Ganguli, J. M.)
The two pilgrims to Kashi and other stories.   (Tucker)
The two rings.   (Chatterji, B. C.)
The two shilling baby.   (Batley)
Two sisters.   (Tagore, R.)
Two stories or mysteries of government service.   (Anon)
Two strong men.   (Grier)
Two tales of the occult.   (Eliade)
The two visions: a novel of hopes and aspirations.   (Surya,
    Rao)
Two women and a maharaja.   (Phillimore)
Tyranny of freedom.   (Savi)

Via Geneva. (Ali, Aamir)
Vice and virtue. (Jag)
Victims of fate and fashion. (Star-Najnin)
Victory of faith and other stories. (Ramabai)
Videhi: a novel of Indian life. (Holden, C. L.)
The vigil. (Ghaduri)
Vijaya. (Chatterji, S. C.)
The village. (Anand, M. R.)
The village had no walls. (Madgulkar)
Village tales and jungle tragedies. (Croker)
Villain. (Varghese)
Virgin and the well. (Chandar)
Virgin Bouquet. (Nathaniel)
A vision splendid. (Bishop)
A vizier's daughter: a tale of the Hazara war. (Hamilton,
     L.)
The vizier's son, or the adventures of a mogul. (Hockley)
A voice of Dashin. (Ganpat)
The voice of God and other stories. (Singh, K.)
Voices in the city. (Desai)
Voices in the night. (Steel)
The volcano. (Sheorey)
The vow of silence. (Perrin)
Voyage to Coromandel. (Leighton)

Wait without hope. (Sinha, K. N.)
Waiting for the Mahatma. (Narayan)
Wanderings and wooings east of Suez. (Redwood)
Wanderings in India and other sketches of Indian life. (Lang)
The wanderings of Asaf. (Afghan)
War and peace: a tale of the retreat from Cabul. (Tucker)
The warden of the marches. (Grier)
Warren of Oudh. (Gamon)
Waters of chastisement. (Ponder)
The waters of destruction. (Perrin)
Way of an eagle. (Dell)
The way of stars. (Beck)
Way of the panther: a romance of India. (Stokes)
The ways of man. (Sankar Ram)
Wazir. (Lyon)
We never die. (Karaka)
Weathered: a P. & O. story. (Hervey)
The web. (Stewart, H.)
Wee Willie Winkle. (Kipling)
The weird dance. (Nahal)
We'll soldier no more. (Burt)

Works of Jules Verne. (Verne)
The workshop of religions. (Lillie)
The world is a bridge. (Weston)
The world of Prem Chand; selected stories of Prem Chand.
     (Prem Chand)
Worthwhile. (Wren)
The wound of spring. (Menon)
A wreath of Indian stories. (Tucker)
The wreck. (Tagore, R.)
Wrexham's romance. (Ganpat)
Written on their foreheads. (Elliot)
Wynnegate Sahib. (Sutherland, J.)

Yachts, hamburgers and a Hindu; a summer escapade.
     (Bhaskara Rao)
Yadnamuh: a chapter of oriental life. (Anon)
A yak for Christams: the story of a Himalayan holiday.
     (Hillary)
Yanks and yogis: sensational stories of eerie events and
     uncanny adventures into yogiland by GI's in India,
     Burma, and Ceylon. (Vaswani)
The years of love. (Runbeck)
The yellow turban. (Jay)
Yet a more excellent way. (Scharlieb)
Yoga mist. (Thorne)
The young cadet or Henry Delamere's voyage to India.
     (Hofland)
Young emperor. (Payne)
Young man in the sun. (Greave)
Young Mr. Kelso. (White, J. D.)
The young rajah: a story of Indian life and adventures.
     (Kingston)
The young stagers. (Wren)
The young zemindar. (Datta, S. C.)
The young zemindar. (Rowney)
The youngest disciple. (Thompson, E. J.)

Zalim Singh the great. (Sladen)
Zarina. (Sadoc)
Zit and Xoe: their early experience. (Curwen)
Zohar: a tale of zenana life. (Anon)
Zohra. (Futehally)
Zora, the invisible. (Wilmot)

PART III

THEME INDEX

THEME INDEX: OUTLINE

Sino-Indian Relations and
   Wars
Sirajuddaullah
Sixteenth Century
Sumroo, Begum of
Thirteenth Century
Thugs
Tipoo Sultan
Vijayanagar Empire
Wellesley, Marquess
World War I
World War II
Yale, Elihu

Indians
   Bureaucratic Life
   Forest and Wildlife
   Interpersonal Relations
   Military Life and Ad-
     ventures
   Modernised
   Plantation Life
   Princely Life
   Race Relations
   Rural and Tribal Life
   Social Work
   Urban Life

Minorities, Indian
   Christians
   Communal Relations
   Gypsies
   Jews
   Muslims
   Parsis
   Sikhs

Miscellaneous
   Fiction for Children and
     Young Adults
   Mysteries

Regional Novels
   Andamans
   Assam and Assamese
   Bengal and Bengalis
   Bihar

Bombay
Goa
Himalayas
Kashmir
Maharashtra and Marathas
North India and North
   Indians
Northwest and the
   Afghans
Panjab and Panjabis
Rajasthan and Rajputs
South India and South
   Indians
Uttar Pradesh
Western India

Religion and Mysticism
   Buddhism
   Hinduism
   Occultism

THEME INDEX

Foreigners in India

86, 1202, 1205, 1210, 1224, 1233, 1295-1303, 1313-14, 1334, 1373, 1404-05, 1412, 1414, 1448, 1486-86a, 1556, 1560, 1604, 1612, 1810, 1852-53, 1886, 1901-03, 1933-35, 2012-13, 2027-30, 2092-93, 2096, 2103, 2108, 2167, 2209-10, 2237-38, 2254-56, 2266-68, 2270. (Also see, Historical Novels)

Nabobery, 10, 26-27, 41, 364, 366, 1000, 1014-16, 1491, 2091.

Race Relations, 12, 24, 35, 103, 121-22, 124, 162, 180-81, 213, 227, 237-38, 276-80, 301, 307, 312, 322-23, 326, 334, 338-44, 346-48, 351-53, 364-66, 371, 377-80, 383, 442-43, 455, 479, 482, 489, 491, 501-04, 515, 522-23, 526, 548, 582, 590, 603, 605, 612, 616, 619-21, 627, 631, 636, 640, 653, 678, 690, 695, 702, 707-08, 710-11, 713, 725, 730, 737, 743, 752, 761, 768, 775, 800, 827, 834-37, 844, 853, 862, 875-77, 881, 883-84, 914-15, 919-20, 930, 938, 956, 984, 987-88, 994, 1021, 1025-27, 1067-68, 1071-72, 1080, 1095-96, 1137, 1141, 1158-59, 1161-62, 1164, 1197, 1200-01, 1214, 1222, 1230, 1236, 1238, 1240, 1255, 1263, 1267, 1270, 1272, 1281, 1288, 1293-96, 1298, 1302-03, 1322, 1330, 1333, 1339, 1352-53, 1360, 1371, 1375, 1378, 1395, 1406-08, 1411, 1430, 1477, 1491, 1493-94, 1498, 1542, 1547-48, 1554, 1556-57, 1561, 1563, 1567, 1570-71, 1574-76, 1578, 1587, 1590-93, 1605, 1617, 1624, 1649, 1652, 1658, 1669, 1705, 1712, 1722, 1726, 1757, 1778, 1786, 1788, 1791, 1793, 1812, 1814-18, 1822, 1841, 1848-52, 1873, 1887-88, 1891, 1902, 1932, 1935, 1984, 1992, 1994, 1999-2000, 2012, 2072, 2076, 2084-89, 2092, 2107, 2112, 2117, 2143, 2163, 2168-69, 2178, 2180, 2184-87, 2191-94, 2197-2200, 2202, 2215-16, 2220-21, 2236, 2240, 2245-46, 2254.

Social Work and Missionary Activities, 59, 141, 183-95, 228, 263-66, 302, 343, 347, 364-66, 454, 465-74, 482, 513-14, 559, 652, 841, 847, 890, 956, 981, 993, 1005, 1031, 1193, 1226, 1234, 1273, 1285, 1376, 1418, 1495, 1498, 1542, 1571-72, 1582, 1596, 1599, 1739, 1828, 1841, 1957, 2123-30, 2212-15, 2219, 2228-31, 2242, 2257.

Station and Club Life, 118, 212, 230-31, 308, 311, 325-26, 445, 531, 545, 597, 690, 749, 757, 917-19, 959, 1009, 1017, 1041, 1144-45, 1230, 1276, 1378, 1729-35, 1750.

Miscellaneous

Regional Novels

PART IV

PRINCIPAL SOURCES

PRINCIPAL SOURCES

Baker, Ernest Albert. <u>A guide to historical fiction.</u> New
    York: Macmillan, 1914.

—————. <u>A guide to the best fiction, English and American,</u>
    <u>including translations from foreign languages.</u> London:
    Routledge, 1932.

Bateson, Frederick Wilse, editor. <u>The Cambridge bibli-</u>
    <u>ography of English Literature.</u> Cambridge: Cambridge
    University Press, 1940-57.

Besterman, Theodore. <u>A world bibliography of bibliographies.</u>
    4th edition, 5 vols. Lausanne: Societas Bibliographica,
    1965-66.

<u>Book review digest.</u>

<u>British book news.</u>

British Museum. <u>Catalogue of printed books.</u>

Cook, Dorothy E., editor, and Isabel Monro, joint editor.
    <u>Fiction catalog.</u> New York: H. W. Wilson, 1951.

Cotton, Gerald Brooks and Alan Glencross. <u>Cumulated</u>
    <u>fiction index, 1945-60.</u> London: Association of
    Assistant Librarians, 1960.

Dixson, Zella Allen. <u>Comprehensive subject index to uni-</u>
    <u>versal prose fiction.</u> New York: Dodd, Mead, 1897.

<u>The English catalogue of books.</u>

Fidell, Estella A. and Esther V. Flory, editors. <u>Fiction</u>
    <u>catalog.</u> 7th edition. New York: H. W. Wilson, 1961.

Hill, Winifred C. <u>The overseas empire in fiction; an an-</u>
    <u>notated bibliography.</u> London: Oxford University Press,
    1930.

Indian national bibliography.

Jain, Sushil Kumar. Indian literature in English.   Part III.
     Tenterden: Published privately, 1965-67.

_____. "A select bibliography of Indian short stories and
     historical fiction in English, " Indian Literature, XII,
     ii (June 1969), 76-92.

Journal of commonwealth literature.

The Library of Congress catalogs.

McGarry, Daniel D. and Sarah Harriman White.   Historical
     fiction guide. New York: Scarecrow Press, 1963.

Nield, Jonathan. A guide to the best historical novels and
     tales. London: Mathews, 1902.

Sahitya Akademi. Who's who of Indian writers.   New Delhi:
     Sahitya Akademi, 1961.

Singh, Bhupal. Survey of Anglo-Indian fiction.   London:
     Oxford University Press, 1934.

Spencer, Dorothy M.   Indian fiction in English. Philadelphia:
     University of Pennsylvania Press, 1960.

Times (London) Literary Supplement.

WITHDRAWAL